THE THEOLOGY OF ACTS
IN ITS HISTORICAL SETTING

THE
THEOLOGY OF ACTS
IN ITS HISTORICAL SETTING

J. C. O'NEILL

SECOND EDITION
REVISED AND
SUPPLEMENTED

LONDON
S·P·C·K
1970

First published in 1961
by S.P.C.K.
Holy Trinity Church
Marylebone Road
London N.W.1

Second revised and supplemented edition published in 1970
Made and printed in Great Britain by
William Clowes and Sons, Limited, London and Beccles

SBN 281 02348 4

To my Wife

CONTENTS

PREFACE TO THE FIRST EDITION

I SHOULD LIKE to acknowledge the help I have received from teachers and friends in Melbourne, Göttingen, and Cambridge: from the Reverend A. L. Burns of the Australian National University, who first set me to work on the Book of Acts; the Reverend Professor J. D. McCaughey, Professor of Biblical Studies and Master of Ormond College; the Reverend J. M. Owen, Minister of Lorne, Victoria; the Reverend H. R. Wardlaw; Professor D. Dr Joachim Jeremias of Göttingen; Professor D. Ernst Käsemann, now of Tübingen; the Reverend J. N. Sanders of Peterhouse; the Reverend Professor C. F. D. Moule of Clare College; the Right Reverend Dr J. A. T. Robinson, Bishop of Woolwich; the Reverend Dr J. Y. Campbell, Professor Emeritus of Westminster College, Cambridge; and the Reverend Professor G. D. Kilpatrick of Oxford, who suggested the theme of Chapter Five. I am very grateful to all these scholars for their criticism and encouragement; none of them, of course, can be held responsible for the positions I have adopted.

Ormond College,   J.C.O'N.
Melbourne.

PREFACE TO THE SECOND EDITION

THIS EDITION is a complete revision of the First Edition. I have
not changed my mind about the second-century date that I
suggested for the composition of Luke-Acts, but I now hold that
Luke was using written sources throughout. This has meant
that I have had to omit the old Chapter Five, "The Titles given
to Jesus", partly because a proper treatment of this theme on my
new assumptions would take up a disproportionate amount of
space, but mainly because Professor Moule in his essay, "The
Christology of Acts", in *Studies in Luke-Acts*, edited by Leander
E. Keck and J. Louis Martyn, has already set out the essential
points. My new assumptions have also meant that I have had
to add a section to Chapter Three, "The Attitude to the Jews",
and rewrite much of Chapter Four, "Jewish Christians and
Gentile Christians". I have added a new chapter on Paul at
Athens.

Despite these changes, the book still maintains the same central
thesis, that Luke was writing a history for the general reading
public in order to convert them to Christianity.

I have learnt much from the reviewers, especially from
Professor Hans Conzelmann, the Reverend Professor H. F. D.
Sparks, and Mr E. A. Judge, although I am afraid I have not
always taken their advice. I renew my thanks to those mentioned
in the Preface to the First Edition. The sad death of Mr Sanders
in December 1961 was a loss to New Testament studies and to his
friends. I now add thanks to Dr theol. Berndt Schaller and
Dr theol. Christoph Burchard of Göttingen.

Westminster and Cheshunt Colleges,   J.C.O'N.
Cambridge.

ABBREVIATIONS

B.J.R.L.	*Bulletin of the John Rylands Library*
Beginnings	*The Beginnings of Christianity, Part I:* 5 vols. ed. F. J. Foakes Jackson and Kirsopp Lake. London, 1920-33
E.T.	*The Expository Times*
Hdb.z.N.T.	*Handbuch zum Neuen Testament,* ed. Hans Lietzmann, Günther Bornkamm
H.T.R.	*The Harvard Theological Review*
J.B.L.	*Journal of Biblical Literature*
J.T.S.	*The Journal of Theological Studies*
N.T.S.	*New Testament Studies*
R.B.	*Revue Biblique*
S.L.A.	*Studies in Luke-Acts: Essays presented in honour of Paul Schubert,* ed. Leander E. Keck, J. Louis Martyn. Nashville, 1966: London, 1968
Th.Wb.z.N.T.	*Theologisches Wörterbuch zum Neuen Testament,* ed. Gerhard Kittel, G. Friedrich
T.U.	*Texte und Untersuchungen,* ed. O. von Gebhardt and A. von Harnack, etc.
Z.K.G.	*Zeitschrift für Kirchengeschichte*
Z.N.W.	*Zeitschrift für die neutestamentliche Wissenschaft*
Z.Th.K.	*Zeitschrift für Theologie und Kirche*

CHAPTER ONE

THE DATE OF ACTS

THE THEOLOGY of Acts is the primary concern of this book, but I want to begin by discussing the date of Acts because the assumptions we have about date and authorship affect the way we think about the theology. Not only that; as soon as these introductory matters are raised theological issues also begin to appear, and we shall soon discover that the only way now left to solve the problem about the date of Acts is to decide where its theological affinities lie.

Neither the theology of Acts nor the date of Acts can be considered apart from the theology and date of Luke's Gospel; "Luke-Acts", to use Cadbury's term, is one work in two volumes. Luke's Gospel has traditionally been held to provide evidence of a *terminus a quo* in its reference to the fall of Jerusalem in A.D. 70. The reference is in Luke 21.20–4, and this was supposed to be a revision of Mark 13.14–20. Immediately theological questions are at stake in the technical discussion about dates; if Luke (as we shall call the author of Luke-Acts without prejudicing the question of his identity) rewrote Mark to make Mark's words refer specifically to an event which had occurred since Jesus spoke, he is without doubt a constructive theologian providing an interpretation of the significance of the prophecies; if, however, he simply chose to employ an alternative source, the question of whether or not he was a theologian remains open, as we have no certain way of telling why he preferred one account to the other.

C. H. Dodd, in an influential article, has restated the arguments of Vincent Taylor and T. W. Manson that Luke did not base his version of the Apocalypse on Mark, and that there is no need to see in Luke any reference to the fall of Jerusalem.[1] He says that both passages, Luke 21.20–4 and Mark 13.14–20, "represent diverse forms which an oracle upon the fate of Jerusalem and the Temple assumed in the pre-canonical tradition, though in the Gospel as it stands the Lucan oracle has been supplemented out of Mark".[2] The heart of Dodd's argument is an attempt to demonstrate that Luke 21.20–4 is independent of Mark. First, he states that verses 21a and 23a were inserted later into the previously existing pattern of Luke's source. He argues that they both break up the sequence of rhythmical couplets; that 21a in Luke's final form is an inadmissible hanging τότε clause in asyndeton; that the αὐτῆς and αὐτήν of 21b must now refer to Judea but can only, according to the sense, refer to Jerusalem.[3] None of these points can be sustained. Verse 21 as it stands may not be a couplet, but it makes a perfectly admissible triplet, and verse 23a is irregular in the same way as verse 24a; in any case the alleged poetic structure of the passage, with or without these two sections, is not strongly marked and cannot be used as the basis of an argument. τότε clauses can stand by themselves quite naturally (cf. Luke 11.26; 21.27). There is no reason why αὐτῆς and αὐτήν should refer to the nearest noun; grammar allows what the sense demands. Second, Dodd argues that the verbal resemblances between verse 20 and Mark 13.14 are too slight to suggest that Mark was the source,[4] and that Luke was too well schooled in his LXX to see in the phrase from Daniel and 1 Maccabees, βδέλυγμα ἐρημώσεως, any reference to the idea of Jerusalem encircled by armies.[5] Against this, it would be surprising if these verbal parallels in the middle of a chapter which usually follows the order and often follows the wording of Mark should be entirely independent. If the chief

---

[1] C. H. Dodd, "The Fall of Jerusalem and the 'Abomination of Desolation'", *The Journal of Roman Studies*, xxxvii (1947), 47–54 repr. in *More N.T. Studies* (Manchester, 1968), 69–83; Vincent Taylor, *Behind the Third Gospel* (Oxford, 1926), 109–25; T. W. Manson, *The Sayings of Jesus* (London, 1949) (originally part of *The Mission and Message of Jesus*, 1937), 328–31.

[2] Dodd, op. cit., 49.   [3] Ibid., 48.   [4] Ibid., 48.
[5] Ibid., 53n.

differences could be explained by supposing that an editor knew that the predictions in Mark had not come to pass, that would be a stronger hypothesis than the complicated set of assumptions Dodd is forced to introduce: that two disconnected phrases from Mark were later inserted, so disturbing both rhythm and grammar, and that Luke suddenly abandoned Mark in favour of another source. All the differences between Luke and Mark in fact follow from Luke's historical standpoint after the fall of Jerusalem. He knew that the attempt to erect Gaius's image in the Temple had failed; he knew that the most important catastrophe in Jewish history had been the fall of Jerusalem in A.D. 70; and he knew that the catastrophe had not been the eschatological climax. It is in perfect accordance with the need to strip the fall of Jerusalem of any strict eschatological meaning that he omits Mark 13.15f and puts it in a context where it can teach that the End will be sudden and unpredictable (Luke 17.31).

The same purpose informs his rewriting of Mark 13.18–20. Dodd makes much of the fact that the references to the siege are vague and derived from the LXX, but this again accords with the assumption that an editor is at work who would avoid making predictions after the event too precise, and who regarded LXX language as the proper medium for prophecy. The very smoothness of the Lucan passage and the subtle allusions to the LXX, which Dodd adduces as reasons for believing that Luke is more primitive than the rough and disjointed Mark, are indications that Luke is later and derivative. Finally, even if Luke did possess the source which Dodd postulates, one must explain why he chose it in preference to Mark at this point; the most likely reason would seem to be that it referred better to the fall of Jerusalem.[1]

If Dodd's argument fails, we are left not only with the certainty that Luke-Acts was written after A.D. 70 but also with the certainty that the author of Luke-Acts had reflected deeply

[1] The Proto-Luke hypothesis, which holds that Luke had written one draft of his Gospel before he discovered Mark, is very doubtful. Luke's Gospel was almost certainly based on Mark from the start. See G. D. Kilpatrick, *J.T.S.*, xliii (1942), esp. 36; S. MacLean Gilmour, "A Critical Re-examination of Proto-Luke", *J.B.L.*, lxvii (1948), 143–52.

on the significance of the events of history since Jesus' death and resurrection, and on the significance of Jesus' eschatological teaching in the life of the Church.[1]

There is strictly no reason why that man should not have been Luke, the companion of Paul, "the beloved physician" (Col. 4.14; 2 Tim. 4.11; Philem. 24), but doubts do begin to arise. Paul's companion, we should expect, would primarily be concerned to transmit to a later generation the excitement of the earlier age when the Apostles were alive and when, perhaps, the hope of the end was still the hope of an imminent end. The Luke of Luke-Acts is, however, a reflective theologian who seems bent on equipping the Church to live in history.

It remains possible simply to accept the second-century tradition that the author of Acts was Luke, Paul's companion, but the doubts that have already been raised, together with Cadbury's reasons for believing that the Church tradition was no more than intelligent speculation based on the internal evidence of Acts alone,[2] lead us to turn to other arguments.

Two ways of dating Acts have been often discussed, but neither has been found universally convincing. The first seeks to show that Luke was dependent on the writings of Josephus, and the main difficulty about the argument is that it turns on the proposition that Luke has misread his source.[3] The second argument is that Acts so misrepresents Paul that it must have been written when accurate knowledge of Paul's life and work had been forgotten.

This is a far more persuasive line of approach, which has been recently restated in a careful way by Ernst Haenchen.[4]

[1] Hans Conzelmann, *Die Mitte der Zeit, Studien zur Theologie des Lukas* (Tübingen, 1954), Eng. tr., *The Theology of St Luke* (London, 1960); *J.T.S.*, N.S., x (1959), 6–9.

[2] *Beginnings*, ii.250–64. The "we"-sections of Acts, which were the basis for the Church tradition, were one source, or part of one source, used by the author of Acts; H. H. Wendt, "Die Hauptquelle der Apg.", *Z.N.W.*, 24 (1925), 293–305, esp. 294ff and 302f.

[3] *Beginnings*, ii.355–8; F. F. Bruce, New London Commentary on Acts (London, 1954), 125 and n 47.

[4] *Die Apostelgeschichte*, Kritisch-exegetischer Kommentar über das N.T. (10th ed., Göttingen, 1956), 102–6; (12th ed., 1959), 99–103.

The difficulty is that it depends on demonstrating a negative proposition, that the author of Acts could not have been Paul's companion, and this negative proposition is in danger of attack from two sides; it can be argued either that Luke did not understand the depths of his master's teaching, or else that he imposed on the account of Paul's activity his own theological interpretation, which was not always compatible with Paul's own views, differing at least in emphasis. Even if this negative proposition can be sustained, as I believe it can, we are not left with much guidance for the dating of Acts; all that can be asserted is that Acts was written some time after Paul's death, which in any case is rarely doubted.

The attempt will be made in this chapter to date Acts by discovering positive theological parallels between Luke-Acts and other early Christian writers. It depends on the assumption that, if it can be shown that two writers shared a whole range of presuppositions and were concerned about many of the same questions, then we may conclude that they belonged to the same generation, provided that one did not employ the other's writings. If this assumption is accepted, the discovery of close kinship between Luke-Acts and some other theologian's work, without literary dependence, will enable us to suggest the period in which Acts was composed.

It has, however, proved surprisingly difficult to discover any parallels to Acts. C. P. M. Jones[1] has drawn attention to the similarities between Luke-Acts and Hebrews in language, Christology, Eschatology, and a number of smaller points, and later we shall see some contacts between Acts and the Epistle of Barnabas, but neither of these books reflects Luke's chief interests. Neither attempts to tell the story of the early days in the life of the Church. "No contemporary and no writer before or after the writer of the canonical Acts had undertaken, as far as we know, to relate both the history of the first Christian Church and the decisive expansion of the Christian faith west-

---

[1] "The Epistle to the Hebrews and the Lucan Writings", *Studies in the Gospels: Essays in Memory of R. H. Lightfoot* (ed. D. E. Nineham, Oxford, 1955), 113-43.

wards in one consecutive narrative" (Dibelius).[1] Furthermore, to extend Dibelius's point, no Gospel writer, apart from Luke, has considered the history of the early days of the Church of comparable importance to the history of Jesus' life, death, and resurrection. Although Luke, when he was writing Acts, had no model to follow as he had had when he wrote his Gospel with Mark in front of him, he has done everything possible to give a similar structure to the Gospel and to Acts. As we shall see in more detail in Chapter Two, Acts is not simply a parallel to the Gospel, ending in Rome as the Gospel has ended in Jerusalem; if it was merely a parallel, it would inevitably be the less important part of Luke-Acts, a shadow of the Gospel original. But Acts is important in its own right as the logical completion of Jesus' journey to Jerusalem. The full significance of the central happenings at Jerusalem is not worked out in history until Paul has reached Rome. Our search for a theologian who shares Luke's presuppositions cannot end until we have found one who assumes that the missionary work of the Apostles is part of the salvation achieved by Jesus Christ in Jerusalem.

The nearest approach to Acts in the first century is in Clement of Rome's Epistle to the Corinthians. "But, to be done with the old examples, let us pass to more recent contenders; let us take the noble examples of our own generation. Because of bitter jealousy the greatest and most righteous pillars were persecuted and contended till death. Let us set before our eyes the good Apostles: Peter, who suffered not one or two but many trials because of evil jealousy and so made his witness and went to the place of glory he had earned. Because of contentious jealousy Paul demonstrated the reward for endurance: he was in bonds seven times; he was driven away; he was stoned; he was a preacher both in the East and in the West, and so he gained a nobler reputation for his faith. He taught the whole world righteousness, he came to the western goal and he made his witness before the rulers, so departing from the world and

---

[1] *Aufsätze zur Apg.* (Göttingen, 1951), 163; cf. 11, 108f, 166; (Eng. tr., London, 1956), 192; cf. 3, 123f, 195f.

being taken up into the holy place, the greatest example of endurance " (1 Clem. 5).

The point of this passage has been obscured by speculation about whether Clement is referring to the journey to Spain, which we know from Romans that Paul contemplated. If the phrase ἐπὶ τὸ τέρμα τῆς δύσεως ἐλθών does mean that Paul reached Spain, Clement is then implying that there was only one Roman visit, which occurred after the Spanish journey; like the writer of the Pastoral Epistles, he knows nothing of a release from prison in Rome, further journeys, and a new imprisonment.[1] Harrison's point that τὸ τέρμα is a very unnatural way to describe Spain (we should expect τέρματα) and that it is another of Clement's athletic metaphors, meaning the winning-post of a race, leads us to conclude that Clement is talking about Paul's arrival in Rome, and in Rome alone.[2] When he had completed his teaching mission, he came to Rome to witness to the rulers and to die a martyr's death.

Once this is established, the parallel with Acts becomes obvious. Clement is not explicit about the bitter jealousy which led to the martyrdom of Peter and Paul, but it seems that it came, in part at least, from the Jews who, more than any other group, had cause to be "jealous" of the Christians.[3] As we shall see in Chapter Three, Acts attributes all the misfortunes of the Church to Jewish opposition. Both Clement and Luke emphasize that wonderful results flowed from this "jealousy"; a witness was made and a glory attained. Both Clement and Acts put forward Peter and Paul as the leading examples, and both give Paul the pre-eminence. Clement knew that Peter was martyred in Rome, but he does not seem to have thought that the place of martyrdom was as important for Peter as it was for Paul, perhaps because Paul's martyrdom in Rome was the

---

[1] Conzelmann in Dibelius, *Die Pastoralbriefe*, *Hdb.z.N.T.* (3rd ed., Tübingen, 1955), 3; cf. K. Holl, *Gesammelte Aufsätze zur Kirchengeschichte*, (Tübingen, 1928), 65f, n 2.

[2] P. N. Harrison, *The Problem of the Pastoral Epistles* (Oxford, 1921), 107f.

[3] Cf. J. A. Fischer, *Die Apostolischen Väter* (Darmstadt, 1956), 33 n 49.

climax of a mission to the whole world (ὅλον τὸν κόσμον). (The reference to Peter's arrival at "the place of glory he had earned" is almost certainly not to the place where he was crucified; τόπος refers to "heaven" a few lines later (5.7), as also in John 14.2, cf. Acts 1.25.)[1] Luke simply ignores Peter's fate, though he must have been aware of the circumstances of his martyrdom, and he puts all the emphasis on Paul's arrival in Rome. He would agree with Clement that Paul's universal preaching (cf. Acts 19.10; 28.28), his arrival at Rome to be martyred, and his witness to the rulers (cf. Acts 9.15 and *passim*) were the most important features of his life. As Clement never quotes or alludes to Acts in his Epistle,[2] these affinities may be important for dating Acts.

The Pastoral Epistles stand in much the same relationship to Luke-Acts.[3] They share with Luke-Acts something of the same atmosphere (for instance, in the use of eschatology to inculcate a morality of steadfastness and temperance, and in emphasizing the importance of being in good standing with rulers). More important, they also assume the same estimation of the significance of Paul's work. Paul is again pictured as the model of perseverance and endurance (2 Tim. 3.10–12), and his arrival at Rome to defend himself before the Roman authorities marks, in some sense, the completion of the preaching to Gentiles. In the passage in question, 2 Tim. 4.16–18, Paul is pictured writing to Timothy from Rome during a break in the proceedings against him.[4] "When I was making my first

---

[1] Cf. the emphasis on Rome as the place of Paul's death in Eus., *H.E.*, ii.25.5; see H. Chadwick, "St Peter and St Paul in Rome etc.", *J.T.S.*, N.S., viii (1957), 31–52 at 44 n 3 for the opposite view.

[2] Haenchen, op. cit., 1f; *The N.T. in the Apostolic Fathers* (Oxford, 1905), 48–50.

[3] C. F. D. Moule, "The Problem of the Pastoral Epistles: A Reappraisal", *B.J.R.L.* 47 (1965), 430–52, has argued that Luke wrote the Pastorals during Paul's lifetime at Paul's behest, and *in part* at Paul's dictation.

[4] The traditional assumption has been, on the basis of 2 Tim. 1.17, that these words were written from Rome. There are difficulties in the way, such as the length of time that has elapsed before the books and cloak are claimed from Troy (4.13) and before Timothy is told of poor Trophimus's illness (4.20), but discrepancies of this sort seem easier to explain in a pseudonymous writing than the blatant contradiction between the assumption of a

defence, no one stood by me. They all left me. (May it not be laid to their charge.) But the Lord came to my aid and strengthened me so that the preaching might be brought to its completion through me and all the Gentiles hear, and I was delivered from the lion's mouth. The Lord will deliver me from every evil thing and will bring me safely into his heavenly kingdom; to whom be glory for ever. Amen."

Contrary to the usual view, it is unlikely that the writer of the Pastoral Epistles knew and used Luke-Acts.[1] If that is so, the Pastoral Epistles may, like 1 Clement, reasonably be supposed to belong to the same period in the Church's life as Acts. But in this case we have an almost certain indication that the Pastorals were written after Luke-Acts: the Pastorals are dependent on a thorough and continuous use of the Pauline collection of letters,[2] and Luke seems to have known none of them.[3] All that we may deduce concerning the date of Acts from the theological affinity between the two sets of books is that Luke-Acts can hardly have been written long before the Pauline collection was published (if that is the right way to describe what hap-

---

Caesarean provenance for 4.9–21 and the explicit mention of Rome in 1.17. The final clause in 4.17 looks forward not to a Spanish journey but to the completion of Paul's defence before the judges and his martyrdom (cf. 4.6–8); he has been delivered from the lion's mouth in the same sense as Christ Jesus was (Psalm 22 and 2 Tim. 2.11), and his salvation through death is certain. If it is still maintained that the author of the Pastorals meant us to understand that these words were written from Caesarea, the completion of the preaching, that all the Gentiles might hear, is still Rome, the city where Paul is to be martyred. See Conzelmann, op. cit., 94–6, where the case for Caesarea is argued; Harrison's theory that this is a genuine fragment is convincingly met by Conzelmann, 4.

[1] The quotation of the saying, "The labourer deserves his wages" in 1 Tim. 5.18 may be taken from Luke 10.7, but it is strange that the one saying of Jesus to be quoted in the Pastorals, and to be quoted as Scripture, should look so much like a common saying put into the Lord's mouth in Luke; see Conzelmann, op. cit., 62. Again, if 2 Tim. 3.11 is a summary of Acts 13.50; 14.5,19, it is strange that the writer of the Pastorals refers only to the parts of Acts where Paul is in Timothy's native area and not to those parts where Timothy was Paul's companion, Acts 16 and 17; Conzelmann, ibid., 89. 2 Tim. 4.20 seems to contradict the information about Trophimus we gather from Acts 20 and 21, especially 21.29.

[2] P. N. Harrison, op. cit., 167–75.   [3] See below, 22 and Chapter Four.

pened), since it has in common with the Pastorals, which were written after that publication, both a general theological point of view and an estimation of the significance of Paul's work.

Clement, Luke, and the author of the Pastorals agree in assuming a certain significance in the history of salvation for Paul's martyrdom in Rome. But neither Clement nor the "Pastor" did what Luke has done, and made the story of Paul an integral part of the central event, the life and death and resurrection of Jesus Christ. For that reason the assumption they share must be judged an important but minor part of Luke's theology. As we shall see in Chapter Two, the fact that Paul's martyrdom is never actually described in Acts indicates that he wished to subordinate the human example of Paul to the central event of salvation which occurred in Jerusalem. In this way he made the second part of his work an integral part of the first, rather than an appendix. The early history of the Church was put beside the Gospel history on equal terms, and so the whole journey from Galilee to Jerusalem and from Jerusalem to Rome was seen as the determinative period in the history of salvation. Clement and the "Pastor's" estimation of Paul's work seems to be accepted by Luke, but he has given it a further significance in the history of salvation which we do not find in them.

The first writer, apart from Luke, to assume that the world mission of the Apostles should be told in the same breath as the history of Jesus' death, resurrection, and ascension is Justin Martyr.[1] In the Apology he writes, "After his crucifixion even all his friends deserted, and denied him. But later, when he rose from the dead and appeared to them, he taught them to

---

[1] In Matthew the world mission is commanded, not related. Marcion's name should also be mentioned here. By publishing his "Gospel" and "Apostle", he linked together the work of Jesus with the work of his Apostle in the same way as Luke and Justin; cf. John Knox, *Marcion and the N.T.* (Chicago, 1942), chap. v. An important anticipation of the same link is found in 1 Cor. 15.1–11; see Peder Borgen, "Von Paulus zu Lukas: Beobachtungen zur Erhellung der Theologie der Lukasschriften", *Studia Theologica*, 20 (1966), 140–57 at 154f. Niels Hyldahl, *Philosophie und Christentum: Eine Interpretation der Einleitung zum Dialog Justins* (Copenhagen, 1966), 261–72, gives an outstanding account of the close theological relationship between Justin and Luke.

read the prophecies in which all these things that had happened were foretold. They saw him return to heaven and believed and, when they had received power which he sent from heaven to them, they went to every nation of men and taught these things, and were called 'Apostles'" (50.12; cf. Dial. 53.5). The missionary activity of the Apostles "from Jerusalem" is as much part of the history of salvation as the work of Jesus. The mission of the Apostles was also foretold in the O.T. To prove this Justin quotes Isa. 2.3f and writes, "And there is evidence to convince you (Trypho) that this has come to pass: for men, twelve in number, went out from Jerusalem into the world; they were uneducated (ἰδιῶται) and not good speakers, but by God's power they made known to every nation of men how they had been sent by the Messiah to teach to all the Word of God . . ." (Apol. 39.2f; cf. 42.4; 45.5; 49.5; 50.12; 53.3; 61.9; 67.3; Dial. 109.1; 110.2).

There are many more parallels, but enough have been given to show that the writer of Acts and Justin share an important theological point of view. Without this theological understanding of the connection between the work of Christ and the work of the Apostles, Luke-Acts would be inconceivable.

This concurrence at a crucial point is backed by a number of other theological and factual agreements. The first passage quoted from Justin, Apol. 50.12, provides evidence of a detailed theology of Jesus' resurrection which in the N.T. is peculiar to Luke-Acts. With it should be compared Dialogue 53.5; 106.1; the chief Lucan passages to compare are Luke 24.25–7 and 44–6. The agreements may be summarized in six points. First, Luke and Justin state that the chief business of the risen Messiah was to persuade the Apostles that his suffering was foretold; in Justin this persuasion is all the more necessary because, after the crucifixion, they had not only deserted but had all denied him.[1] Second, they both greatly elaborate and

---

[1] A. Ritschl, *Das Evangelium Marcions und das kanonische Evangelium des Lukas* (Tübingen, 1846), 150, notes that this is foreign to the canonical gospels. Perhaps it is simply an extension of Mark 14.27,50 and Peter's denial; there may be traces of post-crucifixion denial in the road to Emmaus story.

illustrate the primitive statement that all that had happened
was "according to the Scriptures", and the discovery of relevant passages plays a central part in the theology of both
writers (cf. also Heb. and 2 Pet.). Third, they both state that
during the resurrection discussion Jesus referred back to his
own predictions of suffering (Dial. 53.5; 106.1; a minor point,
and partially paralleled in the angel's words, Mark 16.7).
Fourth, both explicitly record Jesus' ascension (see also Dial.
108.2). Fifth, both state that after the ascension the Apostles
received power from above. Sixth, in both it is said that the
Apostles went into all the world to teach what Jesus had persuaded them was true; in both Luke and Justin this is principally the fulfilment of O.T. prophecy in the events of Jesus'
passion. None of these points, taken singly, is exactly paralleled
elsewhere in the N.T.; that not only the individual points but
also the same combination should be found in Justin is a most
remarkable coincidence. The coincidence is even more significant for our purpose because this theology of the work of Christ
is found at the centre of Luke-Acts and is presupposed throughout, particularly in the speeches in Acts.

A further significant similarity between the two writers is
found in their attitude to Jews and Gentiles. In Acts, as in
Luke's Gospel,[1] it is assumed that the Jews have officially
rejected the gospel and that the Gentiles will receive it[2]—or at
least Luke believes that the Gentiles can be persuaded to receive
the gospel, and he insists that they show no ineradicable opposition to it. That the same position is fundamental in Justin is
shown by the fact that he writes an Apology for the Romans but a

[1] See, for example, the first Amen saying in Luke (Luke 4.24); "The Six
Amen Sayings in Luke", *J.T.S.*, N.S., x (1959), 2–4.
[2] Jacob Jervell, "Das gespaltene Israel und die Heidenvölker: Zur
Motivierung der Heidenmission in der Apg.", *Studia Theologica*, 19 (1965),
68–96, argues that there is no connection in Luke's mind between the
rejection of the gospel by Jews and the Gentile mission (see Chapter Three,
below), but he does nevertheless conclude that "the Apostles have completed
the Jewish mission. They have gathered the repentant Israel and given the
Gentiles a share in the salvation to be received from God's repentant people
... After the ending of the Jewish mission, there began the time of the
Gentile mission, and this time is the time of Luke", ibid., 95.

Dialogue with a Jew.[1] "The Jews", he says, "had the prophecies and were ever expecting the Messiah to be at hand; they
not only failed to recognize him but also ill-treated him. But
the Gentiles, who had never heard anything about the Messiah
until the Apostles came from Jerusalem and told them about
him and imparted the prophecies, were filled with joy and
faith and said farewell to idols and dedicated themselves to the
unbegotten God through the Messiah" (Apol. 49.5). We could
hardly find a clearer statement of one of the leading themes in
Acts: how the Church discovered its proper place in the
Gentile world.

We should conclude by noting six coincidences in detail
between Justin's works and Acts. First, Justin argues from a
Psalm of David to Jesus in the same way as Peter argues at
Pentecost (Acts 2.25–32): "And again in other words, through
another prophet, he (the Spirit) says, 'They pierced my hands
and feet, and cast lots for my clothing.' Now David, the King
and Prophet, who said these things, suffered none of them;
but Jesus Christ stretched out his hands and was crucified by
the Jews who reviled him and denied that he was the
Messiah" (Apol. 35.5,6).[2] Second, both note that the Apostles
were uneducated (ἰδιῶται: Acts 4.13; Apol. 39.3). Third, both
employ the common idea, probably going back to Socrates,
"It is necessary to obey God rather than men" (Acts 5.29;
4.19; Dial. 80.3; 1 Clem. 14.1; 2 Clem. 4.4).[3] Fourth, in Justin
and Acts (and in Ignatius) we find it explicitly stated that Jesus
both "ate and drank" with his disciples after his resurrection
(Acts 10.41; Dial. 51.2; Smyrn. 3.3).

[1] F. Overbeck, "Ueber das Verhältniss Justins des Martyrers zur Apg.",
Zeitschrift fur wissenschaftliche Theologie, xv (Leipzig, 1872), 305–49 at 342:
"So in point of fact it seems that, to Justin, the enmity of the Gentiles and
their government to Christians was something which was scarcely explicable, which was only grudgingly recognized, and which one hoped still to
change (which is, of course, the aim of the Apologies). On the other hand
the antagonism shown by the Jews against Christians is, as it were, a natural
growth; one cannot expect it to be overcome before the end of the present
world-order with Christ's return."

[2] Ibid., 347.

[3] *Beginnings*, iv.45.

Fifth, Justin provides a clue to the riddle of "the Unknown God" in Acts 17.23. It is doubtful whether there was an actual inscription in Athens in the singular but, whatever the historical facts, the widespread literary tradition was that there was an altar in Athens dedicated to "the Unknown Gods".[1] Luke's apologetic purpose would be thwarted if his educated non-Christian readers should at any point in the speech have cause to suspect that Paul was arguing from an assumption which the Athenians did not accept. If the speech was to retain its effectiveness, Luke must have been able to count on his audience accepting the premise that the Athenians (and therefore all men of a philosophical temper) had at least entertained belief in an "Unknown God". Justin Martyr supplies evidence that Christian apologists were able to appeal to such a belief, although his argument is based on the writings of Plato rather than on an inscription. After pointing out that Socrates was accused of the same crime as Christians, that of introducing new divinities, he writes, "But he taught men to escape from wicked demons and those who did what the poets related, and he drove out of the state Homer and the other poets. Instead, he exhorted them to seek full knowledge, by the exercise of reason, of God who was unknown to them (πρὸς θεοῦ δὲ τοῦ ἀγνώστου αὐτοῖς διὰ λόγου ζητήσεως ἐπίγνωσιν προύτρέπετο), saying, 'It is not easy to find the Father and Maker of all nor when he is found is it safe to tell everyone'" (Appendix to the Apology, the so-called Second Apology, 10.6). There is no sign that Justin is here dependent on Acts. One may suspect, without being able to demonstrate it, that Luke used this sort of apologetic argument as one of his starting points in constructing the speech at Athens; he has dramatized the argument by supposing, on the basis of the current story that the Athenians had sacrificed to Unknown Gods, that the

---

[1] K. Lake, *Beginnings*, v.240–6; and B. Gärtner, *The Areopagus Speech and Natural Revelation* (Uppsala, 1955) set out the evidence. It is unlikely that the words of Diogenes Laertius refer to any particular altar inscription; the patristic evidence gives strong support to the general tradition that the Athenians had altars dedicated to "the Unknown Gods".

traditional Platonic monotheism had found expression in an
altar "to the Unknown God". Whether or not this hypothesis
can be sustained, it remains significant that both Luke and
Justin appeal to an Athenian belief in the Unknown God.[1]

Finally, we find in Justin's Dialogue with Trypho 39.4 a
dramatic device similar to that which Luke employs when Festus
intervenes in Paul's speech to Agrippa (Acts 26.25). Trypho
accuses Justin of being beside himself, to which Justin replies,
"Listen, my friend, I am not mad or beside myself", before
continuing his argument. This seems to be a stock apologetic
situation which, no doubt, occurred often enough, but which
may have been a common ingredient in the accounts of debates
held between Christians and unbelievers. It is possible that it
goes back to Paul, but Justin seems to be unaware of any such
association.

In none of these six cases is there any indication that Justin
was dependent on Acts. He makes no reference to the context
in which the statements occur in Acts, and he often uses as his
own the ideas which are ascribed by Acts to Paul and the
Apostles (in the first, third, fifth, and sixth examples above).

The case for literary dependence rests on an examination of
Apol. 50.12, which has been quoted above. Haenchen holds
that this passage proves that Justin knew Acts. "The substance
of Luke 23.49a is cited in the account of the passion story;
Luke 24.25,44f is clearly employed; and the ascension and
gift of the Spirit are reported with verbal reminiscence of Acts
1.8, δύναμιν . . . λαβόντες corresponding to the λήμψεσθε
δύναμιν of Acts."[2] Against this argument there are three
objections. First, Luke 23.49a, apart from the fact that it
uses γνωστοί and not γνώριμοι for Jesus' followers, does not
say or imply that the disciples deserted Jesus and denied him,

[1] See now Chapter Six.
[2] Haenchen, op. cit., 7. Cadbury in his review of Haenchen, *J.B.L.*,
lxxvi (1957), 65, doubts Haenchen's case; see also *The Book of Acts in
History* (London, 1955), 157. H. F. D. Sparks, *J.T.S.*, n.s. xiv (1963), 465f
and Hyldahl, op. cit., 262, support Haenchen's position without further
argument.

as Justin does. Second, the only pair of words common to Luke-Acts and Justin in this passage is δύναμιν λαβόντες. In Acts these words are spoken by Jesus, and it is incredible that Justin should reproduce as his own comment words which were attributed to the Lord in his source. Finally, it is surprising, if Justin knew Acts 2, that he neglected to say that this "power" was the power of the Holy Spirit. There is no evidence that Justin cited Acts or even knew of its existence.

In his discussion of this passage, Overbeck comes to the conclusion that, if it is a citation at all, it is a citation of Luke's Gospel and not of Acts. Despite the absence of evidence, however, he is compelled to hold that Justin knew Acts. "It is impossible to imagine", he writes, "that a man in Justin's position, who made use of Luke's Gospel, could not know something of a book which originally formed the continuation of the Gospel, or at least purported to be its continuation."[1]

There are at least three answers to Overbeck's dilemma. The first is his own. He argues that Justin knew Acts but deliberately rejected it because he had succumbed to Jewish propaganda against Paul and because he was engaged in answering Marcion. Only in this way can he reconcile the fact of the enormous area of agreement between the two writers, in their attitude to heathen culture, to the Jews, and to the Romans, with the determined avoidance of Acts by Justin.[2] The weakness of Overbeck's case is that nowhere does Justin explicitly argue against those Christians who presumably espoused the book. He was not afraid of mentioning differing groups and sects within the Church, but he completely ignores Acts and those who read and treasured it.

The second way out is to suppose that Acts acquired canonical status much later than Luke's Gospel, and was ignored until its association with the third Gospel ensured it a place in the canonical collection.[3] The question at once arises, however, of why Acts should be ignored and the Gospel recognized. There seems to be no reason why Acts should have been judged

---

[1] Op. cit., 316.   [2] Ibid., 343 and *passim*.
[3] Haenchen, op. cit., 7, following Dibelius.

useless for preaching and teaching; if it had no special authority, it was at least edifying, interesting, and relevant to the life
of the Church. If Justin knew of it at all, his own special interests would surely have led him to quote from it or draw on it
in some other way. Despite the weaknesses of the second
argument, however, we should probably have to accept it if no
other possibility could be found.

The third way out of Overbeck's dilemma is to deny his
major premise, that Justin knew Luke's Gospel. The fact that
Justin makes no use of Acts then becomes perfectly explicable;
as he did not know Luke's Gospel, there is no need to be
puzzled by the evidence that he did not use Acts. An Appendix
is devoted to the detailed discussion necessary to prove this
point. The fact that he makes no *use* of Luke, which is all that
is proved in the Appendix, indicates that he had never *known*
Luke; as he at times harmonizes two sources, Matthew and his
other Gospel, he would probably not have objected to harmonizing a third, if it was available. Should it be maintained that
Justin *knew* both Luke and Acts but deliberately ignored them,
the case we are about to put forward would stand: the similarities between Luke-Acts and Justin's writings could still not
be explained on the basis of direct literary influence, but only
on the basis of a common background of ideas. It remains
much more probable that Justin failed to use Luke and Acts
because he had never read them.

Given these two propositions (1) that there is a close similarity in the basic theology of Luke and Justin, as well as in
minor matters like the sort of apologetic arguments they use
and (2) that neither has read the writings of the other, we have
good reason to conclude that they belong to the same generation. Harnack's dating of Justin's Apology and Dialogue is
generally accepted. The Apology (which is one work with an
appendix, not two) he puts "a few years after 150", and the
Dialogue between 150 and 160; he believes that Justin became
a Christian about A.D. 133.[1] I think that these dates are rather

---

[1] *Geschichte der Altchristlichen Literatur bis Eusebius*, Part ii, *Die Chronologie*
(2nd ed., Leipzig, 1897, repr. 1958), 274–84.

late, and that the Apology might well have been written either in the first year of Antoninus Pius's reign (July 138–July 139) as the omission of "Caesar" in Marcus's title in the dedication seems to indicate, or in the first three or four years of the same reign (not later than July 142) as Eusebius maintained in his *Chronicon*,[1] but, whatever the conclusion, Justin's "generation", the generation which formed and shared his Christian theology, can hardly have flourished earlier than about A.D. 115 or later than about A.D. 170. Luke probably wrote Luke-Acts at some time during this period.[2] It is very unlikely that he wrote earlier than 115; he probably wrote some time after this date, because the earlier Luke-Acts was written, the more likely it is that Justin would have heard of the work.

If we can determine the first witness to the existence of Luke's Gospel, we shall be able to put forward an upper dating, and to fix the composition of Luke-Acts within narrower limits. Some scholars have argued that Papias knew Luke's Gospel,[3] but this is an argument from silence. Papias mentions only the traditions about the composition of the Gospels

[1] Ibid., ii.29,57f. Harnack once argued from Justin's silence about Marcion's residence in Rome that Marcion had not yet arrived when the Apology was written; ibid., ii.277 and n 2. That, of course, would conflict with the dating of the Apology which he later adopted (ii.276ff) but, as his case for this dating stands and falls on the assumption that Marcus Aurelius had to be in full philosophical flight and that Lucius, the other person mentioned in the dedication, had to be rather more than eight years old before he could receive a dedication (whereas he seems to be included simply because he was son of the *philosopher*-emperor Aelius Verus as well as adopted son of Antoninus Pius; ibid., ii.280), the late dating is not as obvious as has often been thought. The Appendix to the Apology (the so-called Second Apology) contains a number of indications of a later date, but it is by no means certain that it was first published at the same time as the (First) Apology. J. A. Cramer, *Theologische Studiën*, ix (1891), 317–57; 402–36, has argued that the (First) Apology was written about 140 and the Appendix about 152. He shows, to my mind convincingly, that the references to Marcion in Apol. 26.5 and 58.1–3 were later interpolations; op. cit., 323–33.

[2] Hyldahl, op. cit., 271f, affirms the affinity, but still asserts that there was a temporal distance between Justin and Luke.

[3] Jülicher-Fascher, *Einleitung*, (7th ed., Tübingen, 1931), 312; Westcott; Walter Bauer.

according to Matthew and Mark (Eus., *H.E.*, iii.39.15f), and it is precarious to argue that he omitted Luke because he disapproved of the author's association with St Paul.

With Justin eliminated, the next possible witness to Luke's Gospel is Marcion, who traditionally is supposed to have put forward a drastically edited edition of Luke as "The Gospel". It has, however, been doubted whether Marcion did indeed employ Luke's Gospel, and John Knox has revived the theory that Marcion was using the shorter Gospel which was later expanded into our canonical Luke.[1] There seem to be three preliminary objections which can be made to this theory. First, an objection Knox himself tries to meet.[2] If Luke, and therefore Acts, was edited to meet the claims of Marcion, the fact that Acts makes no use of the Pauline epistles, which Marcion had also edited, becomes even more difficult to explain than before. At any time before Marcion it is conceivable that the Pauline collection could have been unknown to the author of Acts, but after Marcion this becomes almost impossible. I cannot believe that he deliberately ignored Paul's letters.

Second, if Luke's Gospel was finally expanded and edited after Marcion, the Marcionite Christians would be perfectly well aware of the fact. The orthodox defence of the four Gospels as ancient and apostolic would be open to such an obvious rebuttal that it is difficult to imagine it being made in this form at all. If such a defence was possible, then the obvious Marcionite objection cannot have been possible; there is no reason to doubt the statement made from Irenaeus onwards that Marcion's Gospel was based on the Gospel of Luke.

Third, every process of editing a Gospel about which we possess evidence has involved the shortening of the source. Matthew and Luke have each omitted some incidents and sayings from Mark. Knox admits that Marcion, who on his theory was using an earlier and shorter edition of the canonical Luke, omitted some parts of this short edition. It would be very

---

[1] *Marcion and the N.T.; An Essay in the Early History of the Canon* (Chicago, 1942), esp. chap. iv.
[2] Op. cit., 132–9.

3

surprising, then, if Knox's later editor, in producing the canonical Luke, had not omitted something from the shorter Gospel which was his (and Marcion's) source; if he did omit any parts, they would probably be among those which Marcion retained. We should expect, on Knox's theory, that Marcion's Gospel would contain some incidents or sayings which are not found in our present edition of Luke. The fact that Marcion's Gospel (as far as it can be recovered) contains no saying or incident which is not in Luke, in one form or another, counts against Knox's thesis.

There is, however, an important fact about Marcion's Gospel which lends powerful support to the theory Knox has revived, and which the usual interpretation underestimates. A large number of Marcion's changes seem to have no doctrinal motive, and this raises difficulties for a theory which ascribed the changes to an arbitrary desire to alter Jesus' words to fit a particular theological point of view. If a number of important differences between Marcion's Gospel and our form of Luke's Gospel cannot be explained as alterations which Marcion might make in Luke to suit his own theology, it becomes much more of an open question whether Marcion had altered Luke or Luke Marcion. For the reasons given, it still seems more likely that Marcion had altered our Luke, but the investigation of Justin's Gospel sources suggests another answer to the problem. In two cases we have found that Marcion's version of Luke, while retaining traces of the Lucan framework, agrees with Justin.[1] As Justin seems here to be employing his special Gospel source (a source which was probably used by Luke), we should probably conclude that Marcion is editing Luke by means of this older source. Some of the differences between Luke's Gospel and Marcion's version may be due to Marcion's use of sources which he believed were more reliable, in order to correct Luke.

This last point is important for estimating the lowest possible interval between the composition of Luke and the issuing of

[1] The two cases are Luke 10.22; Dial. 100.1; and Luke 18.18f; Apol. 16.7; Dial. 101.2; see Appendix 1 and Tables IV and X.

Marcion's Gospel. Assuming that Marcion's Gospel was published early in the 140's, and that it was a revision of Luke's Gospel, we should be able to fix a time after which Luke could not have been written. On one view of Marcion's work, he has selected the established Gospel which suited his purpose best and arbitrarily changed it whenever he wished. But it is not necessary to hold that Marcion was trying to produce an uncorrupted version of Luke's Gospel as such; it is more likely that he intended to produce a pure version of the most authentic Gospel possible. It is not necessary, that is, to assume that Luke had attained any sort of canonical acceptance: indeed, there is no evidence that any of the Gospels were quoted with canonical authority by this date.[1] We do not know why Marcion chose Luke's Gospel as the basis of his own, but his silence about Lucan authorship is evidence against the theory that he chose it because he believed it was the work of St Paul's companion.[2] There is therefore no need to assume that Marcion's use of Luke implies that Luke has been in circulation for a long time or that it had any strong ecclesiastical authority. Luke-Acts need not have been written very long before A.D. 140. On the other hand we are required to allow at least time for it to have become fairly well known and respected in Christian circles, time for it to have gained the sort of following which would justify Marcion in making it the basis of a new edition. It is hard to imagine this condition being fulfilled if Luke-Acts had been issued less than ten years before Marcion's edition, and we suggest very tentatively that Luke could not have been written later than A.D. 130.

The *terminus a quo* for Luke-Acts is about A.D. 115 and the *terminus ad quem* is about A.D. 130, but the naming of these dates gives an air of precision to the case which is scarcely warranted. More important than the dates are the arguments, that Luke and Justin Martyr held common theological positions without being dependent on each other, and that

[1] H. Köster, *Synoptische Überlieferung bei den Apostolischen Vätern*, *T.U.*, v.10 (=65.Band) (Berlin, 1957).

[2] Cf. H. J. Cadbury, *The Book of Acts in History* (London, 1955), 145f.

Luke-Acts was completed in time for Luke to be used by Marcion.

There remains one important objection to dating Luke-Acts late enough to be part of a theological movement still represented in the writings of Justin Martyr. The writer of Acts seems to know nothing of Paul's Epistles.[1] Some critics have detected traces of influence of the Epistles, but if Luke knew anything at all of any one of them he would almost certainly have made a great deal of use of it, and have looked for others; only slight dependence means no dependence. Luke-Acts must, then, belong to an age when Paul's letters were not generally known. Largely as a result of the work of E. J. Goodspeed, it is now coming to be accepted that the Pauline letters were rescued from obscurity and "published" as a collection about A.D. 90.[2] If Goodspeed's thesis is accepted, Luke-Acts cannot be later than about A.D. 90.[3]

Without entering into a full discussion of Goodspeed's theory, some arguments against this early dating for the formation of the corpus should be mentioned. Goodspeed seems to be on firm ground when he denies Harnack's theory of the gradual building up of the collection of letters, but he has probably placed the date of "publication" too soon.

In attempting to show that "the letters of Paul had disappeared from Christian consciousness" at the time the synoptic Gospels were written and that they suddenly reappeared in all the Christian writings after A.D. 90, Goodspeed and his supporters are forced to rely on an argument from silence. "If failure to quote from a Pauline letter proved ignorance of it, the evidence of the Apostolic Fathers would support Lake and Harrison in the claim that partial collections existed in different centres, before the complete Corpus was formed. It does not, however, prove this. Any one of the

---

[1] This assertion is supported at greater length in Chapter Four below.

[2] E. J. Goodspeed, *An Introduction to the New Testament* (Chicago, 1937), etc. For a favourable British report see C. L. Mitton, *The Formation of the Pauline Corpus of Letters* (London, 1955).

[3] E.g., Haenchen, op. cit. (10th ed.), 106 (not in the 12th ed.); Conzelmann, *Die Apostelgeschichte, Hdb.z.N.T.* (Tübingen, 1963), 2.

Apostolic Fathers may have known all ten epistles without happening to reflect more than one or two."[1] This argument is true as far as it goes: the silence of an Apostolic Father about any of the letters of Paul does not necessarily prove that he did not know it. But we must go on to ask whether there is other evidence to settle the question one way or the other.

The three Apostolic Fathers who particularly concern us are Clement of Rome, Ignatius, and Polycarp. The evidence of the way they use Paul's Epistles suggests that the first two knew only some of them and that Polycarp knew all of them. First, the conclusions of the Committee of the Oxford Society of Historical Theology which investigated the question in 1905 point in this direction.[2] They have classified the degree of probability that an author should have known each book of the N.T. by using the letters A to D, class A at one end indicating that there could be "no reasonable doubt", and class D at the other that "the evidence appeared too uncertain to allow any reliance to be placed upon it".[3] The evidence for the use of Paul's ten epistles by the three authors we are considering may be set out as follows.[4]

	A	B	C	D
1 Clement	Rom. 1 Cor.	—	—	2 Cor. Gal. Eph. Phil. Col.
Ignatius	1 Cor.	Eph.	Rom. 2 Cor.? Gal. Phil.	Col. 1, 2 Thess.? Philem.?
Polycarp	1 Cor.	Rom. 2 Cor. Gal. Eph. Phil. 2 Thess.	—	Col.

On the face of it, this table indicates that there is a high probability that 1 Clement knew Romans and 1 Corinthians and

[1] Mitton, op. cit., 23.   [2] *The N.T. in the Apostolic Fathers* (Oxford, 1905).
[3] Ibid., Preface.   [4] Ibid., 137.

that Ignatius knew 1 Corinthians (and Ephesians?), and a con-
siderably lower probability that they knew the rest; there is a
distinct contrast between the force of the evidence that they
knew one or two epistles and the evidence that they knew the
others, especially in 1 Clement. For Polycarp, on the other hand,
the probability is high that he knew a large number of the
epistles, as most of the evidence is concentrated under categories
A and B, and it shows that he used seven out of the ten.

Second, the manner in which these writers refer to the
Epistles offers some indication of whether they knew the whole
collection or only one or two of the letters.

Clement of Rome refers specifically to 1 Corinthians in his
own letter to the Corinthians. He writes, "Take up the epistle of
blessed Paul the Apostle" (1 Clem. 47.1). If Clement and the
Corinthians had recently witnessed the rediscovery and publication of a collection of Paul's epistles, it seems likely that
Clement would have made his reference to 1 Corinthians more
explicit. He would probably have written something like,
"Take up *your* epistle of Paul." The method he used to refer to
1 Corinthians implies that the Corinthians possessed only one
of Paul's epistles (or one limited group of epistles, those
addressed to them). Similarly, if Paul's letters had recently
been published in a collection, one would expect Clement to
acknowledge any extended quotation from them. Instead,
Romans 1.29–32 is incorporated into 1 Clement 35.5 with no
indication of its source. (The argument is weakened, but not
demolished, if both writers are making independent use of a
common list of vices.)

The one explicit reference to the epistles of Paul in Ignatius
shows the same features. In his letter to the Ephesians, 12.2, he
refers to "Paul . . . who in every epistle mentions you in Christ
Jesus".[1] Paul only mentioned the Ephesians in 1 Cor. 15.32
and 16.8, and this is the one Pauline epistle which it is extremely probable that Ignatius knew.[2] Ignatius's statement

---

[1] See W. Bauer, *Hdb.z.N.T.*, *Ergänzungsband* (Tübingen, 1920), 212.
[2] Cf. the references in Eph.; 1 Tim. 1.3; 2 Tim. 1.16ff; 4.19f.

is pardonable exaggeration only in the writing of a man who knew in general that Paul wrote a number of letters and that he spent some time in Ephesus, without knowing much more; the inaccuracy is extremely difficult to understand in the work of a man who had read the great new collection of Paul's letters, published in his life-time.

When we turn to the epistle of Polycarp, an entirely different picture meets us. Not only are Ephesians, Galatians, 1 Corinthians (and 1 Timothy) explicitly cited but a standard citation formula is employed: εἰδότες ὅτι (1.3; 4.1; 5.1; cf. 9.2; 11.2; 12.1). The use of such a formula implies that the recipients of Polycarp's letter could verify the references for themselves, that they possessed a collection of Paul's letters. "It appears that the collection of the Epistles of Paul was as good as closed by II Polycarp, something that it was not possible to say for Ignatius. . . . Polycarp also assumes that the recipients in Philippi know the collection and recognize it."[1]

If Polycarp is the first of the Fathers to use a published collection of Paul's letters, we are now in a position to suggest a date for the formation of the corpus. P. N. Harrison[2] has put forward a persuasive case for regarding the first twelve chapters of Polycarp's epistle as a later composition. Chiefly on the basis of a reference to Marcion in 7.1 (cf. Eus., H.E., iv.14.7; Iren. iii.3.4), he dates this second letter about A.D. 135.[3]

---

[1] J. A. Fischer, Die Apostolischen Väter (Darmstadt, 1956), 239.

[2] Polycarp's Two Epistles to the Philippians (Cambridge, 1936).

[3] Fischer, op. cit., 234–8, accepts the two-fold division of the epistle, but argues for a date for 2 Polyc. one or two years after 1 Polyc. Peter Meinhold, Article "Polykarpos", Pauly-Wissowa, Realencyclopädie der classischen Altertumswissenschaft, 42. Halbband (Stuttgart, 1952), coll. 1662–93 at 1681–8, supports Harrison's argument that the second letter to the Philippians was written long after the first, as an answer to Marcion. He agrees with Harrison in placing this attack on Marcion after the famous encounter between the two men, which, he argues, occurred in Asia Minor and before Marcion reached Rome. While agreeing that "2 Phil." is an attack on Marcion, I am not sure that it is possible to date it so precisely; it may well have been written later, when Marcion's break with Rome made his threat to the Church's life far clearer and when it was necessary to show that the leaders of the orthodox church made no claim to rival "the wisdom of the blessed and glorious Paul" (Polyc., ad Phil., 3.2).

On the basis of this argument it is no longer necessary to suppose that Luke-Acts must have been written before A.D. 95. Since the first witness to the existence of the Pauline corpus is the second epistle of Polycarp, about A.D. 135, the author of Luke-Acts could still have written in ignorance of Paul's letters between A.D. 115 and 130, the limiting dates which were suggested earlier.

But, it might be asked, is it really possible that the author of Acts could have failed to discover and use at least one of Paul's letters if he was working not long after Clement and Ignatius had used Romans and 1 Corinthians? The Pauline corpus may not yet have been published and made widely known, but is it conceivable that Luke should have been unable to use some of the letters—if indeed he wrote as late as this?

These are difficult questions, but there is evidence that it could have been possible for such a late writer not to have had access to even one Pauline epistle. This possibility existed because there was no universal interest in the work of Paul and because a church which still treasured one of his letters would probably have felt no need to send copies of it to other churches. Proof and illustration is found in the writings of Justin Martyr.

Justin almost certainly wrote after the Pauline collection was published, and not only does he never quote Paul but he never even mentions him. Attempts have been made to explain this silence on the assumption that Justin was familiar with Paul's work and writings; Overbeck[1] argued that Justin had succumbed to the attacks of the Jewish opponents of Paul and that he did not want to prejudice his case against Marcion by quoting the Apostle, while Harnack,[2] in rejecting Overbeck's position, argued that Justin omitted to mention the honoured Apostle because he was able to find nothing of use in Paul's attitude to the Law and Judaism, and consequently, by remaining silent, could avoid bringing down on his own head

---

[1] "Ueber das Verhältnis Justins des Märtyrers zur Apg.", *Zeitschrift für wissenschaftliche Theologie*, xv (1872), 343.

[2] *Judentum und Judenchristentum in Justins Dialog mit Trypho, T.U.*, iii. 9 (= 39.Band) (Leipzig, 1913), 5of.

the whole weight of Jewish prejudice against Paul. Harnack admitted that Justin's silence was possible because Paul's writings were not yet regarded as canonical, but the evidence seems to require a more radical conclusion than that. Both Harnack and Overbeck have advanced reasons why Justin might decide to set aside Paul, but in both arguments it is granted that Paul's position would have been relevant to Justin's case, if not for Justin himself in the first place, for his opponents, and therefore for him to answer in the long run. The only satisfactory explanation of Justin's silence is that Paul was not an influence on his theology; that Paul's writings were not in use in his Church; that Paul was not especially remembered for his missionary work; that Paul was not quoted against Justin's church by Jewish controversialists; and that Paul was not counted as one of the Apostles.[1] Of course this also involves the assumption that Marcion's edition of Paul was not the dominant issue for Justin; but it might not yet have become a dominant issue for Marcion himself, since he seems not to have published his "Gospel" and "Apostle" until the decade after his excommunication in Rome (A.D. 144), and long before then to have worked out his peculiar theological position.[2] It is all the more likely if Marcion had not yet been expelled from the Roman Church when Justin wrote.[3]

[1] This last point is not as scandalous as it sounds, because Acts does not count Paul among the Apostles—meaning the reconstituted Twelve—and calls him an apostle only in a different sense; J. Y. Campbell, article "Apostle", *A Theological Word Book of the Bible*, ed. A. Richardson (London, 1950), 20f; Haenchen, op. cit. (10th ed.), 102f; (12th ed.), 101f. This is one of the soundest reasons for believing that the author of Acts was not Paul's companion.

[2] Clem. Alex., *Strom.*, vii.17.106f; Tert., *de praescr.*, 30; *adv. Marc.*, i.1; iv.4; Harnack, *Geschichte der altchristlichen Literatur bis Eusebius*, ii, *Die Chronologie* (2nd ed., Leipzig, 1897, repr. 1958), 298–310. Harnack later maintained that Marcion prepared his "Gospel" and "Epistle" in Rome during the quiet years before his excommunication (139 to 144), the argument being that only in quiet could one produce such comprehensive and weighty works; *Marcion: Das Evangelium vom fremden Gott*, *T.U.*, iii.15 (=45.Band) (Leipzig, 1924), 25f. The deduction from Tertullian that the heretical works were only published after the excommunication (though they may have been prepared earlier) presumably still stands.

[3] See now J. A. Cramer, op. cit.

The fact that Paul's epistles are quoted in 1 Clement and Ignatius, and that Paul's work is held in high regard by Luke shows that his influence did not entirely disappear, but the absence of reference to him or his position in the first two Gospels, in John, and in the Apocalypse,[1] as well as in Justin Martyr, is proof that it was possible for Christian writers to be ignorant of Paul or to ignore him. Luke seems to be a midway case, in that he has rich sources for Paul's missionary work but has not read his epistles, but the other writers who show no trace of Pauline influence may have been in the same position, as any influence they betray would be not by mentioning Paul's name but by referring to his statements and arguments: they too might have known his reputation as a missionary without having read his epistles.

The silence of Justin about Paul indicates two things: that the hero of one part of the Church could be as good as unknown in another part; and that even the collection and publication of the letters of Paul took time to affect the whole Church. If we are right to assume that, although Clement of Rome and Ignatius used one or two letters of Paul, the Pauline collection was not published until some time before A.D. 135, it is possible in the light of the evidence from Justin to imagine Luke composing his two volumes without having access to any of Paul's letters. Clement and Ignatius were fortunate to have read some of Paul, but both the absence of interest in Paul in parts of the Church and the slowness with which writings treasured in one area were circulated to other areas show that it would have been quite possible for an author writing about Paul in this period to have written without knowing the epistles.

We have used a preliminary analysis of Luke's theology to help fix the date of composition of his writings. Our conclusions must be tested by further discussion of the theology, and by

---

[1] Goodspeed (see Mitton, op. cit., 32f) believes that the seven letters at the beginning of the Apocalypse show the influence of the Pauline corpus of seven, but it is probable that the influence, if any, runs the other way; the author of the Apocalypse is interested in the symbolic significance of seven and, on the other hand, it probably required some juggling to find seven members for the Pauline corpus.

comparing it with the writings of those who, we now have reason to believe, were Luke's contemporaries.

APPENDIX I TO CHAPTER ONE

Did Justin Martyr use Luke's Gospel?

After tracing briefly the history of the discussion of this question, we shall try to establish five points. First, Justin did not use the third Gospel as a source. Second, he employed a source (or sources) also used by Luke. Third, he harmonized his own source with Matthew as he wrote; he was not copying from an existing Gospel-harmony. Fourth, Justin shared with the author of Luke-Acts a number of unwritten traditions. Fifth, a subsidiary point, Marcion edited Luke's Gospel in the light of Justin's other source (or sources).

Albrecht Ritschl, in the first book he wrote, denied that Justin used Luke's Gospel.[1] His case rests mainly on the contradictions between Justin and Luke: Justin's statements that Jesus was born near, not in, Bethlehem (Dial. 78.5) and that he was descended from David through his mother and not through Joseph, and the assertion, in Dial. 103, that no one came to Jesus' aid when he was arrested, which conflicts with Luke 22.49–51.[2] He argues further that, though many of the individual expressions in Justin's citations of the sayings of Jesus tend towards Matthew, the Gospel he remembers best is Marcion's, for it is the order of sayings in Marcion's Gospel which he follows.[3]

The contradictions Ritschl has noted are certainly impressive, but they are not decisive.[4] If the Gospels were not yet canonized,

[1] *Das Evangelium Marcions und das kanonische Evangelium des Lukas* (Tübingen, 1846), especially 135–51.

[2] Cf. Hilgenfeld's point (1850) that it is very surprising that Justin, who was a Samaritan, should have never mentioned any of the Samaritan incidents and sayings in Luke.

[3] See the brilliant discussion of Apol. 16.11,12, op. cit., 150f.

[4] H. F. D. Sparks, *J.T.S.*, n.s. xiv (1963), 465, n 2, does not mention the small discrepancies, and argues that the traditions are so close that Justin must have been using Luke's infancy and passion narratives.

as he rightly points out they were not, there is nothing to prevent Justin preferring his own traditional accounts to those given in Luke or any other of the Gospels—assuming that he had even noticed the contradictions. Ritschl's brief discussion of a group of Jesus' sayings in Justin is much more compelling, and it is in this sort of analysis that we shall find the best proof of our case.

Ritschl's discussion of Justin's sources was only one of many which were written within and outside the Tübingen School at that time. Semisch's attempt (1848) to attribute all the discrepancies between Justin and the synoptic Gospels to Justin's poor memory was almost completely discredited, and Credner's thesis (1832) that Justin was using another Gospel source was followed in general by almost everyone, though conservative critics like Zahn (1889) tried to minimize the extent to which this other source had been employed.[1] E. R. Buckley has more recently added a valuable footnote to this discussion by showing that the form of Justin's citations indicates that he was using a source. This "Gospel" differed in contents and order from the synoptic Gospels, which he also quoted.[2]

By drawing on the rich collection of gospel-citations in the Fathers, Bousset, in the last decade of the nineteenth century, tried to discover more precisely what this other Gospel might be. He came to the conclusion that the source Justin was using for many of his sayings of Jesus was older than the parallels in our Synoptics, and was indeed the collection of the Lord's words used by Matthew and Luke (i.e., Q).

Bousset's seems to have been the last full-scale attempt to argue that Justin's other source material was in any way source material for the canonical Evangelists. The ruling theory to-day is that Justin for the most part relied on a Gospel-harmony. This theory also goes back to the early years of the nineteenth century and took many forms, among which it is

---

[1] See the survey in Wilh. Bousset, *Die Evangeliencitate Justins des Märtyrers in ihrem Wert für die Evangelienkritik* (Göttingen, 1891), Einleitung, 1–9.

[2] E. R. Buckley, "Justin Martyr's Quotations from the Synoptic Tradition", *J.T.S.*, xxxvi (1935), 173–6.

interesting to notice Eichhorn's, that the harmony consisted of Matthew enriched by Luke.[1] Sanday in *The Gospels in the Second Century*[2] concluded that Justin either used the canonical Gospels or a harmony of them, inclining to the second alternative. "This, however, does not exclude the possibility", he wrote, "that Justin may at times quote from uncanonical Gospels as well."[3] Sanday has been followed by Lippelt (1901) and Köster (1957).[4] Köster's pupil, A. J. Bellinzoni, has argued that, with some small exceptions, all the sayings of Jesus are ultimately based on sayings in the Synoptic Gospels harmonized.[5]

There are six passages peculiar to Luke's Gospel and one in Acts where the verbal parallel with Justin is almost exact: Luke 1.35,38, Dial. 100.5; Luke 1.31,32, Apol. 33.5; Luke 6.29, Apol. 16.1 (except for the phrase τὸν χιτῶνα ἢ τὸ ἱμάτιον, in which the order is that of Matt.); Luke 18.27, Apol. 19.6; Luke 20.35,36, Dial. 81.4;[6] Luke 23.46, Dial. 105.4 (a quotation from Ps. 30.6 (31.5) which differs from the form in the LXX); Acts 10.42, Dial 118.1 (plus Barn. 7.2; 2 Clem. 1.1; Polyc. Phil. 2.1; Hegesippus in Eus., *H.E.*, iii.20.4; cf. Acts 17.31; 1 Pet .4.5; 2 Tim. 4.1). The western text of Luke 3.22 is found in Dial. 88.8, 103.6.

These agreements cannot be lightly dismissed, but the case of Acts 10.42, which appears independently in a number of

---

[1] Paulus, Gratz, Storr, and von Engelhardt were among the early advocates of the harmony theory. See Ritschl., op. cit., 139.

[2] London, 1876.

[3] Ibid., 129; cf. 136 n 1.

[4] *Synoptische Überlieferung bei den Apostolischen Vätern*, *T.U.*, 65 (Berlin, 1957), 87–90. The harmony theory has been condemned by G. Quispel, *Vigiliae Christianae*, xi (1957), 140f. He wishes to return to the theory of Credner and Hilgenfeld, that Justin did not know the four canonical Gospels and used the Gospel of the Hebrews.

[5] *The Sayings of Jesus in the Writings of Justin Martyr, Supplements to Novum Testamentum*, xvii (Leiden, 1967).

[6] Sanday, op. cit., 128, argues that ἰσάγγελοι was coined by Luke to represent ὡς ἄγγελοι in Matt. and Mark, and that Justin could only have taken it from Luke. The fact that a word occurs for the first time in Luke does not prove that Luke coined it. It occurs in the works of the fifth-century non-Christian philosopher Hierocles; *in aur. carm.* 4, ἀνθρώπους σέβειν . . . τοὺς ἰσοδαίμονας καὶ ἰσαγγέλους.

other early writings besides Justin's Dialogue, shows that Justin is not necessarily copying from Luke. It is possible that Justin and Luke are using a common source, and that neither has made any change in the source in these quotations. (Luke often changes Mark, the only one of his sources by which we can check his accuracy, but he does not always do so.) As far as we can see, none of the verses above which Justin has repeated bear the marks of Lucan editorial alteration.

In the cases where Justin agrees with Matthew there is little doubt that Matthew is the source; many of the agreements contain obvious Matthean editorial work.[1] It is where Justin seems to be combining material from Matthew with other material that critics have found reason to believe that the other source was Luke. In thirteen instances it seems possible to put this hypothesis to the test.

At the end of the fourteenth chapter of the Apology (the so-called First Apology), Justin says that he is going "to cite a few precepts given by the Messiah himself". The next three chapters contain a whole complex of Jesus' sayings which are of particular interest to us since, though many appear to be summaries of Matthew, the rest often differ from Matthew and converge towards Luke.

Table I shows the parallels to Apol. 15.9,10a in the Dialogue, Matthew, Luke, the Didache, and the Latin Didascalia.[2] The phrase "pray for your enemies" is also found in Apol. 14.3; Dialogue 35.8; 96.3; Syrian Didascalia v.14 (Connolly, p. 184, l.27); Ps. Clem. Hom. xii.32.1 (Behm, p. 190, l.21), and the Oxyrh. Pap. 1224.[3] The frequency with which the phrase occurs by itself, its absence from Luke and the Latin Didascalia parallel, and its position in the Didache (where it looks like an

---

[1] Buckley, op. cit., 173 n 1, notes Matt. 17.10–13 quoted in Dial. 49.

[2] R. H. Connolly, *J.T.S.*, xxiv (1923), 147–57 at 148, argues that the Didascalia is dependent on the Didache. The different order of the clauses counts against direct dependence.

[3] Köster, op. cit., 221; Bousset, op. cit., 75f. Köster, 220–6, discusses in full the parallels between Did., Matt., and Luke, and concludes, after a tortuous and unconvincing argument, that Did. is dependent on Matt. and Luke (230).

insertion)[1] all suggest that it was a common phrase which would soon find its way into this sort of context.

When we compare Justin and Luke, it is soon clear that Justin is as little dependent on Luke as Luke is on Justin. First, we should expect a harmony of Matthew and Luke to follow the order of one or the other, but Justin's order is unique. Second, in Luke 6.32,33,34 we find the generalized expression "sinners" used to describe the outcasts of society who yet know how to love those who love them. Matthew uses Tax-gatherers in 5.46, the Didache has Gentiles like Matthew in 5.47, while Justin has Adulterers first and Tax-gatherers later. It is unlikely that Justin is dependent on Luke, since the Lucan form looks more like an editorial alteration than do the forms in Justin, nor does he seem to have followed Matthew directly. Third, in the Didache and Luke the formula "what credit (χάρις) is that to you?" appears. The parallel in Justin, "what is distinctive (καινόν) about what you do?", is not taken from Matthew (though cf. Matthew 5.47), and it is hard to see how it could be directly dependent on Luke.

Fourth, because Luke has reproduced the Q-phrase "love your enemies" he is forced to fall back on the weak "do good to those who hate you". "Love those who hate you" is found in the Didache and the Latin Didascalia as well as twice in Justin, and is doubtless original. Justin is not dependent on Luke as he does not reproduce the phrase; indeed, if this case were considered alone, it would be possible to argue that Luke was harmonizing Q and Justin! The comparison at this point is one of the most damaging against the theory that Justin is harmonizing Matthew and Luke.[2]

The second case in which it is possible to test whether Justin

---

[1] Köster, op. cit., 223f, suggests that it arose in the Church as a reflection on Matt. and Luke (cf. Pol. Phil. 12.3). It may have been a product of ecclesiastical usage, but there is no evidence to suggest that Matt. and Luke provided the basis for its growth.

[2] H. F. D. Sparks, *J.T.S.*, n.s. xiv (1963), 462, suggests that Luke's περὶ τῶν ἐπηρεαζόντων ὑμᾶς, verse 28, is a Lucanism, and the source of the corresponding clause in Apol. 15.10. It is just possible that προσεύχεσθε περί is a Lucanism (Acts 8.15), but Justin has εὔχ. ὑπέρ.

is dependent on Luke is in the same chapter of the Apology (15.12a, Table II). Further parallel passages are cited by Köster[1] from 2 Clem. 6.2 and Clem. of Alex., *Strom.*, vi.14. 112.3, but they only confirm what can be deduced from the comparison of Matthew and Luke. Justin is probably giving a shortened version of Matthew in the second part of the section, as he does so often elsewhere in this chapter. In the first part his wording follows Matthew exactly, except at one point. He uses the verb ἀπόλλυμι for Matthew's ζημιόω, while Luke uses both verbs. It is unlikely that Justin, using Matthew, decided to avoid Matthew's verb here in favour of one of Luke's verbs. Clement of Alexandria also preserves the saying with ἀπόλλυμι alone, further evidence that Justin may have had his own source.

Justin's treatment of Matthew in the chapter of the Apology we have been considering is almost invariably to abbreviate (e.g. Apology 16.2 is a summary of Matthew 5.22,41,16). If his tendency is to abbreviate, it is unlikely that his longer version of Luke 10.19 in Dialogue 76.6 is dependent on Luke (see Table III). The differences are so marked (Luke: ἰδού, δέδωκα, πατεῖν, omits σκολοπενδρῶν, adds last clause) and the substance so similar that it is almost certain that neither writer was using the other directly.[2]

A discussion of the various forms in which the famous saying "No one knows the Son except the Father " has been transmitted is not an essential part of our case, since the differences between Justin and Matthew are in no way similar to the differences between Luke and Matthew (see Table IV). However, it is an excellent example of Justin's use of an independent tradition and it throws light on Marcion's editorial methods.

All the peculiarities in Justin are found elsewhere—the omission of μου; the reversal of the clauses, Father-Son, Son-

---

[1] Op. cit., 74.
[2] Sanday, op. cit., 125: "The insertion of σκολοπενδρῶν here is curious. It may be perhaps to some extent paralleled by the insertion of καὶ εἰς θήραν in Rom. 11.9." It is easier to explain it as Luke's omission rather than as Justin's addition.

Father; the plural οἶς; the omission of βούληται.[1] Some of these are found in textual variants to Matthew and Luke, but the important reversal of the clauses is not,[2] and it would be false to assume that the differences between Justin and the Synoptics were due to Justin's use of a poor text. The reversal of the clauses shows that Justin is not dependent on the Synoptics at all; he is reproducing another form of the saying which is found, at least once, in the Pseudo-Clementines, Irenaeus, Origen, Eusebius, Epiphanius, and others.[3] In any case he is not dependent on Luke because he does not reproduce the characteristic Lucan τίς ἐστιν. Justin calls his source "the Gospel".[4]

The order of clauses in Justin is harder than the order in Matthew and Luke: the last clause, "and to those to whom the Son shall reveal (him)", is the logical continuation of the clause "no one knows the Father except the Son", but in Justin's text the two logically related clauses are separated from each other by an intruder, the clause that says "no one knows the Son except the Father". It is difficult to imagine anyone changing the order in Matthew and Luke to the order in Justin and the rest. Justin was neither directly nor indirectly dependent on Matthew and Luke.[5]

This is a clear case of Justin's agreeing with a version of a saying that is not Matthew and Luke's version. Not only does this prove that Justin was not using Luke here, but it raises the general probability that he never used Luke in other cases

---

[1] Bousset, op. cit., 100–3.

[2] Bar U b in Luke.

[3] Ps. Clem. xvii.4.3 (Behm, p. 230, ll.27ff); xviii.4.2 (p. 243, ll.2ff;) the Marcosians cited by Iren. i.13.2 (Harvey i.180); iv.11.2 (v. l.) (Harvey ii.159); Iren. ii.4.5 (Harvey i.263); Origen, De princ., ii.6.1; Eus., Dem. Ev., iv.3.13; v.1.25f; De eccles. theol., i.12.7; H.E., i.2.2; Epiph., Anc., 11.3; 19.7; 67.5; Haer, 34.18.16; 74.4.5, etc.

[4] Dial. 100.1, καὶ ἐν τῷ εὐαγγελίῳ δὲ γέγραπται εἰπών. See Buckley, op. cit., 175.

[5] A. J. Bellinzoni, op. cit., 28 and n 3, tries to escape the conclusion by assuming what has to be proved. He assumes that the canonical Gospels had long supplanted the extra-canonical tradition, and that Justin's version of this saying must have gone back ultimately to the Synoptic form.

when his text is much closer to the text of Luke, provided (1) that the agreements are generally not agreements in words that should be ascribed to Luke because he often employs them in a variety of contexts elsewhere, and (2), that it is often more likely that Justin's version and Luke's version were modifications of a common tradition than that Justin's version was a modification of Luke's version.

Marcion is using Luke, since he copies the τίς ἐστιν (Tertull. iv.25). Although the reversal of the clauses may make his own theological point rather better, he is not the originator of the change, as it appears already in Justin and is later reproduced by anti-marcionite writers. Marcion may have been influenced by theological motives—what text-critic is not?—but the problem was not of his own making. It seems that he had in front of him a copy of Luke and a copy of the variant tradition which we can recover from Justin and other sources. The order in Justin, etc., is the harder reading, and probably original, so that Marcion would have had good critical reasons for emending the text of Luke; he was not trying to recover the best text of Luke, but the best text of the original "Gospel."

In the command to love God and love thy neighbour (see Table V), Justin's Dialogue shares two important peculiarities with Luke: the phrase "with all thy strength"[1] and the passing from the first part to the second without a break. It is, of course, possible that Justin twice omitted the "soul" and "mind" phrases in harmonizing Matthew and Luke, but it is far more likely that Luke is the harmonizer.

The woe on those who tithe has been transmitted in two recensions, the "dill and cumin" version in Matthew and the "rue" version in Justin and Luke. Although Justin and Luke both witness to the non-Matthean version, neither is dependent on the other (see Table VI). The different position occupied by the "judgement" in each of them suggests that they have edited their common tradition differently in the light of

[1] Cf. Deut. 6.5, LXX, which has "heart", "soul", and "strength" (δυνάμεως); it does not, however, seem to have played a direct part in the formation of Luke or Justin's versions.

Matthew (and Q). If Justin was harmonizing Luke with Matthew, it is more likely that he would have put the "love of God" clause in Luke's position. Luke's phrase "and every herb" looks more like an editorial harmonization than Justin's omission of everything except "rue".

The woe against those who have the keys and yet shut men out (see Table VII) is obviously taken from a common non-Matthean tradition by both Justin and Luke. Luke has two peculiarities which Justin does not follow: νομικός instead of γραμματεύς and the "key of knowledge" for "the keys". The former may be a Lucan editorial change, as only Luke uses the word νομικός in the Gospels (except for Matt. 22.35);[1] the latter almost certainly is. The change from Justin's form to Luke's is easy to imagine, but it is much harder to see why Justin should change "key" to "keys", even if he wished to suppress the reference to Gnosis.[2]

In the saying "fear those who can cast you into Gehenna" (see Table VIII), it is most unlikely that Justin is dependent on Luke. The saying is preserved in at least two forms, and Matthew is clearly one of them. Matthew has at least three features which are absent in all the others or only present in one or two of them: φοβεῖσθε (lines 1 and 11); ἀποκτεῖναι (line 8); ἀπολέσαι (line 16). The words which stand in place of these four are sufficiently similar for us to assume that they come from one source and not more than one source. All the features which are also found in Matthew are underlined in the other five columns of the Table, and we may assume that some at least are due to the influence of Matthew or Matthew's source Q. Marcion is the writer who shows the least traces of Matthean influ-

[1] See G. D. Kilpatrick, *J.T.S.*, N.S., i (1950), 56–60.

[2] The Gospel according to Thomas provides additional evidence for a tradition containing the plural "keys"; it follows Luke in reading "of knowledge" and Matthew in referring to "the Pharisees" as well as to "the Scribes": plate 88, lines 7 to 10 (Logion 39 in the edition of A. Guillaumont, H.-Ch. Puech, G. Quispel, W. Till, and Yassah 'Abd Al Masîḥ, Leiden and London, 1959): "The Pharisees and the Scribes have received the keys of Knowledge, they have hidden them. They did not enter, and they did not let those (enter) who wished."

ence: ἀπό (line 2), ἀποκτέννειν (line 3), and possibly δυναμένων (line 4). Marcion, however, is dependent on Luke, reproducing Luke's introductory formula, "I say to (you my) friends" (not in the Table), his central bridge-passage (lines 9 and 10), and his conclusion. Since there is no discernible theological purpose at work, we may at least ask whether again he is not emending Luke in the light of another tradition which he believes to be more ancient.

Köster has tentatively suggested that 2 Clement, Justin, and the Pseudo Clementine Homilies are here following a common Gospel-harmony, that is, of Matthew and Luke.[1] If Luke is the other source employed by 2 Clem., Justin, and Ps. Clem., it is hard to see why all have omitted ὑποδείξω, etc. (lines 9 and 10), why 2 Clem. and Justin omit ἀπό (line 2) and τὸ σῶμα (line 3), and why 2 Clem. and Ps. Clem. add πυρός (lines 17 and 18). Each of these separately might be explained away, but together they make it unlikely that they are dependent directly on Luke. If they are all using a Gospel-harmony it is again difficult to explain why they differ from each other and adopt different words from Matthew (e.g. lines 1 and 14).

The only hypothesis left is to suppose that all five were acquainted with another recension of the saying, which each has harmonized in his own way with Matthew or Q. Marcion is perhaps the nearest to the original. The distinguishing marks of this source were that it made no reference to "body and soul" and that it specifically mentioned the ἐξουσία of the opponent Christians must fear.

The parallels to Apol. 16.9–11 have been adduced to prove that Justin was employing a harmony of Matthew and Luke.[2] The case rests on the phrase (Table IX, column iii, line 9) in Apol. 16.10, καὶ ποιεῖ ἃ λέγω, which is a variant of a phrase in Luke 6.46. As can be seen from the Table, Justin has followed Matthew's wording in the "Lord, Lord" saying. The supposition is that, using a harmony of Matthew and Luke, he observed that

---

[1] Op. cit., 94–7. A. J. Bellinzoni, op. cit., 108–11.
[2] Köster, op. cit., 87–90.

the Lucan parallel to Matthew contained an extra phrase. This extra phrase fitted neatly into the next saying, "He who hears me, etc.", and there he put it.

Three comments should be made. First, if this hypothesis is correct, the supposed harmony would probably have been in the nature of a synopsis, since Justin has adopted the extra phrase in Apol. 16.10 and chosen not to adopt it in Apol. 63.5; the phrase had not been completely harmonized in Justin's source. Second, there is no evidence that it was Luke which Justin was harmonizing with Matthew. The evidence goes the other way. The saying in Apol. 16.10 and 63.5 is not found in the best text of Luke; it is substituted for the last clause of Luke 10.16 by D and some codices of the Old Latin, added to the usual text by Θ, family 13, some codices of the Old Latin and two Syriac versions and, in an earlier position, by Ps. Ign. Eph., Cyprian, etc.[1] From the fact that it is lodged in three different ways we should deduce that it was another tradition attracted to Luke 10.16 early in the history of the text.[2] If Justin had been working from a "Western" text of Luke, he would almost certainly have reproduced more of verse 16.

Third, the general character of the context of the sayings in Justin should be taken into account. This is part of the collection of the Lord's sayings which began in chapter 14 of the Apology. As the simplified list given here shows, the Apology provides a continuity which is paralleled now by Matthew, now by Luke.

Matthew	Apology	Luke
7.21	16.9	(6.46)
	16.10	(10.16: D, etc.)
7.22f	16.11	13.26f
13.42f	16.12	13.28
7.15	16.13	

On grounds of *order*, it is easier to suppose that Matthew and Luke have followed a collection of sayings with Justin's order

---

[1] Bousset, op. cit., 86f.   [2] Bousset's conclusion.

than that Justin has jumped hither and thither in Matthew and
Luke to compile a harmonized collection. When we turn to the
wording we find that Justin's wording is mainly Matthean, but
that occasionally a phrase which is also found in Luke appears.
Apology 16.11 (cf. Dialogue 76.5) is an instructive example.
For the most part it follows Matthew 7.22f, but it includes the
words, ἐφάγομεν καὶ ἐπίομεν, which should be compared with
Luke 13.26, ἐφάγομεν ἐνώπιόν σου καὶ ἐπίομεν. It is possible
that Justin has harmonized Matthew with Luke, but the fact
that he does not reproduce the Lucanism, ἐνώπιόν σου,[1] rein-
forces the conclusion we have reached in other passages that
Justin harmonized an unknown source with Matthew, and that
Luke independently employed the same source.

On these three grounds it is unlikely that Justin was here
using a Gospel-harmony of Matthew and Luke, or that the
harmony he made as he went along was based on Luke.

In the dialogue between Jesus and the rich man, Justin is
independent of Matthew (Table X). He has no trace of
Matthew's "Why do you ask me concerning the good?" The
question is whether Justin has used Luke.

First, his omission of the rest of the rich man's question may
not be simply the abbreviation of a source which originally
contained it. There is independent evidence that other
accounts of the incident had separated versions of the two parts
of the question. The Marcosians (Iren. i.13.1; Harvey i.178)
seem to have preserved the question and answer in exactly the
words of the Dialogue version, without the second part of the
question about eternal life, and the Gospel according to the
Hebrews (Origen, *Comm. in Matt.* xv.14; Klostermann, p. 389,
ll.21ff) preserves the second part of the question separately,
ascribing it to "another rich man" (*dixit ad eum alter divitum*).[2]

---

[1] Hawkins, *Horae Synopticae* (2nd ed., Oxford, 1909), 18. This Lucanism
is also absent in the partial parallel, Origen, *Joh.*, 32.8.

[2] Bousset, op. cit., 106, produces a text of the Gospel according to the
Hebrews which contains the question of the *first* rich man (with a form
of Jesus' answer like Marcion's), but I have been unable to trace his
source.

Justin's omission of the question about eternal life may be due to a peculiarity of his source.

Second, although the wording in the Dialogue contains Jesus' counter-question in the form found in Luke (and Mark), and the statement "One is good" is like Matthew, it is very unlikely that Justin is dependent on either of them. The reason is that not only the Marcosians' tradition cited above but also the Gospel of the Naasseni (Hippol., *Philos.* v.7.26) preserves exactly the same wording; it is unlikely that three writers would arrive independently at a wording which, although it contained phrases found in Matthew and Luke, also contained an identical ending not found elsewhere.

Third, Marcion seems to have used a form of the independent tradition preserved in the Dialogue to edit Luke (Marcion according to Epiphanius, Schol. 50). His μή με λέγε ἀγαθόν is supported by Ps. Clem. Hom. xviii.1.3; cf. 3.4: μή με λέγε ἀγαθόν ὁ γὰρ ἀγαθὸς εἷς ἐστιν ὁ πατὴρ ὁ ἐν τοῖς οὐρανοῖς.

Fourth, the form of the question and answer preserved in the Apology is close to Luke (and Mark), but the differences are still great enough to make it impossible to affirm that Luke (or Mark) has been used. Justin does not give Jesus' counter question, and he has μόνος ὁ θεός ὁ ποιήσας τὰ πάντα instead of εἷς (ὁ) θεός. The latter difference may be an anti-Marcionite alteration, but dependence on Luke (or Mark) cannot be proved.

Justin's version of the eucharistic words is closer to Luke and Paul than to Matthew or Mark, but is independent of any of them (see Table XI). This is clear from the order of the "remembrance" phrase over the bread and the omission of any reference to the covenant over the cup. It is incredible that a harmonizer should have omitted so much or changed the order of the parts. The extraordinary thing is that these words, dependent directly on none of our Gospels or Paul, are contained in a passage where Justin claims to be quoting from "the memoirs of the Apostles called Gospels". We are forced to conclude that his other source (whether a Gospel ascribed to the Apostles, or his own Church's eucharistic tradition) is just as authoritative for him as Matthew, the only canonical Gospel we can be sure he possessed.

Justin claims that the tradition about Christ's agony in Gethsemane[1] when he sweated drops of blood is also taken from the memoirs of the Apostles (see Table XII). Here, however, Justin adds that the memoirs were written by those who followed the Apostles as well as by the Apostles themselves.[2] This has been taken to be a specific reference to Luke 1.1,3, and the fact that only Luke records the drops of blood is supposed to clinch the case that Justin used Luke. A number of considerations makes this unlikely. The words about those who followed the Apostles need not refer to Luke, and they could equally well apply to Mark or to any other Gospel which could not claim direct apostolic authorship. If Justin particularly wished to direct attention to Luke's Gospel, he would surely have quoted from it exactly. Earlier in the Dialogue (99.2) he has quoted the words "Let this cup pass from me" almost exactly from Matthew; on the later occasion when he is supposed to be specifically quoting from Luke his version differs greatly: he omits πάτερ and ἀπ' ἐμοῦ, and he adopts neither of the Lucan pecularities, βούλει and παρένεγκε. Perhaps, however, these differences are due to abbreviation and harmonization with Matthew, so we must turn to the words about sweating drops of blood where, according to the theory we are criticizing, he had only Luke on which to rely.

The first thing to notice is that it is by no means certain that Luke 22.44 stood in Luke at all. It is included by ℵ* D Θ 0171 f1 157, etc., Latin, Syriac Curetonian and Peshitta, and Armenian, and omitted by a corrector of ℵ, A B W f13, etc., f, Syriac Sinaiticus, and Sahidic. Family 13 omits it in Luke and puts it after Matt. 26.39. If Justin proves to be a witness to a separate tradition, we should have another example of the extra-canonical source giving rise to textual variants in the canonical Gospels.[3] But to assume that would be to assume what we have to prove. We can only leave open

---

[1] Note that both Justin and Luke omit all reference to Gethsemane as the scene of the agony (Luke 22.40; Dial. 99.2; 103.8).

[2] Dial 103.8: ἐν τοῖς ἀπομνημονεύμασι, ἅ φημι ὑπὸ τῶν ἀποστόλων αὐτοῦ καὶ τῶν ἐκείνοις παρακολουθησάντων συντετάχθαι.

[3] Cf. Matt. 7.22 syrᶜ, Table IX.

the question of whether Justin's text of Luke, supposing he knew Luke, contained this verse.

The most important difference between Justin's citation and Luke is the order; in Luke, the prayer precedes the agony and in Justin it follows. Justin does not have αἵματος after θρόμβοι, has κατεχεῖτο instead of καταβαίνοντες, and omits "upon earth". If there is any dependence of one upon the other, it is slightly more likely that the Lucan text is dependent on Justin; it is more likely that the additional words are the result of editorial expansion than that they are the result of editorial shortening. The differences are too great for this passage to be used to show that Justin was quoting from Luke.[1] Taking all the uncertainties into account, there is a good case for arguing that the verse did not originally belong to Luke and that it was inserted into his text from the tradition which Justin quotes, "the Apostles' Memoirs".

The three predictions of the passion in Justin are so similar that they probably all come from the one source (see Table XIII). That source may have been a harmony of Matthew and Luke, or it may have been an independent tradition. Matthew seems to have exerted no special influence; none of its special features appears in Justin, and anything else they have in common is also found in Luke. The only remaining possibility is that Justin's source is a harmony of the two predictions in Luke. (The other predictions in Matthew and Luke show no particular affinities; this in itself raises the problem of why Justin did not draw on a wider range of sources for his harmony, if he was making a harmony; Matthew 17.22f; Luke 9.44; Matthew 20.18f; Luke 18.31–3.) It is unlikely that he should harmonize by choosing to name only one of the groups which rejected Jesus, the scribes, out of the three available, and then add to them the Pharisees. It is very likely that Justin reproduced an old source which was independent of the canonical Gospels.[2]

---

[1] Sanday, op. cit., 124, holds that the opposite is true.

[2] Bellinzoni, op. cit., 31f and 32 n 1, argues that Luke 24.7 is a Lucan construction, and that only from here could Justin have derived the words καὶ σταυρωθῆναι καὶ τῇ τρίτῃ ἡμέρᾳ ἀναστῆναι. The verb σταυρόω is used in this sort of context in Matt. 20.19; 26.2, and the verb ἀνίστημι likewise

The few remaining passages where there are verbal points of contact between Justin and Luke are such that it is impossible to tell whether Justin was dependent on Luke. None of them repeats Lucan passages which are obviously editorial additions, and three of them occur in Justin's collections of sayings which we have argued could not, at other points, have been dependent on Luke. These passages are: Luke 5.32, Apol. 15.8, where Justin goes on to record a non-canonical saying about repentance; Luke 12.48, Apol. 17.4: "to whom much is given"; and, from the collection in Apol. 15 and 16: Luke 5.35,36, Apol. 15.13, Dial. 96.3;[1] one phrase in Luke 13.26, Apol. 16.11, Dial. 76.5; Luke 13.28, Apol. 16.12; Luke 6.44, Apol. 16.13.

To conclude, the evidence is certainly not strong enough to prove that Justin used Luke's Gospel. There is much to show that Luke employed Justin's special source; that is the simplest hypothesis to explain all the facts.

APPENDIX 2 TO CHAPTER ONE

An Argument from Textual Criticism
Against the Late Dating of Acts

An interesting attempt has been made to show that Acts cannot have been written in the first, second, or third decades of the second century, by arguing that there is visible in the Codex Bezae the work of an interpolator, who could have been revising Acts at any point between about A.D. 130 and 160. A deliberate revision of Acts would imply that Acts itself was written a good deal earlier.

This argument has been advanced by R. P. C. Hanson in a review article of a book on the Codex Bezae in Acts by E. J.

---

in Mark 8.31; 9.9,31; 10.34; Matt. 17.9 (most Mss., although not B D); 17.23 (B 047 f*13* *118*); 20.19 (B D); besides Luke 9.22 (A C D f1 *565*); 18.33; 24.46. The evidence for Justin's dependence on Luke is far too slight to conclude, as Bellinzoni does, that "this use of peculiarly Lucan material excludes the possibility of the use of a pre-Synoptic source here".

[1] Bousset, op. cit., 80–3.

Epp.[1] Hanson is reviving an old hypothesis about the nature of the "Western" text, an hypothesis most fully stated by J. H. Ropes,[2] and he argues that Epp's book, "whether intentionally or not", helps to confirm that a "recognizable interpolator" was at work before A.D. 160.

If there were a consistent theological tendency in the "Western" readings, there would be grounds for concluding that one interpolating editor had been at work. The hypothetical homogeneity of the underlying "Western" text, which cannot be demonstrated from the existing "Western" manuscripts because they differ from one another so much, would become much more likely if we could establish a homogeneous tendency. Epp has set out in full the evidence for more than sixty variants in Acts between B and D, and concludes that "the relatively few D-variants previously recognized as distinctly anti-Judaic have been vastly expanded so that a clear and consistent tendency comes boldly into view".[3] The question is, Has Epp succeeded in demonstrating a deliberate "anti-Judaic" tendency which should probably be ascribed to a recognizable interpolator?

There are three reasons for denying that he has succeeded.

First, all the tendencies (whether "anti-Judaic", or designed to emphasize the universalism of Christianity or the heroism of the apostles) are already present in Acts, whatever text we choose. There is no evidence, and Epp does not attempt to produce evidence, that the tendencies he alleges in Codex Bezae run counter to tendencies present in Codex Vaticanus; the changes are, at best, a heightening of existing tendencies. Consequently, the hypothesis of a creative editor becomes less likely.

Second, most of Epp's arguments to show that the D-text is a theological alteration of the B-text are unconvincing. Hanson has already discussed a dozen or so cases in which Epp's argu-

---

[1] "The Ideology of Codex Bezae in Acts", *N.T.S.*, 14 (1967–8), 282–6 at 286. E. J. Epp, *The Theological Tendency of Codex Bezae Catabrigiensis in Acts*, *S.N.T.S. Monograph Series* (Cambridge, 1966).

[2] *Beginnings*, iii. pages viii, ccxxi–iii, ccxl–vi.

[3] Op. cit., 169.

ments are doubtful. I find only three instances of variants that might possibly be due to a distinct theological tendency which Epp has added to the cases noticed as such by Corssen, Lagrange, Ropes, and Menoud.[1]

Third, the fact that D contains readings which, it could be argued, are alterations of the B-text in a pro-Jewish sense suggests that the hypothesis of a deliberate anti-Jewish tendency is wrong. In 14.19 (cf. 23.12) D carefully notes that *certain* Jews stirred up trouble against the apostles, where B says simply "the Jews" stirred up trouble; and in 17.4f D says that not all the Jews, only the disobedient ones, gathered together agitators to set the city in uproar. But these examples, like most of Epp's, are not really examples of a distinct theological tendency, so much as examples of the activity of scribes who wished to make the text as clear and precise as possible.

I conclude that there are very slender grounds for thinking that the "Western" text of Acts preserves the work of a single creative editor who revised the narrative between about A.D. 130 and 160 according to his theological predilections.

Ropes would agree that there is no clearly discernible theological tendency in the "Western" text: "Of any special point of view, theological or other, on the part of the 'Western' reviser it is difficult to find any trace."[2] Nevertheless he held that this text was "in the main ... due to a single editor trying to improve the book on a large scale" who was at work in the first half of the second century.[3] This theory is difficult to refute, since we do not possess clear enough evidence to establish whether the diverse "Western" group of texts do really go back to one clear recension or not. But we can say that Ropes's theory has not prevailed, and it is usually considered that the "Western" text was "the result of an undisciplined and 'wild' growth of manuscript tradition and translational activity".[4]

[1] These are 10.39, not D; 14.19, the addition in C *81*; 14.19, the reading επισεισαντες in D. The last is possibly original, and therefore not a tendentious alteration.

[2] *Beginnings*, iii. page ccxxxiii.

[3] *Beginnings*, iii. page ccxxiii; cf. pages ccxxi–iv; ccxliv–vi.

[4] Bruce M. Metzger, *The Text of the New Testament: Its Transmission, Corruption, and Restoration* (Oxford, 1964, 2nd ed., 1968), 213.

If we knew how long a text would take to become "wild", and if we could establish with certainty that the text used by the early Fathers, especially Irenaeus, was suitably corrupt, we might establish, even without supposing that one reviser had been at work, that the textual history of the Acts of the Apostles indicated an earlier date for its composition than the date I have put forward. But it is unlikely that we shall ever be able to fulfil these two conditions.

The history of the text of Acts remains a fascinating and important problem, but the results of study of the question do not rule out the hypothesis that Acts was published early in the second century.

TABLE I

Matt. 5.46,44,42	Justin. Apol.15.q10a	Justin. Dial.133.6	Didache 1.3,5	Didascalia (latin) i.2,3 (Connolly, p.7 ll.2f)	Lk.6.33f,27f,30,34
46 ἐὰν γὰρ ἀγαπήσητε τ. ἀγαπῶντας ὑμᾶς τίνα μισθὸν ἔχετε; οὐχὶ κ. οἱ τελῶναι τ.αὐτὸ ποιοῦσιν; 44 ἐγὼ δὲ λέγω ὑμῖν ἀγαπᾶτε τ.ἐχθροὺς ὑμῶν	49 εἰ ἀγαπᾶτε τ.ἀγαπῶντας ὑμᾶς τί καινὸν ποιεῖτε; οὐ κ.οἱ πόρνοι τοῦτο ποιοῦσιν ἐγὼ δὲ ὑμῖν λέγω	[85.7] ἀγαπᾶτ ιν κ. τ. ἐχθρούς	5 ποία γὰρ χάρις ἐὰν ἀγαπᾶτε τ. ἀγαπῶντας ὑμᾶς; οὐχὶ κ.τ.ἔθνη τ.αὐτὸ ποιοῦσιν;		32. κ. εἰ ἀγαπᾶτε τ.ἀγαπῶντας ὑμᾶς, ποία ὑμῖν χάρις ἐστιν... 33. κ.οἱ ἁμαρτωλοὶ τ.αὐτὸ ποιοῦσιν ἀλλὰ ἀγαπᾶτε τ.ἐχθροὺς ὑμῶν
καὶ προσεύχεσθε ὑπὲρ τ.διωκόντων ὑμᾶς	εὔχεσθε ὑπὲρ τ.ἐχθρῶν ὑμῶν κ.ἀγαπᾶτε τ.μισοῦντας ὑμᾶς κ.εὐλογεῖτε τ.καταρωμένους ὑμῖν κ.εὔχεσθε ὑπὲρ τ. ἐπηρεαζόντων ὑμᾶς	εὔχεσθε κ. ὑπὲρ τ.ἐχθρῶν κ.ἀγαπᾶν τ.μισοῦντας κ.εὐλογεῖν τ.καταρωμένους	[κ. προσεύχεσθε ὑπὲρ τ.ἐχθρῶν ὑμῶν] ὑμεῖς δὲ ἀγαπᾶτε τ.μισοῦντας ὑμᾶς κ.εὐλογεῖτε τ.καταρωμένους ὑμῖν κ.προσεύχεσθε ὑπὲρ τ. ἐχθρῶν ὑμῶν ὑπηρετεῖτε δὲ	diligite odientes vos & orate pro maledicentibus vos	καλῶς ποιεῖτε τ.μισοῦσιν ὑμᾶς 28 εὐλογεῖτε τ.καταρωμένους ὑμᾶς προσεύχεσθε περὶ τ. ἐπηρεαζόντων ὑμᾶς
42. τ.αἰτοῦντί σε δός κ.τ. θέλοντα	10a. παντὶ αἰτοῦντι δίδοτε κ.μ βουλόμενον		ὑπὲρ τ. διωκόντων ὑμᾶς κ. οὐχ ἕξετε ἐχθρόν 5 παντὶ τ.αἰτοῦντί σε δίδου	& inimicum nullum habebitis	30 παντὶ αἰτοῦντί σε δίδου κ.ἀπὸ τ.αἴροντος τὰ σὰ μὴ ἀπαίτει
ἀπὸ τοῦ δανείσασθαι μὴ ἀποστραφῇς	δανείσασθαι μὴ ἀποστραφῆτε εἰ γὰρ δανείζετε παρ'ὧν ἐλπίζετε λαβεῖν τί καινὸν ποιεῖτε; τοῦτο κ.οἱ τελῶναι ποιοῦσιν		κ. μὴ ἀπαίτει		34. κ. ἐὰν δανείσητε παρ'ὧν ἐλπίζετε λαβεῖν ποία ὑμῖν χάρις ἐστιν; κ.ἁμαρτωλοὶ ἁμαρτωλοῖς δανίζουσιν ἵνα ἀπολάβωσιν τ.ἴσα

TABLE II

Matt. 16.26	Justin Apol. 15.12a	Lk. 9.25
τί γὰρ ὠφεληθήσεται ἄνθρωπος ἐὰν τ. κόσμον ὅλον κερδήσῃ τ. δὲ ψυχὴν αὐτοῦ ʒημιωθῇ ; * ἢ τί δώσει ἄνθρωπος ἀντάλλαγμα τ. ψυχῆς αὐτοῦ ; * cf. II Clem. 6.2	τί γὰρ ὠφελεῖται ἄνθρωπος ἂν τ. κόσμον ὅλον κερδήσῃ τ. δὲ ψυχὴν αὐτοῦ ἀπολέσῃ ; † ἢ τί δώσει αὐτῆς ἀντάλλαγμα ; † cf. Clem. Alex. Strom. VI.xiv.112.3	τί γὰρ ὠφελεῖται ἄνθρωπος κερδήσας τ. κόσμον ὅλον ἑαυτὸν δὲ ἀπολέσας ἢ ʒημιωθείς ;

TABLE III

Justin Dial. 76.6	Lk. 10.19
δίδωμι ὑμῖν ἐξουσίαν καταπατεῖν ἐπάνω ὄφεων κ. σκορπίων κ. σκολοπενδρῶν κ. ἐπάνω πάσης δυνάμεως τ. ἐχθροῦ	ἰδοὺ δέδωκα ὑμῖν τ. ἐξουσίαν τοῦ πατεῖν ἐπάνω ὄφεων κ. σκορπίων κ. ἐπὶ πᾶσαν τ. δύναμιν τ. ἐχθροῦ κ. οὐδὲν ὑμᾶς οὐ μὴ ἀδικήσει

TABLE IV

Matt. 11.27	Justin Dial. 100.1	Marcion Harnack 2nd ed., 206*	Lk. 10.22
πάντα μοι παρεδόθη	πάντα μοι παραδέδοται	πάντα μοι παρεδόθη	πάντα μοι παρεδόθη
ὑπὸ τοῦ πατρός μου	ὑπὸ τοῦ πατρός	ὑπὸ τοῦ πατρὸς	ὑπὸ τοῦ πατρός μου
κ. οὐδεὶς ἐπιγινώσκει	κ. οὐδεὶς γινώσκει	(κ.)οὐδεὶς γινώσκει(ἔγνω?)	κ. οὐδεὶς γινώσκει
τ. υἱὸν	τ. πατέρα	τίς ἔστιν ὁ πατὴρ	τίς ἔστιν ὁ υἱὸς
εἰ μὴ ὁ πατήρ	εἰ μὴ ὁ υἱὸς	εἰ μὴ ὁ υἱὸς	εἰ μὴ ὁ πατήρ
οὐδὲ τ. πατέρα	οὐδὲ τ. υἱὸν	κ. τίς ἔστιν ὁ υἱὸς	κ. τίς ἔστιν ὁ πατὴρ
τις ἐπιγινώσκει			
εἰ μὴ ὁ υἱὸς	εἰ μὴ ὁ πατὴρ	εἰ μὴ ὁ πατὴρ	εἰ μὴ ὁ υἱὸς
κ. ᾧ ἐὰν βούληται	κ. οἷς ἂν	κ. ᾧ ἐὰν	κ. ᾧ ἐὰν βούληται
ὁ υἱὸς ἀποκαλύψαι	ὁ υἱὸς ἀποκαλύψῃ	ὁ υἱὸς ἀποκαλύψῃ	ὁ υἱὸς ἀποκαλύψαι

TABLE V

Matt. 22.37-9 [4.10]	Justin Apol. 16.6	Justin Dial. 93.2	Didache 1.2	Lk. 10.27 [4.8]
[cf. 22.38] 1a [κύριον τ. θεόν σου προσκυνήσεις κ. αὐτῷ μόνῳ λατρεύσεις] 2 ἀγαπήσεις κύριον τ. θεόν σου ἐν ὅλῃ τ. καρδίᾳ σου κ. ἐν ὅλῃ τ. ψυχῇ σου κ. ἐν ὅλῃ τ. διανοίᾳ σου 3 αὕτη ἐστὶν ἡ μεγάλη κ. πρώτη ἐντολή δευτέρα ὁμοία αὐτῇ ἀγαπήσεις τ. πλησίον σου ὡς σεαυτόν	μεγίστη ἡ ἐντολή ἐστι κύριον τ. θεόν σου προσκυνήσεις κ. αὐτῷ μόνῳ λατρεύσεις ἐξ ὅλης τ. καρδίας σου κ. ἐξ ὅλης τ. ἰσχύος σου κύριον τ. θεόν τ. ποιήσαντά σε	[= Dial. 103.6; 125.4] ἀγαπήσεις κύριον τ. θεόν σου ἐξ ὅλης τ. καρδίας σου κ. ἐξ ὅλης τ. ἰσχύος σου κ. τ. πλησίον σου ὡς σεαυτόν = Dial. 93.3 (om. σου κ.)	πρῶτον ἀγαπήσεις τ. θεόν τ. ποιήσαντά σε * δεύτερον τ. πλησίον σου ὡς σεαυτόν * cf. Barn. 19.2	ἀγαπήσεις κύριον τ. θεόν σου ἐξ ὅλης τ. καρδίας σου κ. ἐν ὅλῃ τ. ψυχῇ σου κ. ἐν ὅλῃ τ. ἰσχύϊ σου κ. ἐν ὅλῃ τ. διανοίᾳ σου κ. τ. πλησίον σου ὡς σεαυτόν

5

TABLE VI

Matt. 23.23	Justin Dial. 17.4	Lk. 11.42
οὐαὶ ὑμῖν	οὐαὶ ὑμῖν	ἀλλὰ οὐαὶ ὑμῖν
γραμματεῖς κ. φαρισαῖοι	γραμματεῖς κ. φαρισαῖοι	τ. φαρισαίοις
ὑποκριταὶ ὅτι	ὑποκριταὶ ὅτι	ὅτι
ἀποδεκατοῦτε τ. ἡδύοσμον	ἀποδεκατοῦτε τ. ἡδύοσμον	ἀποδεκατοῦτε τ. ἡδύοσμον
κ. τ. ἄνηθον	κ. τ. πήγανον	κ. τ. πήγανον
κ. τ. κύμινον κ.		κ. πᾶν λάχανον κ.
ἀφήκατε τ. βαρύτερα τ. νόμου		παρέρχεσθε
τ. κρίσιν	τ. δὲ ἀγάπην τ. θεοῦ	τ. κρίσιν
	κ. τ. κρίσιν	κ. τ. ἀγάπην τ. θεοῦ
κ. τ. ἔλεος		
κ. τ. πίστιν		
	οὐ κατανοεῖτε	

TABLE VII

Matt. 23.13	Justin Dial. 17.4	Lk. 11.52
οὐαὶ δὲ ὑμῖν	οὐαὶ ὑμῖν	οὐαὶ ὑμῖν
γραμματεῖς κ. φαρισαῖοι	γραμματεῖς	τ. νομικοῖς
ὑποκριταὶ ὅτι	ὅτι	ὅτι
	τὰς κλεῖς ἔχετε	ἤρατε τὴν κλεῖδα τ. γνώσεως
κλείετε		
τ. βασιλείαν τ. οὐρανῶν		
ἔμπροσθεν τ. ἀνθρώπων		
ὑμεῖς γὰρ οὐκ εἰσέρχεσθε	κ. αὐτοὶ οὐκ εἰσέρχεσθε	αὐτοὶ οὐκ εἰσήλθατε
οὐδὲ τ. εἰσερχομένους	κ. τ. εἰσερχομένους	κ. τ. εἰσερχομένους
ἀφίετε εἰσελθεῖν	κωλύετε	ἐκωλύσατε
[23.16,24 ὁδηγοὶ τυφλοί]	ὁδηγοὶ τυφλοί	

TABLE VIII

Matt. 10.28	II Clem. 5.4	Justin Apol. 19.7	R. Clem. Hom. xvii.5.2	Marcion Harnack, 2nd ed. 211ff	Lk. 12.4,5
κ. μὴ φοβεῖσθε ἀπὸ τῶν ἀποκτεννόντων τ. σῶμα τ. δὲ ψυχὴν μὴ δυναμένων ἀποκτεῖναι	κ. ἐμᾶς μὴ φοβεῖσθε τοὺς ἀποκτεννοντας ὑμᾶς καὶ μηδὲν ὑμῖν δυναμένους ποιεῖν	μὴ φοβεῖσθε τοὺς ἀναιροῦντος ὑμᾶς κ.μετὰ ταῦτα μὴ δυναμένους τι ποιῆσαι εἶπε	μὴ φοβηθῆτε ἀπὸ τοῦ ἀποκτείνοντος τ. σῶμα τ. δὲ ψυχῇ μὴ δυναμένου τι ποιῆσαι	μὴ φοβηθῆτε ἀπὸ τῶν ὑμᾶς ὑμᾶς μόνον ἀποκτείνειν δυναμένων κ.μετὰ ταῦτα μηδεμίαν εἰς ὑμᾶς ἐχόντων ἐξουσίαν	μὴ φοβηθῆτε ἀπὸ τῶν ἀποκτεννόντων τ. σῶμα κ. μετὰ ταῦτα μὴ ἐχόντων περισσότερόν τι ποιῆσαι
φοβεῖσθε δὲ μᾶλλον τὸν δυνάμενον κ. ψυχὴν κ. σῶμα ἀπολέσαι ἐν γεέννῃ	ἀλλὰ φοβεῖσθε τὸν μετὰ τ.ἀποθανεῖν ὑμᾶς ἔχοντα ἐξουσίαν ψυχῆς κ. σώματος τοῦ βαλεῖν εἰς γέενναν πυρός	φοβήθητε δὲ τὸν μετὰ τ.ἀποθανεῖν δυνάμενον κ.ψυχὴν κ.σῶμα εἰς γέενναν ἐμβαλεῖν	φοβήθητε δὲ τὸν δυνάμενον κ.σῶμα κ. ψυχὴν εἰς τ. γέενναν τ. πυρὸς βαλεῖν ναὶ λέγω ὑμῖν τοῦτον φοβήθητε	ὑποδείξω δὲ ὑμῖν τίνα φοβηθῆτε φοβήθητε τὸν μετὰ τ.ἀποκτεῖναι ἔχοντα ἐξουσίαν βαλεῖν εἰς γέενναν ναὶ λέγω ὑμῖν τοῦτον φοβήθητε	ὑποδείξω δὲ ὑμῖν τίνα φοβηθῆτε φοβήθητε τὸν μετὰ τ.ἀποκτεῖναι ἔχοντα ἐξουσίαν ἐμβαλεῖν εἰς τ. γέενναν ναὶ λέγω ὑμῖν τοῦτον φοβήθητε

unobtrusive: possible influence of Matt, Q tradition.

TABLE IX

Matt. 7.21	II Clem. 4.2	Justin Apol. 16 g f.	Justin Apol. 63.5	Lk. 6.46; [10.16*]
οὐ πᾶς ὁ λέγων μοι κύριε κύριε εἰσελεύσεται εἰς τ. βασιλείαν τ. οὐρανῶν ἀλλ' ὁ ποιῶν τ. θέλημα τ. πατρός μου τοῦ ἐν τ. οὐρανοῖς	οὐ πᾶς ὁ λέγων μοι κύριε κύριε σωθήσεται ἀλλ' ὁ ποιῶν τ. δικαιοσύνην	9 οὐχὶ πᾶς ὁ λέγων μοι κύριε κύριε εἰσελεύσεται εἰς τ. βασιλείαν τ. οὐρανῶν ἀλλ' ὁ ποιῶν τ. θέλημα τ. πατρός μου τοῦ ἐν τ. οὐρανοῖς 10a ὃς γὰρ ἀκούει μου κ. ποιεῖ ἃ λέγω ἀκούει τ. ἀποστείλαντός με		6.46 τί δέ με καλεῖτε κύριε κύριε κ. οὐ ποιεῖτε ἃ λέγω;
			ὁ ἐμοῦ ἀκούων ἀκούει τ. ἀποστείλαντός με	[10.16* κ. ὁ ἐμοῦ ἀκούων (cf. 6.46 above) ἀκούει τ. ἀποστείλαντός με] add [10.16] Θ f13 a b syˢ cf D l l r

TABLE X

Matt. 19.16f	Justin Dial. 101.2	Justin Apol. 16.7	Marcion Epiph. cf. Harnack² 225f.	Lk. 18.18f (cf. Mk.10.17f.)
διδάσκαλε τί ἀγαθὸν ποιήσω ἵνα σχῶ ζωὴν αἰώνιον; † ὁ δὲ εἶπεν αὐτῷ τί με ἐρωτᾷς περὶ τ. ἀγαθοῦ; εἷς ἐστιν ὁ ἀγαθός	διδάσκαλε ἀγαθέ ἀπεκρίνατο τί με λέγεις ἀγαθόν; εἷς ἐστιν ἀγαθός	διδάσκαλε ἀγαθέ ἀπεκρίνατο λέγων	διδάσκαλε ἀγαθέ τί ποιήσας ζωὴν αἰώνιον κληρονομήσω; ὁ δὲ μή με λέγε ἀγαθόν εἷς ἐστιν ἀγαθός	διδάσκαλε ἀγαθέ τί ποιήσας ζωὴν αἰώνιον κληρονομήσω; εἶπεν δὲ αὐτῷ ὁ Ἰησοῦς τί με λέγεις ἀγαθόν;
	ὁ πατήρ μου ὁ ἐν τ. οὐρανοῖς	οὐδεὶς ἀγαθὸς εἰ μὴ μόνος ὁ θεός * ὁ ποιήσας τ. πάντα	ὁ θεός ὁ πατήρ	οὐδεὶς ἀγαθὸς εἰ μὴ εἷς [ὁ] θεός
† cf. Ev. Hebr.: Origen Matt. 15.14	= Marcosians: Iren. i.3.1 (Harvey i.19) τί με...οὐρανοῖς = Gospel Naasseni in Hippol. V. 7.26.	* cf. Dionysius Areop. de div. nom. 315	cf. Ps.-Clem. Hom. xviii.1.3;14	cf. Marcion: Adamantius, Dial. i.1; ii.17 Origen, de princip. ii.5.1.

TABLE XI

Matt. 26.26-28	Justin Apol. 66,3	Lk. 22.19-20	I Cor. 11.23-25
26 ...λαβὼν ὁ Ἰησοῦς ἄρτον κ. εὐλογήσας ἔκλασεν κ. δοὺς τ. μαθηταῖς εἶπεν λάβετε φάγετε	τ. Ἰησοῦν λαβόντα ἄρτον εὐχαριστήσαντα εἰπεῖν τοῦτο ποιεῖτε εἰς τ. ἀνάμνησίν μου τοῦτ' ἐστι τ. σῶμά μου	19 κ. λαβὼν ἄρτον εὐχαριστήσας ἔκλασεν κ. ἔδωκεν αὐτοῖς λέγων	23 ...ἔλαβεν ἄρτον 24 κ. εὐχαριστήσας ἔκλασεν καὶ εἶπεν
τοῦτό ἐστιν τ. σῶμά μου		τοῦτό ἐστιν τ. σῶμά μου τ. ὑπὲρ ὑμῶν διδόμενον τοῦτο ποιεῖτε εἰς τ. ἐμὴν ἀνάμνησιν	τοῦτό μού ἐστιν τ. σῶμα τ. ὑπὲρ ὑμῶν τοῦτο ποιεῖτε εἰς τ. ἐμὴν ἀνάμνησιν
27 κ. λαβὼν ποτήριον κ. εὐχαριστήσας ἔδωκεν αὐτοῖς λέγων πίετε ἐξ αὐτοῦ πάντες 28 τοῦτο γάρ ἐστιν τ. αἷμά μου τ. διαθήκης τ. περὶ πολλῶν ἐκχυννόμενον εἰς ἄφεσιν ἁμαρτιῶν	κ.τ. ποτήριον ὁμοίως λαβόντα κ. εὐχαριστήσαντα εἰπεῖν τοῦτό ἐστι τ. αἷμά μου	20 κ.τ. ποτήριον ὡσαύτως μετὰ τ. δειπνῆσαι λέγων	ὡσαύτως κ. τ. ποτήριον μετὰ τ. δειπνῆσαι λέγων
		τοῦτο τ. ποτήριον ἡ καινὴ διαθήκη ἐν τ. αἵματί μου τ. ὑπὲρ ὑμῶν ἐκχυννόμενον	τοῦτο τ. ποτήριον ἡ καινὴ διαθήκη ἐστὶν ἐν τῷ ἐμῷ αἵματι τοῦτο ποιεῖτε ὁσάκις ἐὰν πίνητε εἰς τ. ἐμὴν ἀνάμνησιν

TABLE XII

Matt. 26.39 (Justin Dial. 99.2)	Justin Dial. 103.8	Lk. 22.44,42
	[γέγραπται] ὅτι	⁴⁴[κ. γενόμενος ἐν ἀγωνίᾳ ἐκτενέστερον προσηύχετο κ. ἐγένετο
	ἱδρὼς ὡσεὶ θρόμβοι κατεχεῖτο	ὁ ἱδρὼς αὐτοῦ ὡσεὶ θρόμβοι αἵματος καταβαίνοντες ἐπὶ τ. γῆν]
προσευχόμενος κ. λέγων πάτερ [μου] εἰ δυνατόν ἐστιν παρελθάτω ἀπ᾽ ἐμοῦ τ. ποτήριον τοῦτο	αὐτοῦ εὐχομένου κ. λέγοντος	⁴¹ προσηύχετο ⁴² λέγων πάτερ εἰ βούλει
	παρελθέτω εἰ δυνατόν τ. ποτήριον τοῦτο	παρένεγκε τοῦτο τ. ποτήριον ἀπ᾽ ἐμοῦ
cf. Justin Dial. 99.2: πάτερ εἰ δυνατόν ἐστι παρελθέτω τ. ποτήριον τοῦτο ἀπ᾽ ἐμοῦ		

TABLE XIII

Matt. 16.21	Justin Dialogue 51.2	Justin Dial. 76.7	Justin Dial. 100.3	Lk. 24.7	Lk. 9.22 (cf. Mk.8.31)
ὅτι δεῖ αὐτὸν εἰς Ἱεροσόλυμα ἀπελθεῖν	ὅτι δεῖ αὐτὸν	δεῖ τ. υἱὸν τ. ἀνθρώπου	δεῖ τ.υἱὸν τ.ἀνθρώπου	τ. υἱὸν τ. ἀνθρώπου ὅτι δεῖ	ὅτι δεῖ τ. υἱὸν τ. ἀνθρώπου
[cf.17.22]				παραδοθῆναι εἰς χεῖρας ἀνθρώπων ἁμαρτωλῶν	[cf. 9.44]
κ.πολλὰ παθεῖν ἀπὸ τ.πρεσβυτέρων κ. ἀρχιερέων κ. γραμματέων	πολλὰ παθεῖν ἀπὸ	πολλὰ παθεῖν κ.ἀποδοκιμασθῆναι ὑπὸ	πολλὰ παθεῖν κ.ἀποδοκιμασθῆναι ὑπὸ		πολλὰ παθεῖν κ. ἀποδοκιμασθῆναι ἀπὸ τ. πρεσβυτέρων κ. ἀρχιερέων κ. γραμματέων
κ. ἀποκτανθῆναι κ.τ.τρίτῃ ἡμέρᾳ ἐγερθῆναι	τ. γραμματέων κ. φαρισαίων κ. σ.σταυρωθῆναι κ.τ.τρίτῃ ἡμέρᾳ ἀναστῆναι....	τ. γραμματέων κ. φαρισαίων κ.σταυρωθῆναι κ.τ.τρίτῃ ἡμέρᾳ ἀναστῆναι	τ. φαρισαίων κ. γραμματέων κ. σταυρωθῆναι κ.τ.τρίτῃ ἡμέρᾳ ἀναστῆναι	κ.σταυρωθῆναι κ.τ.τρίτῃ ἡμέρᾳ ἀναστῆναι	κ.ἀποκτανθῆναι κ.τ.τρίτῃ ἡμέρᾳ ἐγερθῆναι

CHAPTER TWO

THE STRUCTURE OF ACTS AND ITS THEOLOGY

HISTORIANS DO not need to hold definite beliefs in order to do their work, but, when they do believe, their writings inevitably betray that belief. The first clues to a historian's faith are provided by the point at which he chooses to begin his history and the point at which he ends. When Gibbon began his *Decline and Fall of the Roman Empire* with the Antonines in the second century, he revealed his belief that civilizations start to decline when they enjoy an enervating peace in which the "manly spirit of freedom" is dissipated. Or, to take a more recent example, when Tawney ended his *Religion and the Rise of Capitalism* with the state of affairs at the beginning of the eighteenth century, we are left in no doubt of his belief that religion had reached its lowest point when it did nothing but encourage capitalism.

The theology of the author of Acts is strikingly defined by his beginning and his ending. The beginning has added weight because it is also the middle of the complete work, Luke-Acts, but we cannot interpret the significance of the beginning until we know for certain whether the end we have is really the end.

A long line of commentators has found the present ending unsatisfactory because it does not tell us what happened to Paul. They have supposed that Luke had either intended to write a third volume which he never began, or had written a third volume which has disappeared without a trace. The third volume would have chronicled Paul's later journeys, his last trial, and his martyrdom. This is a hypothesis for which there is no evidence apart from Luke-Acts itself, and it is impossible to entertain such a hypothesis unless the existing evidence is otherwise inexplicable. This chapter, and indeed the whole book, is an attempt to show that Acts and its companion Gospel display a clear and coherent pattern and completely serve the purpose of the artist and theologian who wrote them. There is no need to suppose that Luke had not finished his work.

Before we discuss the significance of the end of Acts we must dispose of another attempt to rob it of any particular meaning. In his later writings, Harnack revived the theory that the end of Acts represented the limits of Luke's historical information; he could write no more because he knew no more.[1] This hypothesis fails on two grounds. First, Luke's Gospel was written after the fall of Jerusalem when it is most unlikely that the martyrdom of Paul was unknown. Clement, writing in A.D. 95, knew of it,[2] and there is no reason to suppose that it would be unknown throughout the whole Church, much less unknown to a writer who made St Paul his hero. Second, Acts itself unmistakably indicates that Paul would die in Rome.

Both these grounds have been challenged. The first is challenged by the argument that Luke's Gospel does not, as has long been supposed, refer to the fall of Jerusalem and that there is, therefore, no remaining reason for holding that it was written after A.D. 70; an attempt has already been made to refute it.[3]

It has also been denied that Acts says that Paul would be martyred in Rome. Harnack[4] has argued that the foreboding of death expressed by Paul in his farewell address to the Ephesian elders when he said that they would never see him

[1] *The Date of the Acts and the Synoptic Gospels* (Eng. tr., London, 1911), 93–9.

[2] 1 Clem. 5.7; cf. Conzelmann in Dibelius, *Die Pastoralbriefe* (3rd ed., Tübingen, 1955), 3.

[3] Pages 1–3, above.

[4] *The Acts of the Apostles* (Eng. tr., London, 1909), 293f; *The Date of the Acts* (Eng. tr., London, 1911), 103.

again (20.25,38) was proved wrong by his release from imprisonment in Rome and his new journey to the East. It is no longer possible to hold that Paul wrote the Pastoral Epistles as they stand,[1] and they alone require a release and second imprisonment. The Pastorals themselves mention only one imprisonment, and the need to call this the second springs from an attempt to harmonize the personal references in 2 Tim. 4.9–21 with those in the other letters ascribed to Paul.[2] The foreboding of death in Acts 20, which the author is at pains to underline, would be clearly understood by contemporary readers of Luke's work to have been fulfilled in Paul's martyrdom at Rome.[3]

The fact that Luke made Acts end with Paul's freedom to preach while imprisoned in Rome now appears even more significant. He has put the prophecy of martyrdom as far back as chapter 20 so that it will overshadow the rest of the story, but chooses to conclude not with the martyrdom itself but with the third rejection of the Jews and a period of unhindered preaching to the Gentiles. Paul dominates the bulk of Acts and his death is of great significance, and yet it is less important to portray this death than it is to say that he has arrived and preached in Rome. The end of the history is a place.[4]

We shall not fully understand the significance of Luke's geographical end to Acts unless we take account of the parallel

---

[1] P. N. Harrison, *The Problem of the Pastoral Epistles* (Oxford, 1921).

[2] Conzelmann in Dibelius, op. cit., 3 and 95. 1 Clem. 5.5–7 probably does not imply a visit to Spain and the Muratorian fragment is a speculation based on Rom. 15.24,28; Harrison, ibid., 107f. Ramsay and Lake's attempts to prove that the last verse of Acts implies a release from prison are unconvincing; *Beginnings*, v.319–38; E. Haenchen, *Die Apostelgeschichte* (10th ed., Göttingen, 1956), 657f n 1; (12th ed., 1959), 648ff n 1.

[3] M. Dibelius, *Studies in the Acts of the Apostles* (1951, Eng. tr., London, 1956), 158 and n 1.

[4] *Beginnings*, iv.350. The significance of the geographical data in Luke-Acts has been stressed by R. H. Lightfoot, *History and Interpretation in the Gospels* (London, 1935), and *Locality and Doctrine in the Gospels* (London, 1938); H. Conzelmann, *Die Mitte der Zeit, Studien zur Theologie des Lukas* (Tübingen, 1954) Eng. tr., *The Theology of St Luke* (London, 1960); and W. Marxsen, *Der Evangelist Markus, Studien zur Redaktionsgeschichte des Evangeliums* (Göttingen, 1956).

ending to his Gospel.[1] Acts ends in Rome; the Gospel ends in Jerusalem. It was by no means necessary that the Gospel should end at Jerusalem, and we can see from the way Luke edited Mark that this was the result of a conscious choice. In Mark the angel who announces the resurrection says, "Go, tell his disciples and Peter that he goes before you into Galilee. There you will see him as he told you" (16.7; cf. 14.28). Lohmeyer has suggested that these words refer to the Parousia: "When the disciples go to Galilee, they will there see the Lord, that is, they will experience the Parousia."[2] Whether or not this is so, it is sufficient for us to notice that the saying seems to have become the basis for a number of Galilean resurrection appearances (Matt. 28.16,10,7; John 21; The Gospel of Peter, etc.). Luke takes a more drastic way out than that taken by Matthew. He has removed every trace of a future appearance in Galilee by changing Mark's words to read, "Remember how he said to you while he was in Galilee, 'The Son of man must be delivered into the hands of sinful men, etc.'" (24.6f). Galilee, which in Mark is the place of future revelation, has become the place where Jesus predicted his death and resurrection; it has been put firmly at the beginning of the saga so that Jerusalem should be at the end (cf. Acts 10.37).

There is evidence, then, that Luke wishes his readers to pay particular attention to the place where he ends both his Gospel and Acts. He has confined the resurrection appearances to Jerusalem and its environs at the expense of altering the words of the angel at the Tomb, and he has deliberately omitted the story of Paul's trial and martyrdom so that the fact of his free preaching in Rome will stand out. Jerusalem is more important than Rome, not only because it is the end of Luke's Gospel but

---

[1] J. B. Lightfoot, *St Paul's Epistle to the Philippians* (London, 1868), 3 n 2: "A comparison (of Acts 28.30,31) with the closing sentences of the Gospel shows a striking parallelism in the plan of the two narratives; they end alike, as they had begun alike."

[2] Ernst Lohmeyer, *Galiläa und Jerusalem* (Göttingen, 1936), 10–14. C. F. Evans, "'I will go before you into Galilee'", *J.T.S.*, N.S., v (1954), 3–18, suggests that Jesus was referring to the Gentile mission.

also because it is the mid-point of Luke-Acts.[1] Rome is the goal of the work, but Jerusalem is the centre to which the action of the Gospel proceeds and from which each new advance in Acts begins. Jerusalem is the city which killed Jesus, as it had killed the prophets before him (Luke 13.34; Matt. 23.37); his resurrection appearances took place in and around Jerusalem; he ascended into heaven just outside its walls; the disciples were ordered to remain there until they had received the power of the Holy Spirit. Because Jerusalem possesses this central importance in the history of salvation, it would be a travesty to end with a subordinate death at Rome. Although Paul's martyrdom dominates the last section of Acts, it only dominates it because it reflects the death of Jesus. The ending of Acts teaches that, even though Paul came to Rome to die, he brought with him the victorious gospel which had triumphed at Jerusalem. The reader is told in the clearest possible terms consistent with historical verisimilitude that Paul was going to be martyred in Rome, but no account of the event is given. Rome has not destroyed the gospel in killing Paul, because Jerusalem could not destroy Jesus; Jesus' triumph in Jerusalem has guaranteed the triumph of the gospel in Rome.

Jerusalem clearly has tremendous theological significance for Luke, but the same is also true about Rome. His preoccupation with showing that neither Jesus nor Paul was ever judged guilty by a Roman official and his accounts of the conversion of Roman soldiers betray his desire to win over the Roman Empire to the side of Christianity. Just as Jerusalem at the centre of the story is the place where God's promises are fulfilled despite the rejection of Jesus by the Jews, so Rome at the end is the place where the acceptance of the gospel by the Gentiles can be confidently announced (Acts 28.28).

Because Luke has endowed geographical data with theological meaning we are justified in reopening the question

[1] This is mathematically as well as symbolically true. Cadbury has estimated that the Gospel of Luke is within 3 per cent of the length of Acts; *The Book of Acts in History* (London, 1955), 138.

whether the geographical movement of the story might not provide the clue to the detailed structure of Acts. If we know the limits of the "chapters" into which the book is divided—if it is divided at all—we should be in a position to isolate the central concern of each part and to understand more clearly the theology of the whole.[1]

Other principles of division have had their vogue. C. H. Turner put forward the suggestion that there were six generalizing summaries which divided Acts into six panels, three for Peter and three for Paul (6.7; 9.31; 12.24; 16.5; 19.20; 28.31).[2] These summaries, however, lack regularity of form[3] and, though they are perhaps the most generalized one can find in Acts, there are a number of other summaries dotted around in a way that suggests that Luke does not intend to divide his narrative by a single trick of style. The summaries play no fixed rôle in the book: 9.31 seems to link two sections rather than to divide them, summarizing the results of the missionary work in preparation for the account of Peter's tour of review; 12.24 marks no more than a stage in the story, a general formula expressing optimism at what has just happened, before the work of Barnabas and Paul is taken up again. Luke's Gospel shows even more clearly the varied functions the summaries are able to perform; in 4.14 and 37, for example, they are put to work to mark off one small but significant section.

The untidiness and incompleteness of some of the panels enclosed by the summaries (in 16.5, as Cadoux notes, "the 'rubric of progress' ... comes right in the middle of Paul's visit to the various cities he had already evangelized on his first missionary journey"), have led Cadoux and Bacon to argue that the summaries mark chronological divisions (or at

---

[1] Cf. the interesting suggestion, made first, I think, by F. Delitzsch, that Matthew's Gospel consists of five blocks of narrative and teaching, with an introduction and conclusion; B. W. Bacon, *Studies in Matthew* (New York, 1930).

[2] Hastings, *Dictionary of the Bible*, i.421; *Beginnings*, ii.175–7 and Cadbury's important criticism, ibid. 392–402.

[3] Cf. the standard rubrics in Matt. 7.28; 11.1; 13.53; 19.1; 26.1.

least Luke thought that they marked chronological divisions) of five years each.[1] But if the sections are not complete and coherent in their subject matter, the dividing lines must be drawn particularly firmly and unmistakably in order to be convincing. If Luke had meant to attach this importance to chronology we should expect much more definite chronological notes than the intermittent and unconnected references to time scattered through Acts (years and months are specified in 11.26; 18.11; 19.8,10; 20.3,31; 24.27; 28.11,30, and days much more often, mostly in the "we"-sections). The summaries are not dated, nor are they attached to dated events. We must conclude that Luke did not intend to divide his work by the summaries. A successful hypothesis about the structure of Acts should both take account of the specific indications Luke chooses to give, and separate the narrative, the illustrative incidents, the speeches, and the summaries into natural groupings; a division by summaries alone does not fulfil these requirements.

Jerusalem and Rome are linked together in Jesus' last charge to his disciples: "You will receive power when the Holy Spirit comes upon you, and you will be my witnesses in Jerusalem, in the whole of Judea and Samaria, and to the end of the earth" (1.8).[2] Many commentators have taken this to be a summary of the contents of Acts,[3] but few have pressed it into service to indicate the divisions of the work. Knowling,[4] taking his cue from J. B. Lightfoot, suggests that the contents may be

---

[1] C. J. Cadoux, "The Chronological Division of Acts", *J.T.S.*, xix (1917–18), 333–41; the quotation in brackets, 336. B. W. Bacon, "The Chronological Scheme of Acts", *H.T.R.*, xiv (1921), 137–66, emphasizes that the panels marked 5-year periods in Luke's mind, even though he may have been mistaken.

[2] See Jacques Dupont, "Le Salut des Gentils et la Signification Théologique du Livre des Actes", *N.T.S.*, 6 (1959–60), 132–55 at 140f; repr. in *Études sur les Actes des Apôtres* (Paris, 1967), 393–419 at 402–4, for a good discussion of "the end of the earth" as a designation for Rome.

[3] The first, as far as I know, was Mayerhoff (1835), cited by McGiffert, *Beginnings*, ii.366.

[4] *The Acts of the Apostles* in *The Expositor's Greek Testament* ii (London, 1900), 11.

divided, according to 1.8, into three sections: 2.14—8.1, "in Jerusalem"; 8.2—11.18, "in all Judea and Samaria", and 11.19—28.31, "and to the uttermost part of the earth". With a slight adjustment to make the first part begin with 1.9, immediately after the introduction,[1] and the second with 8.4, so that Stephen's martyrdom is complete in the preceding verse, Knowling's scheme seems to correspond with Luke's indication in 1.8, and to group the events in a natural way. The second and third divisions both begin a new advance by referring back in similar words to Stephen's martyrdom: οἱ μὲν οὖν διασπαρέντες διῆλθον . . . (8.4; 11.19).

If the scheme so well begun is to provide a complete account of the structure of the book it must be extended to supply at least one, and possibly more than one, division in Knowling's long third section. Menoud,[2] after rightly disposing of the attempt to divide Acts at the end of chapter 12 into The Acts of Peter and The Acts of Paul, argues that the real dividing line comes after 15.35. He relies on two arguments: first, by the time of the Council of Jerusalem all the steps have been made in principle to take the gospel to the end of the earth— geographically the gospel has been taken beyond Jerusalem, Judea, and Samaria to Asia Minor, and theologically the Gentiles are admitted on an equal footing into the Church— and second, after the Council Paul embarks on a long journey which bears a new character, and he is now raised to the apostolic dignity of "witness". These arguments seem to be strong enough to justify putting a new division after 15.35, but not strong enough to require making it the division which dominates all other divisions. It is true that the Council of Jerusalem marks the last discussion of the validity of the Gentile mission, but it is not the first. It is nothing to say that in principle the whole of the geographical advance has been made with the preaching of the gospel in Asia Minor, for in principle the geographical movement outside Palestine was made by

---

[1] The introduction does not end with 1.5; Haenchen (10th ed.), 113–18; (12th ed.), 113–15.

[2] "Le Plan des Actes des Apôtres", N.T.S., i (1954), 44–51.

Jesus' prophetic last words to his disciples,[1] and even when Paul comes to Rome the total extent of the movement to the end of the earth is still only in principle accomplished.[2] Paul certainly assumes full control of his missionary enterprise after the Council, but there is no indication that Luke now elevates him to a new status; Paul believes that he has been a "witness" ever since the Lord appeared to him on the Damascus road (22.15; 26.16). Finally, if Paul plays a more important part after the Jerusalem Council, he assumes yet another rôle in the last section of the book, when his journey up to Jerusalem, and from Jerusalem to Rome, is reminiscent of Jesus' journey to his death.[3] We are fully justified in making 15.35 the end of the third division of Acts, but not in regarding it as the only division.

Menoud[4] rightly rejects the old scheme for dividing Paul's missionary journeys into "the first missionary journey" (13–14), "the second missionary journey" (15.36—18.22), and "the third missionary journey" (18.23—21.14 or 16). That scheme not only derives from a missionary practice which had clear ideas about the fixed "headquarters" from which missionaries were sent out, but also ignores the explicit indications of another pattern in Acts itself. It is clear from these that a new stage begins at 19.21.[5] In 19.10 Luke notes that after two years' preaching in Ephesus it could be said that "all those who lived in Asia, Jews and Greeks, had heard the word of the Lord"; the words at the opening of 19.21, "when these things had been completed", refer not just to the events which took place during Paul's stay in Ephesus but to his whole missionary activity in Asia. From the beginning of the section there is a divine compulsion behind every step that is taken. The ambiguous words ἔθετο ὁ Παῦλος ἐν τῷ πνεύματι tell the discerning

---

[1] Paul Wendland, *Die Urchristlichen Literaturformen, Hdb.z.N.T.*, I.iii (2nd and 3rd ed., Tübingen, 1912), XII, *Apostelgeschichten*, 317.

[2] Knowling, op. cit., 12.

[3] R. B. Rackham, *The Acts of the Apostles* (London, 1901), xlvii.

[4] Op. cit., 48f.

[5] *Beginnings*, iv.243: "This is the real beginning of Paul's last journey to Jerusalem."

reader that the Holy Spirit has inspired Paul's resolve,[1] as the word δεῖ, denoting divine necessity, shows: "After I have been there (in Jerusalem), it is necessary for me to see Rome too." We are reminded of the words Ananias heard in 9.16, when the Lord said to him, "I will show him (Paul) how much it is necessary (δεῖ) that he suffer for my name's sake." Again and again in the next chapters the Spirit tells Paul that he will undergo suffering and eventually stand before Caesar in Rome; Paul tells the Ephesian elders about the Spirit's repeated assurance that this will be so (20.22f, 25, cf. 38); the disciples at Tyre warn him against going to Jerusalem (21.4); Agabus prophesies his arrest in Jerusalem (21.10–14), and the Lord confirms his purpose to send Paul to Rome by appearing to him when he is arrested in Jerusalem (23.11: δεῖ), and again during the great storm on his way to the capital (27.24).

There is an unmistakable unity in this last section. The key to its significance is to be found in the way Paul replies to Agabus in 21.13: "Why do you weep and break my heart? I am ready not only to be bound but to die in Jerusalem for the sake of the name of the Lord Jesus." At first sight we are surprised that he should think it likely that he would die in Jerusalem when he has already stated, "It is necessary for me to see Rome" (19.21), but plainly what he means to indicate is that he is willing to follow the pattern of Christ's suffering, who was also delivered up by the Jews into the hands of the Gentiles (21.11).[2] The repeated predictions of his suffering correspond to Jesus' own predictions as he too travelled up to Jerusalem. Paul, however, is rescued from death again and again (21.31–6; 23.12–24; 25.2ff; 27.24,42f; 28.3ff) so that he will at last arrive safely in Rome. There, as Luke clearly tells us, he is martyred, but that is no climax: the climax is his arrival and his unrestricted preaching at the centre of the Empire. The sufferings by which this goal is achieved are literally Christ-like, but if Luke had gone on to recount how Paul died he would have obscured the gospel message: the

---

[1] Ibid., iv.244.
[2] Overbeck; see Haenchen (10th ed.), 542; (12th ed.), 536.

spiritual conquest of the Empire depended on Jesus' death and resurrection in Jerusalem, not on Paul's death in Rome. While it is true that Acts parallels the third Gospel, and in particular the final sections of each correspond, the more important thing to see is that both books hinge on what happened in Jerusalem. Jerusalem is the centre of Luke-Acts, the centre of the history of salvation.[1]

Before we can confidently draw any further conclusions from the suggested division of Acts into five sections, we must see whether these divisions correspond to anything in Luke; it is not necessary that the Gospel and Acts should be constructed in exactly the same way but, if the Gospel appears to be built on entirely different principles from those which we have suggested for Acts, the hypothesis would lose a great deal of its force.

Commentators usually put divisions in Luke's Gospel at three places: the first either just before or just after Jesus' temptations (4.1 or 4.14), the second when he sets his face to go to Jerusalem (9.51), and the third as he prepares for his triumphant entry into the city (19.28). The fact that the long central section, 9.51 to 19.28, is cast in the form of a journey suggests that geographical factors may be as important for the division of the Gospel as they are for Acts.[2] The usual divisions can be defined geographically. After the Temptations Jesus returns to Galilee (4.14) and seems to have used Galilee as his base for preaching throughout all Judea (4.44; 7.17) before withdrawing to Bethsaida in the north of Galilee (9.10) to prepare his disciples for his journey. Apart from an initial incursion into Samaria (9.51–6), the journey itself seems to have taken place mainly in Galilee, or more vaguely "between Samaria and Galilee" (17.11); the only fixed point is the goal, Jerusalem (9.51; 13.22,33f; 17.11; 18.31; 19.11). The factor which defines the shape of the narrative in this long journey section is not the towns through which the travellers pass—

---

[1] Cf. Conzelmann, *Die Mitte der Zeit* (Tübingen, 1954), 8f, *The Theology of St Luke* (London, 1960), 16f.

[2] R. H. Lightfoot; H. Conzelmann.

none is mentioned by name until they approach Jericho (18.35)—but the way Jesus explains to his disciples his own fate, and the way he prepares them for their discipleship. "Jesus' consciousness that he must suffer is expressed in the form of a journey" (Conzelmann).[1]

If this is so, there is good reason for believing that Luke has grouped the teaching contained in the travel narrative into two sections. The division occurs at 14.1. Just before this new section, Jesus defines again his purpose to go to Jerusalem, under pressure of the warning conveyed by the Pharisees that Herod is trying to kill him. Luke has marked the beginning of the journey by stating Jesus' firm intention to go to Jerusalem, but his purpose is not yet fully defined (9.51); at the end of chapter 13 the intention is repeated, and this time it is made clear by the lament over Jerusalem that the city will kill him as it killed the prophets before him.

It would be out of place to attempt to justify the new division in detail, but there are at least three indications that this is the way Luke meant to divide his Gospel.

First, Jesus' answer to the Pharisees who warn him of the danger from Herod suggests that the journey should be divided into two parts: "See, I cast out demons and perform healings to-day and to-morrow, and on the third day I will reach my goal. But it is necessary for me to journey to-day and to-morrow and the next day, because it is not God's will (ἐνδέχεται) that a prophet should perish outside Jerusalem" (13.32f). "The third day I will reach my goal" obviously refers to the last period of his life when he enters Jerusalem, and it is possible that "to-day" and "to-morrow" represent stages in the journey to his destination.

Second, the content of the teaching in the second part of the journey seems to be developed a stage further than it was in the first half. The clue to the difference may be found in the contrast between the two similar parables of the friend at midnight and the importunate widow. Each is constructed

[1] Op. cit., 53, Eng. tr., 65.

according to the same pattern and each teaches the same lesson, but one occurs in the first half of the journey (11.5–8) and the other in the second half (18.1–8). The significant difference is that the first parable concerns the need for bread and the second the need for help in oppression. This distinction seems to be typical of the difference in emphasis in each part: the first part is full of teaching about the nature of discipleship, its duties, hardships, and rewards, while in the second part the opposition to Jesus comes out into the open and the disciples are taught how they must behave under persecution.

Third, the three occasions on which Jesus dines with Pharisees correspond to the three central sections of the Gospel. The first is taken over from Mark (Mark 14.3–9; Luke 7.36–50), but Luke has radically altered its place in the narrative; the second (Luke 11.37ff) contains the Woes from Q, but their setting during a meal with a Pharisee is found in Luke alone; the opening of the third meal (Luke 14.1ff) seems to be a Lucan repetition of an earlier incident (Luke 6.6–11 and par.), an indication that Luke is responsible for the setting here as well. The first meal occurs in the section where Jesus gathers his disciples together, the second in the first part of the journey, and the third in the second part of the journey, and each meal shows a development in the relationship between Jesus and the Pharisees of increasing antagonism, corresponding to the stages on the spiritual journey to Jerusalem.

It is possible, then, to justify a five-fold division of the Gospel: (1) 1.5 to 3.38, Jesus comes to fulfil all the O.T. expectations; (2) 4.1 to 9.50, he preaches in the whole of Judea and Galilee and gathers his disciples; (3) 9.51 to 13.35, he begins his journey to Jerusalem and teaches the nature of discipleship; (4) 14.1 to 19.27, he concludes his journey to Jerusalem and prepares his disciples for the Passion; (5) 19.28 to 24.53, he reigns in Jerusalem by dying and rising again.

Each of the parts is governed by some sort of geographical factor, and always the geographical movement has significance for the history of salvation. The city which appears at every turn of the story is the holy city of Jerusalem, and it is important to note that at each of the breaks between Luke's sections there stands a definitive reference to Jerusalem. At the first Jesus, after his baptism in the Jordan, is led into the desert by the Spirit to be tempted and his last temptation takes place in Jerusalem; his mission is defined near Jerusalem before he returns to Galilee to begin his ministry (4.14). At the second break he steadfastly sets his face to go to Jerusalem (9.51); at the third he renews his purpose to die in Jerusalem and laments over the rebellious city (13.31–5); at the fourth he enters it to die, having warned his disciples that Jerusalem cannot be the scene of the Kingdom's coming until it has been the scene of his death (19.11ff).

The corresponding five-fold division of Acts is this: (1) 1.9 to 8.3; (2) 8.4 to 11.18; (3) 11.19 to 15.35; (4) 15.36 to 19.20; (5) 19.21 to 28.31.

Jerusalem is equally important for this set of divisions. Stephen's martyrdom is the signal to take the gospel from Jerusalem to Judea and Samaria, and to Antioch and beyond, providing both the first and the second break in the story (8.4 and 11.19). At the beginning of each of these second and third sections the Jerusalem Church specifically approves and watches over the new missionary efforts, by sending Peter and John to Samaria (8.14–25) and by sending Barnabas to Antioch (11.22ff). The second section ends with Peter's reporting back to Jerusalem after he has baptized Cornelius, and receiving the blessing of the Jerusalem Church on his work (11.18). The break between the third and fourth sections is marked by the important Jerusalem Council in which, significantly, James, the leader of the Jerusalem Church, and not Peter, the first of the Apostles, takes the principal part. The final section begins with Paul's making his fateful decision to return to Jerusalem and to go from there to Rome.

In the whole of Luke-Acts Jerusalem controls the history.[1] It is at the same time the city which God redeems (Luke 2.38)

---

[1] G. W. H. Lampe, *St Luke and the Church of Jerusalem*, *The Ethel M. Wood Lecture*. London, 1969.

and the city where he is rejected. It becomes the centre of the mission to the Gentiles, but it rejects the gospel for itself. Jerusalem is both the Heavenly City and the Earthly City. The story ends at Rome because Jerusalem has rejected her saviour, but Rome will be the centre of the Church, and Jerusalem will be in subjection, only "until the times of the Gentiles are fulfilled" (Luke 21.24).

The most cogent objection to seeing the structure of Acts in a geographical framework is made by Overbeck. "The view that Acts is intended to describe the passage of the Gospel from Jerusalem to Rome . . . collapses at once before the fact that in 28.15 Acts presupposes the existence of a Christian community in Rome, without having announced its origin. We are not told how the Gospel came to Rome, but how Paul came to Rome."[1]

This objection cannot be avoided by saying that here is another example of the contradiction between Luke's scheme and his sources, his scheme demanding that Paul be the first missionary in Rome, though his sources have stated that there was already a Christian congregation in the city.[2] We are told too often about the Christians already established in the place when Paul first arrives for this argument to succeed. The existence of Christians in Ephesus seems to be assumed, although they are still part of the Synagogue (18.19ff,26; Priscilla and Aquila) and there are "brethren" at Puteoli to greet Paul on his way to Rome (28.13f).[3] In the same way Peter finds Christians already in Lydda and Joppa (9.32,36), and perhaps we should also note that Jesus is greeted by a "crowd of disciples" when he enters Jerusalem, though he has conducted no mission in the city (Luke 19.37). Luke does not seem to be primarily interested in how the gospel was first planted in the cities of the Empire.

[1] F. Overbeck, *Introduction to De Wette's Commentary on Acts* (4th ed., 1870), in the English translation of Zeller, *The Contents and Origin of the Acts of the Apostles, Critically Investigated* (London, 1875), 16; cf. Cadoux, op. cit., 334f.

[2] Cadoux, op. cit., 335.

[3] Haenchen, op. cit., 663.

Another answer is to turn the objection back on those who make it by admitting that Luke emphasizes the arrival of Paul at Rome, and asserting that, if this is not the first occasion, it is the definitive occasion on which the gospel is preached in the capital. Menoud says: "The 'chosen vessel' is not the first to preach the gospel in the city of the Caesars. But in the eyes of Luke it is Paul who, coming from Jerusalem in the fellowship of the Apostles, and invested by Christ himself with the status of witness, is the missionary truly authorized in every respect, the one qualified to carry out Christ's command to proclaim the gospel to the world."[1]

This approach seems to be the right one, but it goes too far. Granted that Paul is the "hero" of Acts, we may doubt whether the mere fact of his arrival in Rome would be sufficient to mark the preliminary completion of Jesus' command in 1.8. The full significance of the geographical stages according to which Acts is constructed cannot be contained in a simple statement that Paul, the foremost missionary, has arrived at his goal, since the geographical forward-movement depends on many others besides Paul, and begins before his conversion. But if Acts is not the story of how the good news was brought from Jerusalem to Rome, and not simply the story of how Paul, as Christ's chief evangelist, reached Rome, what is it?

In Ephesus, the other main city where Paul finds Christians when he arrives, we discover a clue to the decisive nature of Paul's work in Rome. The Christians still seem to have been members of the synagogue, for it was in the synagogue that Priscilla and Aquila heard Apollos teaching a defective doctrine about Jesus (18.24–8), and Paul had already been treated well by the same synagogue a little earlier (18.19–21). When Paul returned to Ephesus he also had to deal with disciples who only knew John's baptism, and he spent three months in the syna-

---

[1] Op. cit., 50; cf. Knowling, op. cit., 13; "The Gospel had come to Rome already, but those who accepted it were only a sect everywhere spoken against; now its foremost representative gains it a hearing from the Gentiles, and that too without interruption or prohibition."

gogue reasoning and trying to persuade the Jews to become Christians (19.8). Only when they proved adamant and began counter-propaganda did Paul feel obliged to separate off the disciples (Jews and Gentiles) and find another preaching-place (19.9). When two years of this separatist preaching had been completed Luke can say that "all who live in Asia, Jews and Greeks, had heard the word of the Lord" (19.10). It seems that Paul's particular work, in Ephesus at least, had not consisted in simply preaching in order to make Christians: Christians there were already; what Paul's preaching to the Jews accomplished was the ejection of the Christians from the synagogue and the founding of a separate Church. A similar scene had been enacted as a result of Paul's preaching in Pisidian Antioch (13.46) and in Corinth (18.6), and was to occur again in Rome (28.28).[1] It is inadequate to say that the theme of Acts is the spread of the gospel from Jerusalem to Rome, because the gospel has run ahead of Paul from Jerusalem to Rome. The decisive effect of his preaching is the establishment of the Church as an institution separate from Judaism. Luke's thesis is that the gospel is free to travel to the ends of the earth only when it is free from the false form which the Jewish religion has taken. Paul is the one figure in the early Church who saw the issue clearly, and that is why Luke makes Paul the central figure in the latter part of Acts. Paul does not attack the Jews—far from it—but when he goes to them and states the issues they eventually turn on him and, as God has fore-ordained, reject the gospel. Right up to the last journey to Jerusalem Paul has regarded the Church as still essentially part of the Jewish nation. The only reference to the collection he brought up to Jerusalem makes this clear: "Now, after some years I came bringing relief to my nation . . ." not, let it be noted, specifically to the Church which can be distinguished from the nation (24.17). At his trials and examinations he emphasizes that he has remained a faithful Jew: "I have not sinned in any respect against the Law of the Jews, against the Temple or against

---

[1] Dibelius, op. cit. (Eng. tr.), 149f.

Caesar" (25.8; cf. 23.6).[1] Yet still the Jews try to kill him and refuse to accept the gospel, so that, with a note of finality, he is at length forced to declare, "Let it be known to you that this, the salvation of God, has been sent to the Gentiles. They will hear" (28.28). The process which first became obvious when Stephen was martyred has come to its ordained conclusion. While the gospel spread from Jerusalem in ever-widening circles until it reached Rome, another process was at work. The gospel was breaking out of its entanglement with organized Judaism and becoming free to be the universal religion. Jerusalem is left behind and Rome is entered.

[1] Jacob Jervell, "Paulus—Der Lehrer Israels: zu den apologetischen Paulusreden in der Apg.", *Novum Testamentum*, x (1968), 164–90, rightly emphasizes that Luke devotes the last part of Acts largely to defending Paul's claim to be a true teacher of Israel, but he underestimates the significance of Paul's final remark in the whole book, Acts 28.28, and the preceding citation from Isa. 6.9f. Paul is the one who is true to the Old Testament, not the official representatives of Judaism; therefore he turns the face of the Church, composed of Jews and Gentiles (and also containing Jewish Christian congregations, represented in the story by James), towards the Gentile world. Luke does not say that the Gentile mission is the result of the reluctance of Jews to hear the message (that mission was always in view from the beginning, Luke 24.44–7); he says, rather, that an independent Church, expecting her great future to lie in the Gentile world, is the result of the reluctance of Judaism to hear the gospel and assume its proper rôle.

CHAPTER THREE

THE ATTITUDE TO THE JEWS

IT WAS suggested in the previous chapter that the movement of the story from Jerusalem to Rome had more than a matter-of-fact significance. Luke means to show that the Church came of age when it finally left Jerusalem behind. In this chapter we shall explore more thoroughly that part of Luke's theology of history which concerns the Jews who have not repented, and try, by referring to historical parallels, to place this theology in the development of Christian thought.

The best starting point for the exploration is Stephen's speech. One of the chief difficulties in understanding Luke's own theology is that one can never be sure that the sentiments he attributed to any of his characters are precisely what he himself believed; he may either have had good historical information about what they said on a particular occasion, or he may have thought that he knew well enough what they would have said without himself agreeing with it all. The best way of discovering his own point of view is by noting, as we have tried to do in the previous chapter, what he chooses to tell and what he omits, where he begins and where he ends. Luke believed that the history of the apostolic period displayed the working of God as directly as the history of Jesus' life had done, and he felt justified in making his second volume balance and complete the first. His theology must be looked for primarily in the movement of his history. If the speeches differ from one another in theological emphasis, we must not expect to hear Luke's voice in one as against the other, but we should look for his theology in the dramatic contribution each of them makes to the progress of the story. The relationship of the speeches to one another in their similarities and differences is more important for our purpose than the contents of each of them taken by itself.

Stephen's speech provides a good place to begin, for two reasons. First, it occurs at the first great crisis of Acts. The martyrdom of Stephen forms the conclusion of the first of the five sections into which it seems that Luke divided his work. It is the last event which takes place while the action is confined to Jerusalem, and the persecution which follows is specifically pointed out as marking the beginning of the next two stages in the story, set first in Samaria, Judea, and Galilee (8.4—11.18) and then in southern Asia Minor (11.19—15.35). Further, it is the event which first involves Saul of Tarsus in Christian history. By the way in which so much of significance is attached to one event we may suspect that Luke is schematizing the history and attributing to one cause what probably should be attributed to many. It would be wrong to call this falsification; rather he is illustrating with one concrete example the historical truth that the indifference and hostility of the Jews led to the spread of the gospel beyond Palestine. But his art betrays his theology.

Second, we begin with Stephen's speech because it is so very different in form and contents from any other speech in Acts. Its theology seems to be unparalleled, and yet Luke thought it sufficiently important to devote more space to it than to any other speech. The source may have been lengthy, but he was free to shorten or omit as he pleased; if his sources did contain reports of speeches, he must have omitted some and shortened others (cf. the summary in one verse of what Paul preached to Felix in 24.25), so that we are obliged to ask what significance Stephen's speech had for Luke. We shall be nearer the answer if we can understand the part played by the speech in the development of Acts as a whole.

The first question, however, concerns the point of the speech at the trial. The commentary on Stephen's speech in *The Beginnings of Christianity* asserts uncompromisingly that "this is

not a rebuttal of the charges brought against him".[1] In a sense
this is true—Stephen does not defend himself by disposing of
the indictments like a man who wants to save his life—but it is
false if it suggests that there is not a complete correspondence
between the charges and the defence.[2]

The answers to the two charges in the speech are very clear;
the confusion arises only because there seems to be so much
else besides. The answer to the first charge, that Christianity
was attacking the Temple, was that the Temple was not God's
dwelling place, as the O.T. prophets had already made clear.
Jesus was not going to destroy the Temple; if it was destroyed,
the implication is, that would be due to the rebelliousness of
the Jews who built it and claimed that God lived there. Similarly, not Christianity but Judaism has been disobedient to the
Law of Moses, as shown in the rejection of the prophets culmi-
nating in the rejection of Jesus. In both cases Stephen turns
back the charge on to the Jews, and demonstrates that they,
and not the Christians, have disobeyed God and Moses. "The
true representatives of the religion of Abraham, Moses and the
prophets are not the Jews, ever stubborn and rebellious, but
the Christians."[3]

Commentators have attempted to find more in Stephen's
speech than this. They have hoped to discover an esoteric
theology in the seemingly harmless details of O.T. history. It
is true that there are differences between the story as given by
Stephen and as recorded in the O.T., but these differences are
not significant theologically. They provide one more piece of
evidence that Luke is indebted to Hellenistic Jewish sources;
most of the discrepancies can be found in Philo and Josephus.[4]
The history is not told in order to illustrate the general lesson

---

[1] *Beginnings*, iv.69; cf. Wendland, *Hdb.z.N.T.*, I.iii (Tübingen, 1912),
265; F. J. Foakes Jackson, *J.B.L.*, 1930, 283–6; Bo Reicke, *Glaube und
Leben der Urgemeinde* (Zürich, 1957), 133, who states that the speech is
primarily a sermon and only "indirectly intended as a speech in defence".
[2] B. S. Easton, "A Note on Stephen's Speech" at the end of "The
Purpose of Acts" in *Early Christianity* (London, 1955), 115–18.
[3] Loisy, *Les Actes des Apôtres* (Paris, 1920), 320.
[4] H. J. Cadbury, *The Book of Acts in History* (London, 1955), 102–4.

that God is not tied to one special Holy Land, for there is no attempt to avoid mentioning God's promise that Abraham's descendants would inherit Palestine;[1] there is not enough evidence to prove that Luke held some rudimentary version of a theory of biblical "couples", Moses-Aaron, David-Solomon;[2] nor is Stephen represented as a typologist except in so far as he takes Moses' words about "a prophet like me" to refer to Jesus, and regards the way the Jews treated Jesus as typical.[3] As Dibelius has emphasized, the very neutrality of the O.T. narrative is part of Luke's counter to the charges made against Stephen and against Christianity. The first open attack on the Jews is made by a pious Hellenistic Jew, who uses an orthodox O.T. narrative to do it.[4]

How do the answers to the two charges compare with the answers given in the rest of Acts and in Luke's Gospel? Is Stephen's speech almost completely aberrant, and does it "conflict with the basic attitude of Acts"?[5]

At first sight Stephen's attitude to the Temple seems to be shared by no one else in Luke-Acts. Jesus is presented at the Temple according to the Law governing the first-born male; he goes up with his parents when he is twelve; he cleanses the Temple; and he spends the last period of his ministry teaching day after day in the Temple (19.47—21.38). After the ascension the disciples pray continually in the Temple and teach the people there; Paul, according to one account of his conversion, received his commission to go to the Gentiles while he was praying in the Temple (Acts 22.17); and on his last visit to Jerusalem he punctiliously fulfils Temple ceremonial and

---

[1] Bo Reicke, op. cit., 134 and *passim*.

[2] Marcel Simon, *St Stephen and the Hellenists in the Primitive Church* (The Haskell Lectures, London, 1958), 57.

[3] R. P. C. Hanson, *Theology*, 50 (1947), 142–5.

[4] *Aufsätze* (Göttingen, 1951), 143–6; Eng. tr., *Studies* (London, 1956), 166–9. Haenchen (10th ed.), 246ff; cf. (12th ed.), 238–41, follows Dibelius in arguing that Luke has employed a source. Luke's only additions to the source are the polemic sentences at the end of the sections on Moses and Solomon. See now R. Storch, *Die Stephanusrede: Apg. 7.2–52*, Dissertation, Georg August University, Göttingen (1967), and the discussion below.

[5] Marcel Simon, op. cit., 43; and "Saint Stephen and the Jerusalem Temple", *J.E.H.*, ii (1951), 127.

sponsors four others who had taken a vow (21.23ff). Paul speaks not only for himself but for the whole Christian community when he denies the ridiculous charge that he had tried to profane the Temple (24.6,17–19) and says, "I have committed no offence against either the Law of the Jews, the Temple, or Caesar" (25.8).

On closer examination, however, it appears that Luke is well aware that the Temple is to be destroyed and that the piety centred on the Temple will fail. In the cleansing of the Temple he removes the last part of the quotation from Isa. 56.7 on Jesus' lips: "My house will be a house of prayer" (Luke 19.46), not "My house will be called a house of prayer for all nations" (Mark 11.17).[1] The destruction of the Temple has made it no longer possible to regard it as the place where Gentiles will come to pray. Nor is it without significance that Paul is arrested and accused of profaning the Temple at the very moment when he is paying particular attention to its purificatory requirements. Just as God had told him to go to the Gentiles as he was praying in the Temple, so he is arrested and begins his fateful journey to Rome when he is about to complete the days of purification. It seems that God himself is driving Christians out of the Temple, and showing that they cannot confine themselves to its limitations.

So Luke is able to do justice to the faithfulness of the primitive Church to its Jewish background, while showing at the same time that God is at work in its history to force it out into the Gentile world. Luke uses Stephen's prophetic words before he dies to proclaim God's ancient judgement on the Temple, which the Church only learnt for itself by bitter, but providential, experience.

Stephen's views on the Law are not so strikingly different from those expressed by other Christians in Acts.[2] He is certainly not saying that the Law is an enemy from whom

---

[1] The same omission is made by Matt. (21.13), probably for the same reason; Kilpatrick, *The Origins of the Gospel according to St Matthew* (Oxford, 1946), 118.

[2] For the whole subject of the Lucan attitude to the Law see the excellent discussion in Leonhard Goppelt, *Christentum und Judentum im ersten und zweiten Jahrhundert* (Gütersloh, 1954), 231–3.

Christians have been freed, as Paul says in his Epistles. He simply states that the Jews themselves have not kept the Law, and implies that they, not he, have attacked it in attacking the prophets and the Messiah. There is no suggestion in the speech that the Jewish charge of antinomianism is justified. It is true that Peter is aware that all Jews, Christian and non-Christian, find it impossible to keep the Law perfectly,[1] and both he and Paul know that keeping the Law is not sufficient for salvation (15.10f; 13.38f), but they never say that Jews are now free to disregard Moses. Paul readily accepts James's plan for publicly demonstrating that he has never tried to turn the Jews of the Dispersion away from that allegiance (21.20–6). On one point God himself has had to intervene to make it possible for Jewish Christians to associate with Gentiles in order to preach the gospel to them. He sent to Peter a vision of unclean beasts and commanded him to eat them. This same precedent is invoked in chapter 15 to justify not asking Gentile Christians to be circumcised and fulfil all the special Mosaic practices, but the Jerusalem decree does ask them to accept some limitations: to refrain from eating food offered to idols, strangled animals and blood, and from indulging in fornication (15.20,29; 21.25).[2] The argument for specifying these restrictions seems to be that Mosaic morality is not a purely Palestinian thing, but is well known throughout the Gentile world because of the existence of synagogues in every city.[3] Some parts of the Law of

[1] If the words in 15.10, "which neither our fathers nor we were strong enough to bear", are not a gloss.

[2] The reading of Codex Vaticanus should be accepted; the omission of και της πορνειας by p[45] at 15.20 is an omission of the unlike term; the Western reading is an attempt to make the Decree into a purely moral requirement; see C. S. C. Williams, *Alterations to the Text of the Synoptic Gospels and Acts* (Oxford, 1951), 72–5. Hans Waitz, "Das Problem des sog. Apostel-dekrets, usw.", *Z.K.G.*, Dritte Folge vi (1936), 227–63 at 227–31, suggests that it is an application of the Levitical requirements for "the stranger within the gate" to the relations between Jewish and Gentile Christians. This interpretation was anticipated by A. Ritschl, *Theologische Jahrbücher* vi (1847), 301. (Now see Chapter Four in this 2nd ed. for a slightly different suggestion about the text of the Decree.)

[3] This seems to be the meaning of that difficult verse, 15.21. See Haenchen (10th ed.), 396f; (12th ed.), 391f; but see Chapter Four for a slightly different view, which I have adopted for the 2nd ed.

Moses are particularly Jewish, but one may distinguish between those customs (ἔθη) and the universal morality which
it contains. All Christians should accept Moses as their moral
guide.[1] It seems then that Stephen's defence of Christianity,
with its reverence for the Law "received at the command of
angels", is not untypical of the attitude to the Law in the rest
of Luke-Acts.

His attack on the Jews for themselves not keeping the Law
is no fiercer than Paul's when he rebukes the High Priest
Ananias for ordering him to be struck on the mouth. "God is
going to strike you, you white-washed wall. You sit there
judging me by the Law and do you break the Law (παρανομῶν)
by ordering me to be struck?" (23.3).

On both the points of Stephen's speech we must conclude
that his defence fits perfectly the theology of the rest of Acts.
Stephen's manner of speaking is quite different from that
adopted by Peter and Paul and James, or any other spokesmen
for Christianity; he comes out with propositions which could
never be attributed to them, and he leaves unsaid things which
they would say, but he makes his special contribution to the
total consistent theology of the whole book. This theology is
not a propositional theology, but a theology of history which
has room for certain divergencies and even disagreements,
provided they all contribute to showing how God's purpose for
the Church is worked out in the end.

We are now in a position to see Stephen's speech as part of
the developing pattern of Acts, and to draw some conclusions
about Luke's estimation of the place of the Jews in salvation-
history.

Stephen's speech is an attack on the Jews rather than a
measured defence; both charges are thrown back on to the
accusers. The heart of the counter-charge is that the Jews have
killed the Messiah, and if we examine all the references to the
guilt of the Jews for Jesus' death in Acts we shall see how Luke

[1] Goppelt, op. cit., 232f; "Perhaps Luke is trying to help the Church to
understand what is still applicable to their moral behaviour when he
alone among N.T. writers distinguishes the ceremonial Law in the νόμος by
a special term, the ἔθη of Moses".

expounds a single view of the place of the Jews in God's plan by means of the divergent ideas expressed by his historical characters.

Luke is always at pains to emphasize that "Herod and Pontius Pilate, with the Gentiles and the people of Israel" (4.27) each played their part in killing Jesus. It is true that in the account of Jesus' trial he shows that Pilate, in condemning him, was doing it in surrender to the will of the Jews (Luke 23.24f; cf. Mark 15.15), but this does not imply that he believed Pilate guiltless.[1] The factual statements in Acts 2.23 and 3.13 make Pilate's part clear, though this is played down in deference to the Romans, particularly in Peter's speech before Cornelius (10.39).[2] Luke's primary theological interest, however, is to show how the Jews rejected each opportunity to repent of what they had done. In each successive speech that drama is taken to a new point, and Stephen's speech is the end of a climax.

In the speech at Pentecost Peter contents himself with a bare recital of the facts, set in a strong framework of divine inevitability: ". . . him, delivered up in the fixed plan and foreknowledge of God, you nailed up and killed by the hands of lawless men" (2.23). The Jews he is addressing are clearly told of their responsibility and are offered repentance, but no special prominence is given to the matter. The next speech, in chapter 3, is markedly more irenic than the formal statement appropriate to Pentecost. There is no compromise on the need for repentance—"everyone who does not hear that prophet will be rooted out from the people" (3.23)—but the guilt of cruci-

[1] Conzelmann's attempt, op. cit., 75–8, Eng. tr., 90–3, to show that Luke in Acts 2.23 is really referring to the Jews and not to the Romans is unconvincing. He argues that there is a tension between the sources, where the Romans and Jews are blamed alike, and Luke's own view, where only the Jews are guilty. I agree that Luke has emphasized the guilt of the Jews, but there is no evidence that he believes it is an exclusive guilt.

[2] Luke is anxious to demonstrate that Pilate believed Jesus innocent (Luke 23.4; Acts 3.13; 13.28), and this is part of his whole case that Christianity is a law-abiding religion, but the question here is somewhat different: it is whether Pilate himself was guilty, rather than whether he judged Jesus guilty.

fying an innocent man is put down to their ignorance, at the time, of the true status of him whom "the God of Abraham and Isaac and Jacob, the God of our fathers has glorified". "And now, my brothers, I know that you acted in ignorance, like your rulers" (3.17). Although this appeal leads to the conversion of many of the audience, it is also the cause of the first arrest. At his appearance before the rulers, elders, and scribes, Peter is able to stress the exclusive claims of Jesus more strongly than in the previous speech: "In no one else is there salvation, for no other name under heaven is given to men which you must use to be saved" (4.12). After the second arrest the moment of decision for the Jerusalem rulers has drawn another stage nearer, as has the moment when the young Church must decide between loyalty to the religious leaders of its own people and loyalty to God. "One must obey God rather than men ... to the obedient God has given the Holy Spirit" (5.29,32). Pilate's part in the crucifixion is not mentioned, and the Jews are confronted with their own guilt as simply as possible: "You laid hands on him and hung him on the tree" (5.30).

Jerusalem has been given a full opportunity to repent of what it has done but, despite some measure of success, Stephen's arrest and trial and lynching mark the final failure of the mission to the capital. Stephen's speech is a commentary on the significance of his own death; he announces that there is now no turning back from the fatal course of Jewish history inaugurated when the people first rebelled against Moses. Up to this point in Acts the O.T. has been used to show that the prophets had looked forward to Jesus; now it is employed to prove that the Jews have never accepted the prophets. Their guilt has culminated in the murder of Jesus, and they have again refused to repent. "Which of the prophets did your fathers not persecute? And they killed those who announced beforehand the coming of the Righteous One, whom you have now betrayed and murdered" (7.52).

The martyrdom is, as we have already argued, the end of the climax in the first section of the Book of Acts. The mission to Jerusalem is no longer the concern of the author, though he provides evidence that it still continues (21.20); he means us to understand that God's judgement has finally been pronounced on Jerusalem at the murder of Stephen. Stephen is vindicated and sees a vision of the Son of Man, but the city as a whole has lost its chance, though individual Jews might still repent. The mission now goes to Samaria, Judea, and Galilee (8.4—11.18) and to southern Asia Minor (11.19—15.35). At the beginning of each of these two sections stands a reference to the impetus given by the persecution which followed Stephen's martyrdom, showing that the obduracy of the Jerusalem Jews has only furthered the spread of the gospel.

The next time Jews are addressed is by Paul in the synagogue at Antioch of Pisidia. The question of guilt for Jesus' death is again raised, but in the presence of these Dispersion Jews it is specifically laid at the door of the inhabitants of Jerusalem. He stresses that it is now the turn of the Dispersion to accept the promises of God and escape the consequences of disbelieving what God has done. "For the inhabitants of Jerusalem and their leaders did not recognize him and fulfilled the words of the prophets, which are read every Sabbath, condemning him, and though they unearthed no capital crime they (still) asked Pilate to have him executed. . . . And we are now telling *you* the good news, the occurrence of what the Fathers were promised" (13.27f,32). Like Peter in chapter 3, Paul is trying to leave every way open for his audience, not blaming them for what has happened. They, too, fail to respond. His appeal is no more successful than the prolonged campaign in Jerusalem, and he renounces the Jews, formally turning to the Gentiles. "It was necessary for the word of God to be first spoken to you. Since you reject it and deem yourselves unworthy of eternal life, see we turn to the Gentiles, for so the Lord has commanded us" (13.46f). It is no accident, as Dibelius has pointed out,[1] that a formal statement of rejection is delivered three times to the Jews of the Dispersion, once in each main area of mission: in

---

[1] *Aufsätze*, 129; *Studies*, 149.

Asia Minor, in Greece, and in Rome (18.6; 28.25–8). The last rejection sums up the verdict of God on all the Jews, a verdict painfully discovered by the Church throughout the whole of Acts: "Therefore let it be known to you that this salvation of God has been sent to the Gentiles; they will hear" (28.28). Whether Luke means this rejection of the Jews to be final in God's purpose, it is hard to say; certainly the conversion of the people as a whole is no longer to be considered by the Church as part of its mission (cf. 1.6f).[1]

Stephen's speech is not aberrant. It is used by Luke to present an important element in his theology, and foreshadows the position to which God has driven the Church as a whole. In the context of Acts the speech is "a theoretical justification in advance for Christianity's turning away from the Jews to the Gentiles, made in terms of the stubbornness of the Jews. This is, from the point of view of the author of Acts, the chief purpose of the speech" (Overbeck).[2]

The speech as a whole fits into Luke's theological pattern, but it remains true that Stephen expresses his point of view in an extreme way, without the qualifications which the other historical characters in Acts must supply. He says that the Jews built the Temple under a misconception; they expected that God would dwell there whereas "the Most High does not dwell in things made with hands". What he does not say is that the Temple is a perfectly acceptable "house of prayer", as Jesus did, and as the Apostles showed they believed by their practice.

The martyrdom of Stephen and the supporting speech is a pivotal point in Acts. Stephen adumbrates a theology of the Temple that has yet to be worked out in the experience of the Church's history in Acts. That fact might suggest that Luke

[1] Goppelt, op. cit., 231 n 3, says that Luke never indicates whether the "time of the Gentiles" will end with the conversion of Israel (Luke 21.24). It seems to me that this verse and Acts 1.6f; 3.19–21 do imply that Israel will return in the end, but Luke is at pains to stop speculation on this point; the immediate mission of the Church in history is to the Gentiles.

[2] Quoted by Joh. Weiss, *Ueber die Absicht und den literarischen charakter der Apg.* (Göttingen, 1897), 13; cf. Preuschen, *Die Apg., Hdb. z. N. T.* (Tübingen, 1913), 38.

himself had provided the theology, and I argued something very close to this position in the first edition of the book;[1] but, if so, the question remains, If Luke was content to show the Church slowly discovering what God really meant about the Temple, why did he bother to construct an elaborate foretelling of this and insert it so early? If Luke has constructed Stephen's theology for him (using traditional material, to be sure), why does there not appear in Stephen's speech some inkling that his martyrdom is to lead to the Gentile mission? Saul's approval of Stephen's death is emphasized, but the speech of Stephen contains no suggestion that the continual opposition of the people to the Holy Spirit is to lead to a new movement out into the Gentile world.

Finally, it is strange that only the apostles escape a persecution that scatters "all" who belonged to "the Church" (8.1). Wellhausen may be right in suggesting that only the Hellenists were affected, but why did Luke not say so?[2]

Luke's mastery of his material has already been sufficiently demonstrated but, until we can see just what his material was, we are not able to give a complete account of his theology.

The first clue to the mystery of Stephen lies in 8.2. The "pious men" who gathered up Stephen for burial were not apostles, and were possibly not even Christians.[3] Their presence is a salutary reminder that all sorts of synagogues existed in Jerusalem, and that the division between those that believed Jesus was Messiah and those that did not was not nearly so sharp as it eventually became. Possibly many pious Jews could admire Stephen without precisely sharing his beliefs. Joseph of Arimathea played the same role for Jesus as these pious men played for Stephen.[4] Yet the situation has changed, and those who believe in Jesus Christ are now numerous and well-organ-

---

[1] See E. Haenchen, "Judentum und Christentum in der Apg.", *Z.N.W.*, 54 (1963), 155–87 at 165, for a similar position.

[2] Julius Wellhausen, *Kritische Analyse der Apostelgeschichte* (Berlin, 1914), 14.

[3] *Beginnings* iv. 87.

[4] Mark 15.42–7; Matt. 27.57–60; Luke 23.50–4; John 19.38–42; only Matthew and John make him a disciple.

ized. Naturally they would have to fear identification and persecution if they ventured to bury Stephen and publicly lament his
death, but so would any Jew have to be afraid of being identified
with a teacher who aroused such fury.

The puzzle about the identity of the "pious men" raises in
my mind the question, Was Stephen a Christian?

If he was not a Christian, the difficulties set by this verse and
the preceding verse immediately disappear. The ἐκκλησία in 8.1
which suffers such persecution that "all" were scattered was not
the Jerusalem Christian Church but simply the synagogue that
had gathered around Stephen. Luke has added the words
τὴν ἐν Ἰεροσολύμοις, because he assumes the existence of only
one Church, the Christian Church, in Jerusalem. Luke also has
added the note that the apostles did not leave Jerusalem when
"all" were scattered; this was the smallest change he could make
to reconcile one source, which said πάντες δὲ διεσπάρησαν, with
another source, which said the apostles were in Jerusalem to
hear of the success of the mission to the Samaritans (8.14). The
"pious men" who buried Stephen may well have included
Christians, for now we are taking this as a note from a non-
Christian source.

But surely it is too fantastic to suppose that Stephen was not a
Christian! Surely his martyrdom hinges on his following Jesus
of Nazareth!

However, when we examine the text, the Christian references
are found to be insecurely anchored, and few in number. When
they are set to one side as later interpretations of the significance
of Stephen's death, some of the puzzles that had led a previous
generation of scholars to conjecture that Luke had employed
two sources are put in a different light.[1]

The only references to Jesus in the section 6.8—8.3 occur in
four places, 6.14; 7.52; 7.55b; and 7.59. Let us examine them
one by one.

---

[1] P. Feine, *Vorkanonische Überlieferung des Lukas in Evangelium und Apostelgeschichte* (Gotha, 1891); F. Spitta; J. Weiss, J. Jüngst; A. Hilgenfeld. See
H. H. Wendt, *Die Apostelgeschichte* (4th ed., Göttingen, 1913), 134 n 2; 150
n1; *Beginnings*, ii.147–52.

In 6.14 the false witnesses put forward at the meeting of the Sanhedrin introduce a new element into the charge that had previously been circulated among the people, "We have heard him speaking blasphemous words against Moses and God" (6.11). The new element is that they had heard him saying that *Jesus* would bring an end to the Temple and change the Law (6.14). Yet this is strange. There was a tradition, brought up at Jesus' trial and repeated by mocking bystanders as he hung on the cross, that Jesus had said, "I shall destroy this sanctuary made with hands and in three days I shall erect another not made with hands" (Mark 14.58; 15.29; cf. Matt. 26.61; 27.40; cf. John 2.19). In the first edition of this book I argued that Luke had deliberately cut Mark's version off at the end of the negative part, and transferred the charge to Stephen's trial in order to answer it at greater length.[1] Now I am very doubtful whether Luke's copy of Mark yet contained this pericope. Nevertheless, Luke could well have known the tradition that Jesus had been accused of promising to destroy the Temple. But there was no tradition that Jesus had said, "I shall change the customs that Moses delivered to us", nor is it likely that any such saying could have been ascribed to him. The reason is not so much the content, as the future tense of the verb, "I shall change". He could have promised the future destruction of the Temple, but if he thought the Law should be abrogated he would have proceeded to do so straight away. And the word "change" is an odd one to use. All these difficulties fall away if we suppose that the words ἀκηκόαμεν γὰρ αὐτοῦ λέγοντος ὅτι Ἰησοῦς ὁ Ναζωραῖος are an interpretative addition. They echo verse 11, "we have heard him saying", and they ascribe to Jesus what tradition has already suggested he was charged with saying against the Temple. But originally Stephen was the one accused of teaching in such a way that all good Jews could see that, if allowed to go unchecked, "he will destroy this place and change the customs that Moses delivered to us". The second part of the charge is now perfectly fitting as a prediction others could

[1] 73f.

make about the effect of Stephen's work. The word οὗτος referred originally to Stephen, but naturally a Christian editor would see a hidden reference to Jesus.

The second reference to Jesus occurs at the end of Stephen's speech, in the section 7.51–3. It is noteworthy that at the beginning of verse 51 and at the end, in verse 53, the audience is addressed as an inseparable part of the Jewish people; anything the fathers did, they did, and anything the fathers received, they received. The second person pronoun embraces every generation and includes the audience sitting there. At the end of verse 51 and in verse 52, however, the fathers and the audience are distinguished, and the point is that what the fathers did in persecuting the prophets and killing those who foretold the coming of the Righteous One has been continued by this generation, who became his betrayers and murderers. This distinction, although on the surface a natural one, in fact disturbs the grammatical unity between verse 51a (ending ἀντιπίπτετε) and verse 53 (beginning οἵτινες). That unity consists in the fact that "you" embraces and is not distinguished from "the fathers". The simple explanation seems to be that the section made up of verses 51b and 52 is a very appropriate piece of traditional polemical material inserted into the source to bring out a Christian interpretation of Stephen's prophetic attack on his people.[1] Without this section, the two charges against Stephen stand out perfectly clearly and are answered with devastating effect; he did indeed say that God needed no Temple and, far from his wishing to change the Law, he could prove from Scripture that the people had constantly failed to keep its commands.

The third reference to Jesus is found at the end of 7.55. The description of what Stephen saw ("he saw the glory of God and Jesus standing at the right hand of God") is obviously an interpretation of what Stephen said he saw: "Behold, I see heaven open and the son of God standing at the right hand of

---

[1] The tradition is also preserved in 1 Clement 17.1; Polycarp, *Phil.*, 6.3; Irenaeus, *adv. Haer.*, I.ii (Harvey i.90); *Acta Philippi*, 78. See G. D. Kilpatrick, "Acts 7.52 ΕΛΕΥΣΙΣ", *J.T.S.* xlvi (1945), 136–45.

God" (7.56).[1] The interpretation identified the Messiah, and the identification would be all but self-evident to a Christian editor, but the fact remains that Stephen's words are not necessarily Christian, and, if the rest of my argument holds water, the words show he was not a Christian. The extraordinary possibility begins to open up that a Hellenistic Jew was able to express *in these terms* what he saw in a vision. Such a possibility cannot be ruled out, since 4 Ezra 13 records such a vision, and in verse 35 speaks of God's son standing upon the summit of Mount Sion.[2]

The final reference to Jesus occurs in Acts 7.59, in the words, "Lord Jesus, receive my spirit". Harnack argued that verses 59b and 60 were doublets,[3] but it is important to see that the doubling is not exact, and is only one of a number of such doublings in the same context. The small section, beginning from the mention of the witnesses in 7.58b to the end of verse 59, contains three doublings: the stoning is repeated, having already been mentioned as accomplished in verse 58a; Saul is said to guard the clothes of the witnesses, only to be mentioned again later as having consented to the killing, in verse 60; and Stephen makes a prayer for himself, to be followed, in verse 60, by a prayer for his executioners. I do not think these doublets are good evidence for the weaving together of two sources, since each of the three doublings is a comment upon and explanation of the details given in the surrounding verses. The stoning is mentioned again to try to show that this was a judicial execution, in which the witnesses rolled stones down on the man they had first thrown over the cliff. Saul is made guardian of the clothes of the witnesses to represent by a vivid pictorial touch the bare fact recorded in verse 60, and the detail is slightly wrong, for probably the only clothes to guard would have been the clothes of the

---

[1] G. D. Kilpatrick, *Theologische Zeitschrift*, 21 (1965), 14, has argued that the reading θεου of p[74] 614 bo (2 Mss) old Georgian is to be preferred.

[2] See G. H. Box in Charles, *Apocrypha and Pseudepigrapha* (Oxford, 1913), ii.618.

[3] *Beiträge zur Einleitung in dem N.T., III: Die Apostelgeschichte* (Leipzig, 1908), 171; English tr., *N.T. Studies, III: The Acts of the Apostles* (London, 1909), 221 (where 59a should read 59b).

victim rather than of the witnesses.[1] The rest of the passage makes Stephen's death look more like a lynching than a judicial execution. Finally, the prayer for the reception of Stephen's spirit, which would possibly be expected to come after the prayer for the executioners, makes explicit that the "Lord" in the second prayer is Jesus. I conclude that 7.58b–59 is a commentary added to the source to make explicit what the editor saw in the material that had come into his hands.

With a great deal of hesitation I conclude that all four references to Jesus have been added to the original source by a later editor.

Before we can draw even tentative conclusions from this evidence, we have to try to decide whether or not Luke was responsible for the additions.

The first thing to notice is that each addition is a literary addition, not a change that occurred during oral transmission. Indeed, the detection of the additions as additions depended on observing seams in the narrative which would not have persisted had not the editor scrupulously preserved the wording of his source.

If the additions were made by a literary editor, there seems no good reason to deny that they were made by Luke—provided we can imagine the document's circulating in Christian circles without such addition. We can, I think, imagine this. In 11.19f we are told that some Cypriots and Cyrenians among those scattered by the tribulation that had befallen Stephen and his "church" came to Antioch and spoke to Greeks[2] as well as to Jews, "preaching the Lord Jesus". It seems quite credible that these followers of Stephen had drawn the conclusion from his

[1] Mishnah, *Sanhedrin* 6.3f.

[2] The meaning of the word ἑλληνιστής is still in dispute. Cadbury, *Beginnings*, v.59–74 at 71, is right in suggesting that the third instance, Acts 11.19f, should be taken as the starting point. (The reading of B E *614*, etc., should be preferred.) Here the word means "Greeks". In 6.1 and 9.29 it is clear that a longstanding division between Jews is involved (against Cadbury) which probably showed itself in the language they commonly spoke; the word still means "Greeks", though in the context it implies "Greek-speaking Jews". It had no pejorative force. Cf. C. F. D. Moule, "Once More, Who Were the Hellenists?" *E.T.*, lxx (1958–9), 100ff.

theology that the Gentiles must also be spoken to, and had discovered the good news that the Son of God whom Stephen had seen as he died was Jesus.

This is supposition, with no explicit support in the text, but we have an account which quite explicitly tells us how one man came to make the same identification. This man was, of course, not a disciple of Stephen, but Saul, "who had consented to his killing" (7.60). The heavenly figure appeared to him on the Damascus road, and in answer to the question, "Saul, Saul, why are you persecuting me?" Saul asked the question Stephen's disciples must also have asked themselves, "Who are you, Lord?"[1]

In short, the account of the martyrdom of Stephen and a record of his speech could well have survived among Christians without an explicit literary addition. Stephen was a Christian without knowing it, and would have been honoured as such.

Whether or not it was Luke who made Stephen explicitly preach Jesus and die with his name on his lips, Luke almost certainly identified the Stephen in the list of the seven Hellenists who were ordained by the apostles to look to the needs of the widows (6.1–6) with Stephen the prophet. The name is "frequently found".[2]

What can we conclude about Luke's theology? First, Luke is a good historian in that he reproduces verbatim his sources. He is right to give Stephen such a prominent place in his work, because Stephen's disciples did become some of the first Christians to make a policy of preaching to Gentiles as well as Jews, and also because Saul of Tarsus was made to look for the exalted Son of God by acquiescing in Stephen's death.

But secondly, Luke has brought Stephen into the framework of his narrative in a way that confirms what we have already been able to discover about his theology. Stephen is ordained by the apostles, and his disciples who preach so successfully to

[1] The way Paul describes his conversion in Galatians 1.15 is fully in accord with the theological questioning that lies behind the Acts account. Note Paul uses the term "Son of God" (cf. Acts 9.20).

[2] Bauer-Arndt-Gingrich, s.v.

THE ATTITUDE TO THE JEWS

Gentiles in Antioch have their work confirmed by Barnabas who comes as an envoy of the church in Jerusalem (11.22). Stephen's prophetic denunciation of God's people for their continual resistance to the Spirit is probably formalized by being made part of a trial scene, but, more important, never afterwards does Luke let Jerusalem be offered the gospel, although he knows that a successful mission to the Judeans has been carried out from that city (21.20).

Luke is a good historian, but nevertheless the incident of Stephen is set firmly as part of a theological pattern. A line runs from Jerusalem to Rome, and all Luke's material has been subordinated to that scheme. Stephen may not have been a Christian, and he certainly had not seen the possibility of a mission to Gentiles, but Luke, knowing the end from the beginning, has constructed a pattern whose formalities betray a set of theological presuppositions. Stephen's martyrdom has become the archetypal rejection of the gospel by Jerusalem.

Acts presents a theology in which the Church has abandoned the People and appropriated the Book.[1] The salvation of Israel as a whole is no longer a living possibility, and the Church is shown to be at last facing the destiny to which God was leading it, by finally turning from the Jews to the Gentiles. Christian theology did not come to this point of despair easily; it is possible to discover the period in which the momentous change took place and so obtain another indication of the historical setting for the theology of Acts.

It is the enduring contribution of Professor Johannes Munck to Pauline studies to have demonstrated that Paul's mission to the Gentiles was no alternative to the mission to Israel.[2] His argument may be briefly summarized as follows. Paul believed that he had been called to preach to the Gentiles as a necessary

---

[1] Cf. Goppelt, op. cit., 228–31. I do not wish to deny that for Luke the O.T. is "not only the inspired book . . . but also the historical source of the first epoch of redemptive history"; Conzelmann, *S.L.A.*, 309.

[2] "Israel and the Gentiles in the N.T.", *J.T.S.*, N.S. ii (1951), 3–16; *Paulus und die Heilsgeschichte* (Acta Jutlandica, xxvi, Aarhus, 1954) Eng. tr., *Paul and the Salvation of Mankind* (London, 1959); *Christus und Israel; eine Auslegung von Röm.* 9–11 (Acta Jutlandica, xxviii, Aarhus, 1956).

step towards the conversion of the Jews. Romans 9–11 is not an insignificant piece of self-justification, but the key to Paul's understanding of his mission. What divided Paul and the earliest Apostles was not a conflict between an exclusive desire to keep the gospel for Israel and a doctrine of universalism, but a difference of emphasis: the earliest Apostles were working with Israel for Israel and the Gentiles, whose salvation would follow the conversion of the Jews, while Paul was working with the Gentiles for the Gentiles and Israel. The question of the foreseeable salvation of Israel has not been excluded from the discussion as it has in Luke-Acts, and Paul is constantly working with this end in mind. He is still actively hoping for the salvation of Israel; "my grief is great, and there is ceaseless anguish in my heart", he wrote; "for I could even wish that I myself might be anathema and cut off from Christ for my brothers, my fleshly kinsmen . . . Brothers, my heart's desire and my prayer to God for them is for their salvation" (Rom. 9.2f; 10.1). Peder Borgen finds evidence in Paul that he turned to the Gentiles because of the hardening of Israel (esp. Rom. 11.7–8,11,25).[1] There is truth in this exegesis, but that truth should not, I think, be allowed to overshadow the clear evidence of the opening of Romans 9 that Paul, although disappointed at the obduracy of Israel, still hoped for Israel's conversion.[2] Paul supported the direct mission to Israel, while carrying on his own direct mission to the Gentiles (Gal. 2.9). Borgen emphasizes that Luke has carried further forward ideas that are

[1] "Von Paulus zu Lukas: Beobachtungen zur Erhelling der Theologie der Lukasschriften", *Studia Theologica*, 20 (1966), 140–57.

[2] It is true that two verses in 1 Thessalonians (2.14–16) seem to contradict all that has been said: whatever the precise sense of εἰς τέλος in the last sentence, ἔφθασεν δὲ ἐπ' αὐτοὺς ἡ ὀργὴ εἰς τέλος, it does not offer much hope for the Jews. But these two verses cannot be pitted against the three chapters in Romans as representing Paul's considered view of the destiny of his own people; either they are not his genuine words, or they represent a justifiable outburst of anger with no serious theological implications, or they state only one side of the paradox which is to be fully expounded in Romans. The first explanation is that of the Tübingen school; for the second see Jülicher-Fascher, *Einleitung* (7th ed., Tübingen, 1931), 61f; for the third see Goppelt, op. cit.,112–25 and *passim*.

already present in Paul;[1] I am arguing that Luke has made two missionary impulses, which were originally parallel, logically successive.

We may conclude that, historically, the salvation of Israel was a central concern for St Paul, and that, if the salvation of Israel was a central concern for St Paul, it was much more the central concern of all parts of the early Church. Despite the hostility of the Jews towards the Christians, the Church continued to work for their redemption.

After A.D. 70 Jewish hostility towards the Church increased and steps were taken to exclude Christians from the synagogues. The Gospel according to St Matthew reflects the point of view of a Church which has been forced to define its opposition to Judaism and its mission to the Gentiles without finally abandoning the hope that Israel would repent. The opposition between the Church and Pharisaism is still seen as an opposition within Judaism.[2] The Didache, which belongs to a similar tradition, shows the process taken to the point when the breach is open and irrevocable. The Jews are now simply "the hypocrites", whose religious behaviour the Church must on no account follow (8.1–3).[3]

Both Matthew and the Didache, however, have come to their position in debate with Rabbinic Judaism, from which they have both learnt so much. The Lucan position has closer affinities with the Epistle of Barnabas and the writings of Aristides and Justin Martyr, where Rabbinic tradition is unimportant. The traditional methods of expounding the Septuagint which they have taken over from Hellenistic Judaism show that this is the principal influence. The Epistle of Barnabas explains the breaking of the tablets of the Law by Moses as the final breach of the covenant.[4] From that point onwards the Jewish history is no longer the history of God's covenant with his people, and the significance of the records of this history in the

---

[1] Op. cit., 157.
[2] See G. D. Kilpatrick, *The Origins of the Gospel according to St Matthew* (2nd ed., Oxford, 1950), especially chapter VI; Goppelt, op. cit., 178–85.
[3] Goppelt, ibid., 186–9.   [4] Ep. Barn. 4.6–8; 14.1–5.

O.T. lies solely in the fact that they foretell Christ and provide lessons for the Church. The Apology of Aristides, which perhaps belongs to the same period, puts the Jews almost on the same level as the heathen; they think that they are worshipping God, but in fact they only worship the angels.[1] In Justin Martyr the O.T. has become a book of riddles to which the right answer in every case is Jesus the Messiah, and his long and patient dialogue with Trypho the Jew is principally concerned with showing that this is true. There is no sense that Jews and Christians share a common history; what they possess in common is a religious book which the Christians understand and the Jews do not.[2] Justin's special efforts to convert Trypho do not seem to spring from a view that it is more important to convert Jews than Gentiles; the only difference is that it is harder. Justin believes that Christians are bound to refute all men who contradict the Scriptures, on pain of being judged guilty of negligence at the day of judgement, and it is for this general reason that he conducts the dialogue with a Jew.[3]

The general position which the Church had reached in its relations with the Jews may be summed up in Ignatius's dictum: "For Christianity has not based its faith on Judaism, but Judaism on Christianity, into which has been gathered every tongue that believes in God" (Magn. 10.3).[4] The prophets of the O.T. "lived according to Christ Jesus", and so Judaism is a misguided derivative from Christianity (Magn. 8.2; 9.2).[5]

Acts stands in this tradition. It traces back to the apostolic age the rejection of the gospel by the Jews. It shows how the People, despite all the efforts of the early Christian preachers and the persuasiveness of their arguments from Scripture, rejected the gospel; it argues that this rejection was long ago foretold in the Book, to which Christians alone—pious men like

[1] Apol. Aristides 14, Syrian text, tr. by J. Rendel Harris, *The Apology of Aristides* (Cambridge, 1891), 48; cf. the Greek text.

[2] Goppelt, op. cit., 284–301, especially 288.

[3] Dial. 82.3f; 38.2; 44.1; see Harnack, *Judentum und Judenchristentum in Justins Dialog mit Trypho*, T.U., iii.9 (= 39. Band) (Leipzig, 1913), 82–4.

[4] Cf. K. Lake's tr. (Loeb Classical Library, London, 1912).

[5] Bauer, *Hdb.z.N.T.*, *Ergänzungsband* (Tübingen, 1920), 228.

Stephen—now hold the key. The Lucan interpretation of the history of the establishment of the Church reflects a theology which developed in the second century, and all the elements which go to make up his story, though they are derived from a variety of traditional sources, must be seen in relation to the standpoint of a second-century theologian.

CHAPTER FOUR

JEWISH CHRISTIANS AND GENTILE CHRISTIANS

IN THE last chapter it has been argued that the theology of Acts consists not so much in the doctrines which are put into the mouths of the chief historical characters as in the movement of the history. God was leading the Church to understand his will in its historical experience, as it was driven out of Jerusalem and towards Rome. For that reason it is more important in studying the theology of Acts to investigate the history of the developing relationship between groups—between the Church and the Jews, and between Jews and Gentiles within the Church—than the classical doctrinal questions like the relationship between Gospel and Law.

The present question, that of the agreement reached concerning the status of Jews and Gentiles in the Church, has in fact been taken by the Tübingen school as the key to the purpose of Acts. In 1836 Schrader and F. C. Baur revived the hypothesis that Acts was an attempt to reconcile the supporters of Paul and the Judaizers by making Paul as Petrine and Peter as Pauline as possible.[1] Few scholars would now accept Baur's picture of the early Church, divided into Judaizers led by Peter and universalists led by Paul, but, leaving that question aside for the moment, his thesis remains important because it raises the issue: what was Luke's theological purpose in presenting the historical discussion of the steps by which Gentiles were admitted into the full fellowship of the Church in the way he did?

This problem can only be avoided if it can be shown that

[1] See the admirable summary by A. C. McGiffert, *Beginnings*, ii.367–9.

Luke is writing an accurate account of the meetings which were held and the decisions which were taken by the Apostles and the Jerusalem Church in consultation with Paul and Barnabas. That is no longer possible. This does not mean that Acts is historically worthless. It is still necessary to correlate the historical data presented in Acts with the other extant accounts, particularly with the opening chapters of Galatians, in the continuing search for the historical truth of the matter, but the present results of that investigation show that Acts is mistaken at one point or another.

If we can discover the precise reason for Luke's mistakes, we may be able to advance a little further towards understanding his theology.

Baur and the early members of the Tübingen school deduced from the fact that Luke's account of the negotiations was inexact the conclusion that he had deliberately constructed a tendentious narrative in order to reconcile the opposing parties. It was soon pointed out by Baur's younger followers that it was very improbable that the author of Acts would have been aware of what he was doing, and have deliberately falsified the story of the events to produce a compromise. If the supposed two parties were still conscious of the points of disagreement, any attempt to blur the issue would be bound to fail; it is much more likely that Luke wrote at a time when the original debates had been forgotten.[1]

The Tübingen school took it for granted that Luke knew and used Paul's letters, and this view is still advanced.[2] If that were so, we should be able to see Luke's bias very clearly in the way he selected some incidents, omitted some, and put a different interpretation on others. But there are very good reasons for

[1] E.g., A. Ritschl, "Das Verhältniss der Schriften des Lukas zu der Zeit ihrer Entstehung", *Theologische Jahrbücher*, vi (1847), 293–304 at 300; and cf. Overbeck.

[2] F. C. Baur; F. Overbeck; W. Soltau, *Z.N.W.*, 4 (1903), 128–54; Carl von Weizsäcker, *The Apostolic Age of the Christian Church*, i (London, 1894), 208ff; Morton S. Enslin, "'Luke' and Paul", *Journal of the American Oriental Society*, 58 (1938), 81–91; Günter Klein, *Die zwölf Apostel* (Göttingen, 1961), 189–90; John Knox, most recently in "Acts and the Pauline Letter Corpus", *S.L.A.*, 279–87.

denying that Luke used Galatians as a source for his long account of the Jerusalem Council. The chief reason is that he could scarcely have allowed Paul's visit to Jerusalem that he records in Acts 15 remain Paul's third visit to the city after his conversion if he saw from Galatians that this visit was only the second. Galatians is quite explicit, and we cannot regard this detail as one that would escape a cursory reader.

Luke may have thought (or known) that Galatians had been written before the third visit, but in that case he would have seen that what he thought happened on the third visit—the approval by Jerusalem of the Gentile mission—had really happened on the second visit. Whether or not J. B. Lightfoot was right in arguing that the conferences in Acts 15 and Galatians 2 were historically the same,[1] it is difficult to imagine an ancient historian who had both accounts before him as sources not asking himself whether they weren't the same, and adjusting his narrative in some way or other. There is no trace of any such adjustment. Luke would therefore almost certainly have thought Galatians was written after the council he wished to record in Acts 15, so that the original difficulty we have been discussing remains.

I can see no strong doctrinal or tendentious reason that would have caused Luke to contradict his source; Jerusalem was certainly important for Luke, but Paul's two visits would have made that point just as well as three. I shall argue later that Luke has in fact constructed a visit of Paul to Jerusalem that never happened. This constructed visit fits into Luke's theological emphasis on the importance of Jerusalem, but it certainly did not arise as a deliberate attempt to alter information available to him from the Epistle to the Galatians.

If we reject the hypothesis of those scholars who would argue that Luke was deliberately rewriting Galatians, we are left with a number of possible explanations of Luke's "mistakes", and not each explanation allows us to draw the same conclusions about Luke's theology. If Luke was Paul's companion, he could have made mistakes because he did not understand from talking with Paul the point of the meeting Paul recorded in Galatians

[1] *St Paul's Epistle to the Galatians* (10th ed., London, 1890), 123–8.

2, and then we might have to conclude that his theological bias was unconscious, and perhaps not very interesting, being the bias of a man who did not care very much for the facts. But if we are able to discover approximately the information Luke had available, and to see how he used that information, we may be able to discover something more about Luke the theologian, and the historical setting in which he wrote.

Our task is twofold: to show that Luke has made some significant mistakes in his account of Paul's relations with Jerusalem, and to show exactly how those mistakes arose. Only then can we draw conclusions about Luke's theology.

WHERE LUKE IS CORRECT

Before I discuss the two significant mistakes Luke made, it would be well to list the two important matters on which he was not historically mistaken.

First, Luke was correct in stating that the church authorities at Jerusalem did not at any time demand that Gentiles who believed in Jesus Christ should be circumcised. In this they were following a possible, if disputed, contemporary Jewish practice concerning proselytes.[1]

The Epistle to the Galatians provides good evidence of this, because Titus was not circumcised. The argument that he was circumcised turns on the omission by D*, vg(1), Iren.^{lat}, Tert., Ambst., Pelag., of the words οἷς οὐδὲ in Gal. 2.5; it then proceeds to reinterpret verse 3 to mean, "Titus was not *compelled* to be circumcised (but nevertheless he agreed to it of his own free will)." There are many objections to this argument, but two seem to be decisive. The first is J. H. Ropes's: "Paul might have admitted that he 'yielded', but never that his yielding was a 'subjection'!"[2] The second is made by Lietz-

---

[1] Josephus, *Ant* xx. 2. 3ff = §§34–53, esp. §41.

[2] *The Singular Problem of the Epistle to the Galatians* (Cambridge, Mass., 1929), 31f n 10. The words τῇ ὑποταγῇ are omitted by p^{46}. Perhaps this is the original text, and the words were added to allow for the circumcision of Timothy (Acts 16.3), which was done freely; note then that the original text must have stated that Titus was not circumcised, if the addition was to have had any point.

mann: "And supposing the original text had read πρὸς ὥραν εἴξαμεν, it is understandable that an οὐδέ might have been added, but not an οἶς, which needlessly changes a smooth construction into an intolerable anocoluthon."[1]

Not only was Titus not circumcised, but it could be argued, from the form in which Paul reports the fact to the Galatians, that he would have allowed Titus to be circumcised had that been required: ἀλλ᾽ οὐδὲ Τίτος ὁ σὺν ἐμοί ἠναγκάσθη περιτμηθῆναι. In other words, Paul recognized the jurisdiction of Jerusalem, at least in Jerusalem, and regarded the issue as in principle open—although he would hardly have taken Titus with him if he had had any serious reason to doubt what the attitude of the Jerusalem authorities would be.

Luke does not mention Titus—something impossible to imagine if he had known the epistles of Paul—but he does report that Timothy was circumcised, Acts 16.1–3. Is this a mistake? Paul continuously and resolutely opposed agitators who tried to persuade Gentile Christians to be circumcised;[2] but Timothy was a legitimate exception, being by Jewish Law a Jew. We could only conclude that nevertheless Paul would not under any circumstances have circumcised Timothy if not to circumcise any Christian were for Paul a matter of principle. It has been suggested that 1 Cor. 7.18 is such a principle.[3] To this there are two replies: first, the next verse states that neither circumcision no uncircumcision is a matter of principle (ἡ περιτομὴ οὐδέν ἐστιν, καὶ ἡ ἀκροβυστία οὐδέν ἐστιν, 1 Cor. 7.19; cf. Gal. 5.6; 6.15); and second, the passage in question, 1 Cor. 7.18–24, is probably not by Paul.[4] Circumcision was no empty sign for Paul, but I can find no evidence, in the parts of the letters ascribed to him that are genuine, that he ever argued

[1] *Galaterbrief, Hdb.z.N.T.* (2nd ed., Tübingen, 1923), 11.

[2] Gal. 5.11 does not imply that Paul had at any time since his conversion preached circumcision.

[3] E.g. by Haenchen, op. cit. (10th ed.), 427; (12th ed.), 422.

[4] It clearly turns aside from the matter in hand, marriage, to lay down general maxims. The form is poetic. Beza argued that 1 Cor. 7.17–22 was misplaced, and G. Baljon, *Theologisch Tijdschrift*, 21 (1887), 432–40, that it was a non-Pauline interpolation.

that Jewish Christians should give up the observance of the Law. Timothy need not have been circumcised when he became a Christian, but he could have been circumcised, before becoming a partner in Paul's mission to the Gentiles, for the sake of the Jews, as Luke's source said.

Acts does, however, report that the question of whether or not Gentile Christians should be circumcised was a matter of dispute. Again, there is no reason to doubt that Luke is historically accurate. Paul had to oppose Christians who came in to the Galatian churches from outside to persuade the Galatian Christians that they needed to be circumcised; he faced similar trouble at Philippi; and the Epistle to the Romans perhaps shows that the issue was not dead even then. Luke reports that the advocates of circumcision who troubled the church at Antioch were Judeans (15.1), and he further reports that a group of converted Pharisees in Jerusalem proposed for discussion the proposition that it was necessary that they should proclaim the keeping of the Law of Moses (Acts 15.5).[1] Paul is not specific about the origin of the agitators who were troubling the Galatian churches, but we may deduce from his insistence that the Jerusalem leaders fully approved his course of action, even though he had adopted it quite independently, that he is opposing men who claimed to represent in some way the best thought current in the cradle of Christianity. The "false brethren" mentioned in Gal. 2.4 might be assumed to parallel the believing Pharisees of Acts 15.5, but the mysterious vagueness of the whole reference makes this a difficult piece of evidence to handle.

We can conclude, then, that Luke's reports about the issue of whether or not Gentile Christians should be circumcised are in general reliable.

[1] The infinitive περιτέμνειν and the consequent τε are glosses, the result of the incorporation of a marginal note first made to explain that keeping the Law of Moses implied circumcision. The word αὐτούς in our present text has always caused difficulty, because there is no explicit antecedent to it in the previous clause. When the gloss is removed, αὐτούς refers quite naturally to the Jerusalem church. There is a parallel to the construction παραγγέλλειν τηρεῖν in 2 Chron. 36.22; Acts 4.18; 5.40; 1 Clement 27.2.

Second, there are good reasons for relying on his reports that the early churches had discussed how best to enable Gentile Christians and Jewish Christians to eat together, and that the Decree transcribed in Acts 15 was in fact made by Jerusalem at some stage in the discussion. But we must be cautious, and not claim too much for Luke, because I wish to argue later that Luke's first significant historical mistake is over Paul's relation to the Decree. Nevertheless, Paul in general supplies confirmation that the issue of how Jewish Christians could eat with Gentile Christians was a live issue at the time, and we can leave aside for the moment the question concerning Paul and the Decree. The fact that Peter changed his policy about eating with Gentiles is all we need to know to support the general proposition that the issue was being urgently debated (Gal. 2.11ff).

Luke gives two different accounts of the terms in which the issue was discussed. The first is the story of Peter's vision, which is embedded in the narrative of Cornelius's conversion (Acts 10.9b–16; 11.5–10), and which Luke explicitly reports as deciding the question about eating with Gentiles: no meats are unclean, and therefore a Jew may eat with a Gentile without hesitation (11.3). In the context of the story of Cornelius, the vision is meant to show that Gentiles have a full and equal place with Jews in the company of those who hear and receive the word of God, but historically it is doubtful whether the issue of fellowship at table had to be settled before Gentiles could be admitted to the congregations, and Cornelius, who was already a pious man who feared God with all his house, who gave alms liberally to the people, and who continually prayed to God, may well have known already how to entertain a Jew without causing offence. Bauernfeind has suggested that the vision of Peter can be isolated from the story of Cornelius's conversion, and his suggestion seems plausible.[1] In that case Peter's vision came to Luke as an isolated tradition, possibly in two forms.

[1] O. Bauernfeind, *Die Apostelgeschichte* (Leipzig, 1939), 145; M. Dibelius, *Aufsätze zur Apg.* (Göttingen, 1953), 98f; *Essays* (London, 1956), 111f; Jacques Dupont, "Les Problèmes du Livre des Actes entre 1940 et 1950", repr. in *Études sur les Actes des Apôtres* (Paris, 1967), 77f.

Luke's second account is found in Acts 15, where James's suggestion that Gentile Christians be asked to abstain from the pollutions of idols, from unchastity, and from blood, is accepted and sent out to the Gentile Christians in Antioch and Syria and Cilicia (Acts 15.20, 28f; 21.25)[1]

All three requirements would have a bearing on whether or not Jewish Christians could invite Gentile Christians to their houses for a meal and whether or not they could accept invitations to dine with Gentile Christians. The Jewish Christians would shrink not only from eating food or drink that might have been offered to idols, or meat not kosher killed, but they would be reluctant to allow their dishes to be touched by Gentiles whose lips might have tasted such food. They would also find it difficult to dine with Gentile married couples who were related within one of the forbidden degrees.[2] Admittedly the Decree does not explicitly ask Gentile Christians to abstain from unclean meats, but in practice it is unlikely that pork, the main unclean meat, would be kosher killed,[3] so that the provision against eating blood would probably cover the other case. Possibly Gentiles in this region did not normally eat unclean animals. We know that the Egyptians did not eat pigs except at the Dionysian feast, and the practice of abstaining from pork may have been general.[4] In other words, the Decree may not

[1] The three-fold form of the Decree found in Tertullian, de Pudicitia 12, is probably the original. The words καὶ πνικτοῦ (note the absence of an article, against the presence of articles for the other terms in 15.20) were a perfectly correct gloss on καὶ τοῦ αἵματος. The omission of καὶ τῆς πορνείας by p⁴⁵ was the omission of what was (wrongly) thought to be a non-cultic term, and the addition of the negative Golden Rule in D was an attempt to complete the Decree in a moral sense. The case for the three-fold text is best stated by J. Wellhausen, Kritische Analyse der Apostelgeschichte (Berlin, 1914), 28, briefly, and, more fully, by J. H. Ropes, Beginnings, iii. 265–70. The case for the four-fold text was presented in a footnote to Chapter Three of the 1st ed. of this book, and has been retained in the 2nd ed. for interest.

[2] Paul uses πορνεία in this sense in 1 Cor. 5.1. Wellhausen, ibid, argues that this is the required sense in the Decree.

[3] There is a general reference in Josephus, contra Apion, ii.282, to the fact that there is no city, Greek or barbarian, where the Sabbath, fasts, lighting of lamps, and "many of the prohibitions as to our food" (πολλὰ τῶν εἰς βρῶσιν ἡμῖν νενομισμένων) are not observed. This is too slender evidence from which to conclude that unclean animals would be kosher-killed.

[4] Herodotus, ii. 47f; Origen, contra Celsum, v. 34, 41.

have needed to take into account the possibility that Gentile Christians might eat unclean meat, as little as the regulations about strangers living in Palestine in Leviticus 17.10–16, the ultimate source of the Decree, had to. We cannot decide this issue without knowing more about the food customs of Antioch and Syria and Cilicia. Nevertheless, we can maintain that there is no formal contradiction between Peter's vision and the terms of the Decree: the distinction between clean and unclean meats could have been abolished and the restrictions of the Decree enforced at the same time.[1] Of course the spirit of Peter's vision was lost once the Church started to make cultic regulations regarding food, but perhaps it was possible that the practical and tactical reasons for the regulations may not have been felt to count against the general import of the vision. The fact that the vision was used to adorn the principle that Gentiles were to be admitted to the body of believers on equal terms with Jews is evidence that the vision lived on, although the practical consequences that should have flowed from it were being eroded.

The questions now arise, Are both these accounts accurate historical reports of the positions held by Peter and James, or is only one of them accurate, or is neither of them accurate?

Peter's vision, confirming that God made no distinction between clean and unclean meat, represents a reliable tradition, which probably goes back to Jesus himself. The sayings of Jesus in Mark 7.14–23; Matt. 15.10–11, 15–20 seem to sweep away all regulations touching food. They were possibly not present in the earlier and shorter form of Mark used by Luke, but there is some evidence that Paul knew the tradition, for he says, "I know and am persuaded by the Lord Jesus (ἐν κυρίῳ Ἰησοῦ) that nothing is common (i.e. unclean) in itself."[2] Paul and the Pauline

---

[1] W. Schmithals, *Paulus und Jakobus* (Göttingen, 1963), 84; *Paul and James* (London, 1965), 100, tries to argue that the Decree was inappropriate as a basis for table-fellowship because it would not exclude wine that had come from a libation, or pork. The terms τῶν ἀλισγημάτων τῶν εἰδώλων or εἰδωλοθύτων would exclude wine as well as meat; the verb θύω is used of cheese, for instance, *Odyssey* 9.231.

[2] B. Weiss, Zahn, and Jülicher argue that Paul is appealing to a saying of Jesus, but most other commentators (from Lipsius on) are doubtful.

tradition is clear that this general position stands firm (1 Cor. 10.25ff; 1 Tim. 4.4; Titus 1.15).[1] Negatively, I know of no evidence that Christians kept the distinction between clean and unclean meat, although some abstained from meat altogether (Rom. 14.2,21).[2]

But the evidence is equally strong that the terms of the decree reported in Acts 15 were also observed in at least some parts of the Church.[3]

In Revelation 2.14,20 the Seer charges the churches at Pergamum and Thyatira with harbouring some who hold the teaching of Balaam or Jezebel, and describes the teaching in both cases as being to commit adultery and to eat food offered to idols. The same combination of charges is made against the Valentinians by Irenaeus, i.6.3 (Harvey i.55ff). The Syriac version of the *Apology of Aristides* 15 states that Christians "do not eat of the meats of idol sacrifices";[4] Justin condemns Christians who do so (Dial. 35f); Didache 6.3 rigidly forbids eating what is offered to idols, although it says about other food regulations, "bear what you can"; and Clement of Alexandria says περὶ τῶν εἰδωλοθύτων that Christians should abstain, although there is no power in such food to be feared (*Paed.*, ii.8.3ff, citing 1 Cor. 10.20; 8.7f; Matt. 15.11; 1 Cor. 9.4f).

Abstinence from meat with the blood in it is attested as a Christian custom by Tertullian, *Apology* 9.13; Minucius Felix 36.6; and Biblis in Eusebius *H.E.* v.1.26.

The nearest we get to a collection of precepts in which all three of the decrees are combined is in the Pseudo-Clementine literature.[5] The cultic requirements to be observed by those who

---

[1] The distinction of meats is explicitly said to be abolished, *Didascalia Apostolorum*, 26 (vi.16) (Connolly, 219 l.18).

[2] This custom was practised by some Greeks, and by the Therapeutae (Philo, *de vita contemplativa*, 37), and is ascribed to James (Eusebius, *H.E.* ii. 23.5), and, by the Ebionites, to Peter (Epiph. 30.15.3). It was adopted by Tatian's Encratites. See Lietzmann, *An die Römer*, Hbd. z.N.T. (3rd ed., Tübingen, 1928) to Rom. 14.

[3] C. K. Barrett, "Things Sacrificed to Idols", *N.T.S.*, 11 (1964–5), 138–53.

[4] Tr. by J. Rendel Harris, *Texts and Studies*, i (Cambridge, 1891), 49.

[5] A. F. J. Klijn, "The Pseudo-Clementines and the Apostolic Decree", *Novum Testamentum*, x (1968), 305–12.

would belong to this church always include not partaking of the table of demons (Homilies vii.4.2–3; vii.8; viii.19.1; viii.20.1; viii.23.1–2; ix.14.3–4; ix.23.2; xiii.4.1–3; Recognitions iv.36.1–5; vii.29.1–3). Usually there is added to this prohibition the prohibition against eating blood (Hom. vii.4.2–3; vii.8.1–3; Rec. iv.36.1–5), and in two of these three cases abstaining from "things sacrificed to idols" is offered as an interpretation of what is meant by not partaking of the table of demons, and stands at the head of the list of prohibited foods: for example, "to abstain from the table of demons, that is, from food offered to idols, from dead carcases, from animals that have been suffocated or torn by wild beasts, and from blood" (Hom. vii.8). Refusal to sit at meals where pagan gods ("demons") are honoured would not necessarily imply that one should refuse to eat meat that had once been offered to an idol, but it did imply this in the Pseudo-Clementine church, because of their theory that demons had the power "to convey themselves by means of meats and drinks consecrated to them into the minds and bodies of those who partake of it" (Rec. iv.19.6).[1] Occasionally certain ablutions are also added to the lists of cultic requirements (Hom. vii.4.2–3; vii.8.1–3; cf. xi.28.1; xi.30.1; xi.33.4; Rec. vi.10.5; vi.12), but it is very unlikely that these are what is meant by the prohibition of πορνεία in the Apostolic Decree.[2]

We conclude that the Jewish Christian church whose traditions are preserved in the Pseudo-Clementine literature strictly forbade taking part in meals at which pagan gods were honoured; interpreted this as also excluding any consumption of food offered to idols; and observed the Jewish food laws about meat. There is no sign that the actual terms of the Apostolic Decree had an influence on their practice.

In the first edition of this book I argued that the absence of

---

[1] I think that the prohibition of εἰδωλοθύτα followed logically from the prohibition of sitting at the table of demons, and does not reflect the influence of the terms of the Apostolic Decree; against Klijn, op. cit.

[2] An argument put forward by H. J. Schoeps; Einar Molland, "La circoncision, le baptême et l'autorité du décret apostolique (Actes 15.28 sq.) dans les milieux judéo-chrétiens des Pseudo-Clémentines", Studia Theologica, ix (1956), 1–39; opposed by Klijn, op. cit., 310f.

evidence that all the terms of the Decree were in force at the one place and the one time indicated that a council at Jerusalem had never promulgated the Decree. Schmithals has now taken this line of argument even further, and has argued that the second-century parallels to the terms of the Decree are accidental: the struggle against Gnosis led to the prohibition of meat sacrificed to idols; the resistance to pagan accusations of murdering and consuming children led to the insistence that Christians ate only kosher-killed meat; and the observance of Roman law led to the avoidance of marriage within the prohibited degrees.[1] This argument of course will not do. It is impossible to imagine Christians adopting the practice of eating kosher meat in order to rebut the charge that they ate children; only if the practice were well established and attested would it be a good answer to the imputation, and, in any case, this would be an absurd way to try to meet the charge of cannibalism, a charge that probably arose from a misunderstanding of the Eucharist. Similarly, we should have to ask *why* some Christians regarded other Christians as heretical because they ate food offered to idols. It is very unlikely that the "orthodox" decided to abstain from food offered to idols simply because the "gnostics" were indifferent to what food they ate. Paul's epistles show that in the early days of the Church there were Christians who had strong scruples about idol meat, and it is possible that the "gnostics" decided to eat idol meat on principle, in order to assert their freedom—proof that the custom of abstaining from idol meat was already in existence. The Church's struggle against πορνεία, whatever precisely that meant, cannot be simply written off as an obedience to Roman Law. Probably all the Christian marriage ideals can be paralleled in parts of Judaism, in Greek philosophy, and in the Roman law, but that in no way diminished the achievement by which these ideals were carried out by Christians as a general rule.[2]

---

[1] *Paulus und Jakobus* (Göttingen, 1963), 82ff; *Paul and James* (London, 1965), 99f.

[2] Herbert Preisker, *Christentum und Ehe in den ersten drei Jahrhunderten: Eine Studie zur Kulturgeschichte der alten Welt.* Berlin, 1927.

There is no reason to doubt that the three terms of the Decree go back to the earliest days of the Church; certainly it is never suggested in the second-century evidence that any of them is an innovation. Not all three are mentioned together in any of our sources, but this, I think, is easily explained. First, the Decree was specifically directed to "Antioch and Syria and Cilicia". The naming of Syria and Cilicia, about which nothing had so far been reported in Acts, shows that Luke is quoting a source, as Wellhausen saw.[1] The Decree was meant for one area, and the Jerusalem authorities did not think of themselves as making canon law for a Catholic Church. Second, circumstances would alter, and regulations required for one church need not necessarily be the ones required for other churches. In fact the relations between the Jewish Christians and Jews who did not accept Jesus as Messiah changed very rapidly, and the circumstances that led James to suggest his working arrangement did not hold for very long. The eating of kosher meat by Christians, for example, lasted far beyond the time when its practical advantage, of not scandalizing Jewish converts or potential converts, had passed.

Not all the problems raised by the comparison of our two sources, Acts and Galatians, are yet solved, but there is a *prima facie* case for allowing that the reports both of Peter's vision and of the Jerusalem Decree are accurate.

LUKE'S ERRORS

Nevertheless Luke is wrong in two important respects.

First, he reported that Paul promulgated the terms of the Jerusalem Decree beyond the area to which the original letter had been directed (Acts 16.4). In fact Paul never referred to the Decree in his epistles, and gave rulings that differed from the provisions laid down at Jerusalem. He allowed Christians to eat food that had been offered to idols with a clear conscience, provided only that they did not scandalize their fellow-Christians by doing so (Rom. 14; 1 Cor. 8). He never referred to the prohibition on eating blood, but clearly he would not have

[1] Op. cit., 28.

objected to the eating of meat which had not been kosher-killed in principle, but only if thereby a fellow-Christian who had scruples would have been offended.

The evidence from Paul is backed by evidence in Acts itself. When Paul returned to Jerusalem for the last time he was welcomed and then addressed by James. After drawing Paul's attention to the large numbers of Jews zealous for the Law who have believed, and warning him of the bad effect reports were having that he had taught that believing Jews in the dispersion need not circumcise their children nor observe other customs, James went on to suggest a way Paul could demonstrate his own loyalty to the Law of Moses. Then, in 21.25, James says, "Concerning Gentiles who have believed, we have written giving our judgment that they should keep themselves from things offered to idols and from blood and from unchastity."

I argued in the first edition of this book that this scene could be taken as the plea of minority Jewish Christians to Paul, representing the majority Gentile Church, for permission to continue observing their customs.[1] The argument is as follows. The author of Acts believed that the working arrangement between Jews and Gentiles in the Church should be maintained whereby neither side attempted to impose its view on the other. The seal of this agreement was the abstinence of the Gentile Church from food offered to idols, meat with the blood in it, and the forbidden degrees of marriage. In return, the Gentile Church would protect the rights of the Jewish Christians to maintain the Mosaic Law among themselves as far as that was possible.

When did the situation implied by this reading of Luke's text exist?

The Epistle of Ignatius to the Philadelphians 6.1 provides us with the first clue. "If any one discourses to you on Judaism, do not listen to him. For it is better to listen to Christian teaching from a man who is circumcised, than to Judaism from one who is not. But if neither speaks about Jesus Christ, I hold

[1] F. Overbeck, "Ueber das Verhältniss Justins des Märtyrers zur Apg.", *Zeitschrift für wissenschaftliche Theologie*, xv (Leipzig, 1872), 335f.

them pillars and tombs of the dead, bearing only the names of the dead." Ignatius is facing a strong Judaizing movement which wanted to observe the Sabbath instead of Sunday, revered the High Priest to the point of forgetting the pre-eminence due to Jesus Christ, and tended to put the O.T. above the gospel (Magn. 9.1; Philad. 9.1f; 8.2).[1] The members of this movement seem, from the passage quoted, to be Gentiles who are not circumcised and do not ask for circumcision.[2] What is important for our question is that, even though Ignatius is opposing these Judaizers so strongly, he yet continues to recognize that there are Jewish Christians who have a right to exist. It seems that the ingredients of the situation we have seen presupposed in Acts are already being assembled. The extent to which Gentile Christians should observe the Jewish cultic practices is a live question, although the Judaizers in this case are not asking for circumcision, and there still exist groups of Jewish Christians who have continued to circumcise their children and who are tolerated by the dominant Gentile part of the Church.

In Justin's Dialogue with Trypho we find a much closer parallel to Acts, particularly in chapter 47.[3]

Trypho asked whether a man who had acknowledged that Jesus was the Messiah and trusted in him, but still wished to observe the Mosaic Law, would be saved.

Justin replied, "In my opinion, Trypho, such a man would be saved, but only as long as he did not try to persuade others— I mean Gentiles who have been cut off from error through the Messiah—to observe the things he observed. That is, he must not tell them that they will only be saved if they observe these things. . . ."

---

[1] See discussion in W. Bauer, *Hdb.z.N.T.* (Tübingen, 1920), 239f.

[2] See J. B. Lightfoot, *Apostolic Fathers*, Pt. 2, sect. 1 (London, 1885), 263f.

[3] The similarity was first pointed out by Schwegler (1846); see *Beginnings*, ii.374 n 2. See also the articles by A. Ritschl and F. Overbeck already cited. The fullest discussion of Justin's evidence (without, however, mention of the possible relationship to Acts) is by A. Harnack, *Judentum und Juden-christentum in Justins Dialog mit Trypho*, *T.U.*, iii.9 (=39. Band) (Leipzig, 1913), 47–92.

Trypho: "Why did you say, 'In my opinion such a man will be saved'? There must be some who deny that these people will be saved."

"There are," I replied, "and they refuse to engage them in conversation or invite them into their homes, but I do not agree with them. It is because of a weakness in understanding that the Jewish Christians want to keep as much of the Law of Moses as is possible under the present circumstances;[1] we know that it was imposed because of the hard-heartedness of the people. However, if they wish to go on holding to it alongside of their hope concerning this Messiah and the natural and supernatural moral and religious demands, and as long as they choose to live with Christians and the faithful without, as I have said, urging them to be circumcised like them or to keep the Sabbath or to do anything else they observe, then I maintain that they should be received into our fellowship and treated like kinsmen and brothers."

"But if, Trypho," I continued, "these compatriots of yours who claim to believe in this Messiah compel Gentiles who have likewise believed to live in all respects by the Mosaic Law and will not otherwise associate with them, I too will not recognize them."

"Those they succeed in persuading to submit to the observance of the Law while continuing to confess God's Messiah may perhaps, in my opinion, be saved. But those who had once confessed and recognized that this man (Jesus) was the Messiah and, for whatever reason, have gone over to the observance of the Law and have denied that he was the Messiah will, in my opinion, have no chance of salvation unless they change their minds before they die."

This extract shows again that the problem of the extent to which one should keep the Law of Moses was still alive. Some Gentile Christians were being persuaded to join the Jewish Christians in following the full range of Mosaic practices, and some were even going so far as to apostatize completely to

[1] In chap. 46 Trypho has admitted that it is now impossible to perform the Mosaic sacrifices, because there is no Temple.

Judaism. Justin firmly condemns any Jewish Christians who encourage Gentile Christians to observe the Law, but he adopts a tolerant attitude to Jewish Christians who are content to live with the rest of the Church without frightening their fellow Christians with the prospect of losing salvation for not keeping the Law. Justin admits that other Gentile Christians are not as tolerant as he is; they deny that the Jewish Christians who continue to observe the Law are Christians at all. As Harnack has pointed out, Justin would scarcely have admitted that the other view existed if his own view had not been in the minority, or at least under heavy fire.[1] This, however, is almost the only difference one can detect between Justin's position and Luke's, and it may be accounted for by the fact that the unsuccessful Bar Cochba revolt has occurred between Luke's time and Justin's.[2] The *modus vivendi* which was established in Luke's time, or which he believed should have been established, may well have been challenged when the Jewish people fell into deeper disgrace after the revolt had failed. The arrangement was otherwise the same as the one Justin was advocating. Attempts from the Jewish Christian side to impose the Law of Moses are as firmly squashed in Acts as in Justin. On the other hand, the right of the Jewish Christians to continue the observance of the Mosaic Law, as far as one could (Acts 15.10), was fully and freely granted by Paul himself who, as a Jew, never deviated from its observance (Acts 25.8 etc.).

It has been argued in Chapter One that Justin had not seen Luke-Acts. Even if he had, the agreement with Luke on this issue could scarely be due to Justin's copying Acts, since both Trypho and Christian readers of the Dialogue would know if the situation he presented did not correspond to conditions at the time. Nor should it be forgotten that Justin never once mentions Paul's name, here or anywhere else.[3] The close agreement between Acts and Justin's Dialogue on this question of the status

---

[1] Op. cit., 86 and n.

[2] Overbeck, op. cit., 337f, adds that in Acts the observance of the Law is obligatory for Jewish Christians and in Justin, optional.

[3] See 26–8 above.

of Jewish Christians within the Church is one of the most compelling arguments in favour of the second-century date for Acts.

But is my reading of Luke's understanding of the point of James's speech correct? I think it must stand, because Luke could hardly have overlooked the fact that he has said not only that Paul was present at the Council when the Decree was formulated, but also that he had carried the Decree out to the churches he visited after leaving the area to which the Decree was first addressed. Luke must have seen the Decree as the sign of a pact.

However, the wording of Acts 21.25 shows that those commentators who argue that Luke is here employing a source are also correct. Luke believed that Paul carried the terms of the letter by word of mouth to other churches outside Syria and Cilicia, but James, in 21.25, clearly states that the Council's judgement was conveyed by letter, and implies that its terms applied only to believing Gentiles under its jurisdiction, not to the Gentiles who were members of the churches Paul had been visiting. There is no need to be pedantic and to read James's words as implying that Paul did not know about the Decree at all—many things known to everybody present have to be said again on formal occasions—but the manner in which James introduces the matter, at the end of his remarks, suggests that he cites the Decree not as a rule for all Gentile Christians but as an arrangement agreed upon for the restricted group of Gentile Christians under the jurisdiction of Jerusalem.

Luke possibly took his source in a different sense in order to apply it to his own situation, but the wording of his report indicates that the source supports the picture of Paul's relation to the Decrees that we gather from his own epistles. The source implies that Paul and his churches were not bound by the Decree, and that the terms of the Decree were not imposed on all the Gentile Christians as a condition for avoiding circumcision.

The second historical point on which Luke is wrong is in his general assertion, often illustrated, that Paul went to the Gentiles only when forced to do so by the hostility of the Jews. In fact, as Galatians makes perfectly clear, Paul deliberately chose, as his God-given vocation, to preach to the Gentiles. No doubt he looked for his first Gentile converts in synagogues, if there were synagogues in the towns he visited, but his aim was to set up purely Gentile congregations. Of course the synagogues that believed in Jesus Christ would continue to attract and hold Gentiles, but Paul's strategy was the entirely new one of setting up purely Gentile churches to be representatives of the great return of the Gentiles promised in Scripture.

Again, the sources Luke was employing give evidence that this was in fact how Paul worked, although Luke himself does not understand the picture in that way at all.

In Acts 18.1–18, for example, there is an account of how Paul on his arrival at Corinth first stayed with the Jewish couple Aquila and Priscilla, and then moved to the house of Titius Justus, a Gentile who worshipped in the synagogue. The move is of crucial importance for Luke. It is the second of the three occasions when Paul is forced by the Jewish hostility to his preaching to turn to the Gentiles. "Your blood be on your head. I am guiltless. From now on I shall go to the Gentiles." He moves to the house of a Gentile, and Luke understands that Aquila and Priscilla come to the new meeting place with him, as does Crispus, another Jew who believed. The Gentile's house next to the synagogue is the centre of a new entity, a church composed of Jews and Gentiles existing outside the synagogue system.

But, when we come to examine the passage more closely, Luke's reading of the move raises difficulties. If Paul was forced out of the synagogue, why did he not gather together a new synagogue in Aquila and Priscilla's house? Jews and Greeks worshipped in the first synagogue; why should not Jews and Greeks who believed that Jesus was Messiah worship in a new place that would still be Jewish? We know from 1 Cor. 16.19 that Aquila and Priscilla did have a church in their house.

The problem is sharpened when we observe that Acts 18.7, when read by itself, seems to be describing a move of residence. Codex Bezae takes the verse in that sense, having μεταβὰς [ἀπὸ τοῦ] Ἀκύλα instead of καὶ μεταβὰς ἐκεῖθεν,[1] and this reading

---

[1] E. J. Epp, *The Theological Tendency of Codex Bezae Cantabrigiensis in Acts* (Cambridge, 1966), 91f.

may well be the original, since it fits the natural sense of the rest of the sentence, and is yet the harder reading in the context of verse 6.

Notice, further, that the passage contains two descriptions of Paul's preaching. In verse 4 "he discoursed in the synagogue every Sabbath and tried to persuade Jews and Greeks". His message must have been about Jesus, but in verse 5, when Silas and Timothy arrive, he begins to be engrossed in "witnessing to the Jews that the Messiah was Jesus".[1] The activity is basically the same, but the Jews are singled out, whereas before it had been "Jews and Greeks", and the message is made explicit. But the singling out of the Jews and the elaboration of the message are signs that an editorial hand is at work; we are being prepared for the moment when the Jews will turn against Paul.

If we bracket off the words διαμαρτυρόμενος τοῖς Ἰουδαίοις εἶναι τὸν χριστὸν Ἰησοῦν in verse 5 and the whole of verse 6, we are left with a straightforward account. Paul at first worked at his own trade while staying with Aquila and Priscilla. Every Sabbath he preached about Jesus in the synagogue. When Silas and Timothy came, he was able to give up work and devote himself entirely to preaching. He moved to the house of Justus, a Gentile God-fearer who had believed in Jesus. Crispus ὁ ἀρχισυνάγωγος (probably a Gentile of rank in the affairs of the city rather than a Jewish ruler of the synagogue)[2] and many other Corinthians also believed.

Paul's move from Aquila's house probably did imply that he began to gather a new synagogue, without breaking off his good relations with Aquila and Priscilla, in whose company he was eventually to leave the city (18.18). The reason he did not simply establish the new synagogue in Aquila's house seems to be that he wanted to gather Gentiles as Gentiles, without their having to become adherents of a Jewish synagogue. Indeed, we can hardly understand the source, without the editorial addition, in any other sense, because we possess Paul's epistles, and know

---

[1] See *Beginnings*, iv.224.

[2] Moulton and Milligan, *The Vocabulary of the Greek Testament Illustrated from the Papyri and Other Non-Literary Sources* (London, 1914–30), 82, cite an inscription from 80–69 B.C. that shows that the word could be used of pagans.

of his mission to Gentiles as Gentiles. Luke, however, could not imagine Paul, the ever-faithful Jew, as voluntarily leaving the synagogue to live and preach in a Gentile's house, unless official Judaism had compelled him to leave. He interpreted the source in the only way open to him, but he retained the words of the source embedded in his own narrative, so that we are able to reconstruct it and to interpret its meaning correctly in the light of our greater knowledge.

A further example where Luke's source preserves the true nature of Paul's missionary strategy occurs in the speech from the Temple steps, Acts 22.17–21, in which Paul implies that he was sent only to the Gentiles.[1] The source for the speech before Agrippa in Acts 26 probably also contained the same idea, but Luke has added his own interpretation, that Paul himself always went first to the Jews before turning to the Gentiles (verses 17 (?), 20, 23).

WHY LUKE ERRED

How did it come about that Luke made these two mistakes, the mistake about Paul's promulgating the Decree, and the mistake about the reason for Paul's mission to the Gentiles?

There is a whole scale of possible answers, from Luke's ignorance at one extreme, to his theology at the other extreme. But before we can dogmatize about either his ignorance or his theology, we should do well to attempt to provide a detailed explanation of how he compiled his narrative from the sources he did have.[2]

From the fact that Luke is a skilful story-teller we cannot legitimately conclude that he did not employ documentary

[1] J. Jervell, "Paulus—Der Lehrer Israels", *Novum Testamentum*, x (1968), 177f.

[2] This theory about the structure and composition of Acts 15 is based on the work of Hans Waitz, "Das Problem des sog. Aposteldekrets und die damit zusammenhängenden literarischen und geschichtlichen Probleme des apostolischen Zeitalters", *Z.K.G.*, Dritte Folge vi (1936), 227–63. Cf. Johannes Weiss's earlier two-source hypothesis, *Das Urchristentum* (Göttingen, 1914), 195ff; *The History of Primitive Christianity* (London, 1937), i. 259–63 (*Earliest Christianity*, New York, 1959).

sources. Nevertheless, the way in which the story in Acts 15 is told may indicate that Luke has written up the narrative on the basis of general information, and not constructed the account out of one or more sources which he copied more or less word for word. Ernst Haenchen has argued strongly that Luke had no continuous source or sources, and has repeated and strengthened his argument in answer to Rudolf Bultmann's criticism of the first edition of his commentary on Acts.[1]

Haenchen argues, first, that the speeches ascribed to Peter and James are mutually dependent, that Peter's words are only understandable in the light of the story of Cornelius, a Lucan construction, and that the point of James's speech depends on a quotation from the LXX, which could not be made from the Hebrew text. He argues, second, that such features as the double origin of the debate (verses 1 and 5) and the marginal rôle of Paul and Barnabas are readily explicable when we understand the end Luke had in mind and his literary skill, as, third, is the seemingly restricted and unexpected address on the Decree, to which Bultmann (like Wellhausen[2]) had attached so much significance as indicating a source.

Haenchen's second and third arguments are a matter of judgement, and depend on whether one is convinced that alleged unevennesses and difficulties indicate the faithful following of documentary sources or whether they indicate a more subtle and contriving writer than the surface simplicity had led one to expect. But his first argument is refutable. Granted that the speeches of Peter and James are dependent on one another, does Peter's fit so closely into the Cornelius incident, and in such a way, that we must ascribe it to Luke, and does James's point really depend on the LXX alone?

Whether or not dependence of Peter's speech on the Cornelius

[1] Ernst Haenchen, "Quellenanalyse und Kompositionsanalyse in Act. 15", in *Judentum—Urchristentum—Kirche: Festschrift für Joachim Jeremias*, ed. Walther Eltester, *Beiheft zu Z.N.W.* 26 (Berlin, 1960), 153–64. R. Bultmann, "Zur Frage nach den Quellen der Apostelgeschichte", in *New Testament Essays: Studies in Memory of T. W. Manson 1893–1958*, ed. A. J. B. Higgins (Manchester, 1959), 68–80; reprinted in *Exegetica* (Tübingen, 1967), 412–23.

[2] Op. cit., 28.

incident would indicate a Lucan construction, it is unlikely that the speech is so dependent as has been maintained. The main point Peter made was that God showed his willingness to "take from Gentiles a people for his name" by bestowing the Spirit on them without distinction, and this point is echoed by James. Of course Cornelius's conversion is a striking example, but both Peter and James are arguing from general and repeated experience (as Paul was to argue later in Gal. 3.1ff). When we see that this is the point of both speeches, it is possible to see that the two references to the conversion of Cornelius are more likely than not to be additions made by Luke to link the speeches into his particular narrative, where the conversion of Cornelius is made to occupy a typical rôle, and to stand for a whole series of events. The first reference back, διὰ τοῦ στόματός μου in verse 7, rather awkwardly cuts across the main thrust of the sentence, which emphasizes that "God has chosen *you* that the Gentiles should hear the word of the gospel and believe", ἐν ὑμῖν ἐξελέξατο ὁ θεός ... The awkwardness has helped lead to various readings in place of ἐν ὑμῖν (p74 ℵ A B bo; ημιν D *614*; εν ημιν after the verb EHLPS; om. *69* sa). Peter is arguing primarily that the existence and activity of the Jerusalem church has led to numbers of Gentile conversions, and I find it easier to hold that Luke added the specific reference to Peter's part in this work, than that Peter's original speech contained a distraction from the main argument, which depended for its force on being a convincing appeal to the universal experience of the church. The second reference back, πρῶτον in verse 14, is also, strictly speaking, superfluous; James's point is not how God acted at first, with respect to Cornelius, but how he has acted in gathering a Jewish church that would be the catalyst for winning from Gentiles a people for his name.

Haenchen is right to notice that Luke ties the speeches closely to the Cornelius incident, but on closer examination these ties look very much like the additions a skilled narrator would make, a narrator who constantly worked by using specific incidents to indicate a general trend.

James's citation from Amos 9.11f seems to depend for its force on the LXX mistranslation of the Hebrew, and since James would almost certainly have used the Hebrew Scriptures in preference to the Greek, we might have to conclude that James's speech was the work of a Greek-speaking writer, who could just as well be Luke himself. However, the citation from Amos is not uniformly from the LXX, but the first part, a rendering of Amos 9.11 in Acts 15.16, is a free and independent translation from the Hebrew.[1] This must indicate that a citation, originally wholly independent of the LXX, was partly "corrected" by reference to the LXX; I can see no other plausible conclusion. What Haenchen takes to be a clinching argument that Luke, who (it is assumed) knew only the LXX, wrote the speech, turns out to be fairly strong evidence that Luke used a source. The source presumably continued to give a free rendering of the Hebrew of Amos 9.12: "'... that they may possess the remnant of Edom and all the nations who are called by my name', says the Lord who does this." James was arguing that Scripture had foretold that the restoration of the tabernacle of David would be accompanied by the chosen people's possession of all the nations called by the Lord's name, in other words, that when God sent the Messiah to Israel, the Gentiles God had designated would flock to put themselves under the Son of David's rule. The LXX mistranslation is politer to the Gentiles and seems to be more appropriate—that is why Luke or a later scribe substituted it—but it does not really make James's point so well; he is arguing that *God* has brought these Gentiles in (verses 8, 18[2]), not that they seek the Lord of their own free will.[3]

[1] Most recently, Traugott Holtz, *Untersuchungen über die Alttestamentlichen Zitate bei Lukas*, T.U., Bd. 104 (Berlin, 1968), 21–6. Max Wilcox, *The Semitisms of Acts* (Oxford, 1965), 49, 158f, 177, argues that "an originally circulating element has been adapted somewhat to a new context". It is unlikely that the Hebrew text behind the Greek is especially related to the text cited in CD VII. 16, 4Q Flor I.30. See J. A. Emerton's criticism of Wilcox and Rabin on this point, *Journal of Semitic Studies*, 13 (1968), 288.

[2] In verse 18 the reading of A D Hcl^ms, etc., γνωστον απ αιωνος (εστιν) (τω κυριω) το εργον αυτου is preferable to the reading of B.

[3] See C. C. Torrey, *Composition and Date of Acts* (Cambridge, Mass., 1916), 39; Floyd V. Filson, *Three Crucial Decades: Studies in the Book of Acts* (1963, London, 1964), 79.

Before we leave Haenchen's attempt to show that Luke wrote these two speeches, we should examine another argument that would suggest that Peter's speech was made up later. In verse 10 Peter seems to argue that, because the Law was an intolerable burden on Jews, which they and their fathers were unable to bear, it should not be imposed upon Gentiles. This argument would naturally lead to the conclusion not just that Gentiles need not keep the Law, but that Jewish Christians, too, need not, because they could not. Such an argument must stem from a time when the Church has finally separated from Judaism, and is scarcely credible as an utterance of Peter.[1] But the argument, besides being anachronistic, does not fit its context. Peter is arguing in verses 7–10a that the Jerusalem church must not tempt God by adding additional requirements to the Gentiles after they have already clearly received the Spirit in exactly the same way as the Jewish believers. Whether or not the Jews had kept the Law is irrelevant; even if the Jews had found their strength unequal to the task of keeping the Law, Peter's opponents could argue that the struggle was a necessary part of worshipping God. Peter's point is complete when he has said, "Now therefore why do you tempt God by imposing a yoke on the neck of the [new] disciples?"[2] Verse 10b looks very much like a later addition, due either to Luke himself, or, more likely, to a later scribe. James could scarcely have allowed this additional argument to go by default—even if Luke had been making up his speech for him (cf. Acts 21.20–5)—but, instead, James accepts Peter's main point, that God has been calling the Gentiles as Gentiles, but suggests in effect that a few sensible regulations, which would not infringe their status as Gentiles, need not be interpreted as putting God to the test by going against his revealed good pleasure.

Whenever we can test Haenchen's arguments, they point in exactly the opposite direction from the conclusions he wishes to draw, and we are now at liberty to go forward to attempt to isolate Luke's source or sources.

[1] Hans Conzelmann, *Hdb.z.N.T.* (Tübingen, 1963), 83.
[2] I am not sure whether verse 11 belonged to the original speech or to the addition in verse 10b; a decision does not affect my main point.

LUKE'S SOURCES

The double origin of the discussion is a good place to start. In Acts 15.1ff the Christians at Antioch, having been disturbed by Judeans who taught that circumcision was necessary to salvation, decided to send a delegation to Jerusalem to find out if the church there, with the apostles and elders at her head, thought that this was so. In verse 5 some Pharisees who had believed raised the issue as to whether or not it was necessary to proclaim to believing Gentiles that they keep the Law of Moses.

It is very strange that, as the narrative now stands, the delegates from Antioch seem to forget their mission when they arrive in Jerusalem, and that Barnabas and Paul appear, without our hearing quite how they got there, as witnesses for Peter's position, in an assembly of the apostles and presbyters.

There is a further small oddity, which helps to put us on the right track. In verse 27 the Jerusalem church writes to Antioch to say that they have sent Judas and Silas with Barnabas and Paul to convey by word of mouth the same message (ἀπεστάλκαμεν οὖν 'Ιούδαν καὶ Σείλαν, καὶ αὐτοὺς διὰ λόγου ἀπαγγέλλοντας τὰ αὐτά), and that message can scarcely be anything but the message already written in verse 24: the Judeans who have troubled you and perverted your lives were not acting under our orders. Of course Luke goes on to give a further message, the message about the new Decree, but verse 27 refers back.[1] In fact, the message in verse 24 is quite sufficient to solve the problem at Antioch, and needs nothing further to be said. Since Paul never suggests in Galatians or elsewhere that the freedom of Gentiles from circumcision and their obligation to keep certain cultic regulations are in any way connected, we are

---

[1] Haenchen, op. cit. (10th ed.), 399; (12th ed.), 394, makes the illuminating comment on τὰ αὐτά: "The reader already knows what the Decree will contain, but the recipients of the letter do not. One sees that the composition of the letter goes back to Luke." I should argue, on the contrary, that the letter has already given a message which could be confirmed by the oral testimony of the bearers, and that Luke is forced, rather awkwardly, to append the terms of the Decree, from the letter in his other source, after τὰ αὐτά. The awkwardness is a positive sign that Luke did not compose the letter; a letter composed by one hand is likely to be entirely smooth.

justified in drawing a line under verse 27, and asking whether Luke has not combined two things that were once separate.

I suggest that Luke was combining two distinct sources, which can be reconstructed as follows:

Antioch Source: verses 1–4; 12 (καὶ ἤκουον . . . δι' αὐτῶν); 22; 23 (γράψαντες διὰ χειρὸς αὐτῶν); 24–7; 30–4.
Jerusalem Source: verses 5–11; 12 (ἐσείγησεν δὲ πᾶν τὸ πλῆθος); 13–21; 23 (οἱ ἀπόστολοι . . . χαίρειν); 28 (om. γάρ); 29.

One of the marks of the Antioch source is the naming of Barnabas before Paul (verses 12b, 25; cf. 13.7; 14.14), but we must not conclude that those verses where the order is "Paul and Barnabas" belong to a different source (verses 2, 22; cf. 35). They are probably additions inserted by Luke in order to make his own hero Paul a little more prominent in the story that the Antioch source had done. Verse 22 certainly reads more smoothly if the words σὺν τῷ Παύλῳ καὶ Βαρνάβᾳ are set aside, and I conjecture that verse 2 in the source originally read, γενομένης δὲ στάσεως καὶ ζητήσεως οὐκ ὀλίγης, ἔταξαν ἀναβαίνειν τινὰς ἐξ αὐτῶν πρὸς τοὺς ἀποστόλυος κτλ, "When strife and not a little controversy had arisen, they appointed some of them[selves] to go up to the apostles and elders in Jerusalem about this question". This conjecture removes the absurd possibility, which is raised by the usual text, that it was the trouble-makers from Judea who had appointed envoys to Jerusalem.[1]

The Antioch source, then, describes a visit to Jerusalem by a delegation in which Barnabas and Paul are members, but not so much representatives of the church, resident at Antioch, as men whose experience further afield is a valuable adjunct to the Antiochine case. That explains why they are not mentioned in the source until after the general delegation has started its plea in verse 4; Barnabas and Paul add their special testimony afterwards, in verse 12b. It also explains why Barnabas and Paul are singled out in the letter from Jerusalem as "men who have devoted their lives for the name of our Lord Jesus Christ", and are said to be sent back with the two leaders from Jerusalem,

[1] This possible interpretation is seriously canvassed in *Beginnings*, iv.170.

Judas and Silas, to Antioch. It is as though their special work has been adopted by Jerusalem, and as though they are now being commended to Antioch by Jerusalem. In other words, Barnabas and Paul were not an integral part of the Antiochine delegation, although the church at Antioch was proud to be associated with their work and knew that their testimony would add force to its own plea that Gentiles who had been converted need not be circumcised. And Jerusalem recognized the independent nature of Barnabas and Paul's work, commended them for it, and was glad to adopt them as co-messengers of comfort to go back to Antioch with the news that the troublemakers from Judea were not authorized teachers.

The events described in the Antioch source therefore correspond very well to the second visit to Jerusalem recorded by Paul in Galatians.

The Jerusalem source concerned a dispute that arose within the Jerusalem church about how Gentiles who joined the synagogues under their jurisdiction were to be treated, whether or not they were to be told to keep the Law of Moses. That the discussion concerned only a limited geographical area is clear, not only from the address of the letter to the Gentile brethren of Antioch and Syria and Cilicia (verse 23b), but also from James's statement that "Moses has from generations of old had those who proclaim him *in every city*" (verse 21). There were not synagogues in every city of the Mediterranean world, but there were more likely to be synagogues in every major city of Syria and Cilicia.[1]

This Jerusalem source contains a speech by Peter, which seems to argue that nothing more should be asked of the Gentiles who had believed than had already been asked of them— presumably, to believe that Jesus was the Messiah, and to worship the true and living God who had sent Jesus. James accepted Peter's main argument, which he believed God had foretold in

---

[1] The cities known to have Jewish Colonies (outside Palestine) are underlined in the map of the Eastern Mediterranean at the time of Paul in the *Biblisch—Historisches Handwörterbuch* (Göttingen, 1962), reproduced as a supplement to Conzelmann, *Hdb. z.N.T.* (Tübingen, 1963).

Scripture, but he thought it prudent to ask these Gentiles to observe certain cultic restrictions. Why?

The quotation from Amos gives us the first clue. James must have cited Amos because he believed that the coming of the Messiah and the conversion of Gentiles was part of the restoration of the tabernacle of David. The cultic requirements were simply what Leviticus 17 and 18 demanded of the "stranger within the gate", as I have argued in Chapter Three.[1]

The second clue lies in verse 21. James is clearly arguing that the scruples of Jews who do not yet believe in Jesus Christ are to be taken into account; if believing Jews were going to cities where there were no synagogues already established, they might ask no cultic observances from the Gentile converts, but there were always old-established synagogues in the area they were speaking of, and the susceptibilities of those synagogues had to be respected. James is assuming that all Gentile converts will be members of Jewish synagogues, synagogues where all would believe in Jesus Christ, but that they would *ipso facto* be associated with the loose confederation of Jews in that place, many of whom belonged to synagogues that had not yet been convinced that Jesus was indeed the Messiah. James is speaking out of a situation where there was no organizational division between Jews who believed and Jews who did not believe; the freedom of belief from synagogue to synagogue was great enough to allow those who believed in Jesus to remain in uneasy communion with those who did not. But in that situation it was important, for cultic reasons, that the Gentiles who had attached themselves to the converted synagogues should observe the minimum cultic requirements, so as not to endanger the communion of the Jews who believed in Jesus with their fellow-Jews; cultic differences were far more serious, at this stage of history, than creedal differences. The Jerusalem church still hoped to be the nucleus of the Jewish people who would all finally recognize the Messiah.

The Jerusalem source, then, tells how Peter's principle and James's prudential advice are accepted by the Council of the

[1] 82 and n; 108.

Jerusalem church and embodied in a letter to the Gentile converts in Antioch and Syria and Cilicia.

If I have correctly isolated and expounded the two sources, what was the historical relationship between them?

Many scholars have argued that the matter discussed in the Jerusalem source must have arisen out of Paul's clash with Peter in Antioch, that is, after Paul's second visit to Jerusalem (Gal. 2.11ff).[1] If that is so, the Jerusalem source must be untrustworthy, because it definitely makes the controversy originate in Jerusalem. But I am inclined to place the events described in the Jerusalem source a long time before the visit described in the Antioch source and in Gal. 2.1–10. Unless there had been such a discussion and decision, I can hardly see how Paul would have dared to take Titus, an uncircumcised Gentile, with him to Jerusalem on his second visit. Paul seems to have acknowledged the right of the Jerusalem church to insist on the circumcision of Gentile converts in Jerusalem, if they had decided that this was right (Gal. 2.3), so that he must have been confident about the line the Jerusalem authorities would take.

To the objection that Peter would hardly have withdrawn from eating with Gentile Christians at Antioch if the Jerusalem Decree was in force, I should answer that the hypothesis of the existence of the Decree provides a better explanation for what happened, than the hypothesis that the Decree had not yet been made. The existence of the Decree would explain why Peter was formerly happy to eat with Gentiles, and Peter's withdrawal from eating with them is understandable against the knowledge we have been able to obtain from the Jerusalem source about the reason for adopting the Decree in the first place. The Decree was adopted for the sake of the as yet unconverted Jews. The Jews in Antioch—for it is they, and not the Jews in Jerusalem, who are referred to by the clause φοβούμενος τοὺς ἐκ περιτομῆς in Gal. 2.12—were unhappy with the state of affairs in Antioch, and were putting pressure on the Jews who believed in Jesus Christ. They could have been unhappy either with the regulations laid down in the Decree

[1] E.g., K. Lake in *Beginnings*, v.204–10.

or with the scrupulousness with which the Gentile converts in Antioch were observing the Decree's provisions. If that were so, Peter could have felt himself bound to suspend the sharing of meals until matters were improved. Peter's action was justifiable, and convinced even Barnabas; and he could still maintain that he had no wish to require Gentile converts to become Jews.

All this is, of course, conjecture, because Peter's answer to Paul is never given. However, the evidence we have does not rule out the possibility that the Decree was promulgated from Jerusalem to the Gentiles of Antioch and Syria and Cilicia before Paul's second visit to Jerusalem, and before Paul's attack on Peter in Antioch. In some ways this possibility explains the evidence a little more plausibly than the hypothesis that the Decree was made after the clash between Paul and Peter over Peter's withdrawal from eating with Gentiles. We may even venture the guess that Paul's attack on Peter—which is very obscurely expressed—included the demand that he should stick to the terms of the Decree, whatever the Jews in Antioch said.

The greatest objection to the assumption that the Decree preceded Paul's second visit is the fact that Paul never mentions its terms, and does not adopt its provisions.

In answer I should repeat the earlier argument, that the Decree was promulgated by the Jerusalem Council to apply to a specific area and to perform a specific task. The provisions of the Decree were designed to enable Gentile converts to be attached to Jewish synagogues without rousing the wrath of other Jewish synagogues that had not yet accepted Jesus Christ. Paul, on the other hand, was adopting an entirely new strategy. He was establishing separate Gentile churches, alongside Jewish Christian synagogues in some places, but, in other places, in isolation, where there were no synagogues of any kind. He always allowed for the possibility that food taboos and scruples held by some Christians might force other Christians to abstain from food and drink they would otherwise be free to take, but he was under no pressure to make general regulations in the way the Jerusalem Council had felt bound to do. In fact, the Jerusalem leaders had specifically sanctioned Paul's separate strategy, as it is now clear not only from Gal. 2, but also from the Antioch source that Luke has reproduced in Acts 15. The Decree had nothing to do with Paul's strategy, and there is no suggestion that the Jerusalem leaders expected Paul to adopt its terms. The manner in which James introduces the Decree in Acts 21 suggests to me, as I have argued earlier, not that Paul had never heard of its provisions, but that James is reminding Paul of the separate circumstances under which the Jerusalem church is attracting Gentiles, with the implication, fully agreed to by Paul, that the Jews who believed should continue in the strict observance of the Law.

I conclude that, soon after the believing synagogues in the sphere of the Jerusalem church began to attract Gentile converts, the decision was taken in Jerusalem that these converts were not to be required to keep the Law of Moses, but three cultic observances alone, to avoid scandalizing the as yet unconverted Jews.

Some time later, Paul and Barnabas, who had been experimenting with a mission to Gentiles as such, which did not envisage their joining a Jewish synagogue, went up to Jerusalem along with a delegation from the Antioch church, the church that had first commissioned them to their work. The occasion of the delegation was the arrival in Antioch of Judean Christians who preached that circumcision according to the Law of Moses was necessary to salvation, but Paul and Barnabas were glad to take the opportunity to see whether the Jerusalem leaders would accept their new strategy. This they did, and adopted Paul and Barnabas as co-representatives alongside their own representatives to carry to Antioch the assurance that there was no change in their policy, and that any Judeans who advocated circumcision were acting entirely without authority from the Jerusalem church.

Later still, Peter came to Antioch and decided to discontinue his practice of sharing meals with Gentile believers, because of Jewish pressure. Paul openly opposed him for his change of practice.

10

It has been necessary to attempt this reconstruction of the events in order to see precisely where Luke has gone wrong in his narrative. Before we attempt to draw conclusions about Luke's theology from these "mistakes", we must attempt to deal with one last difficulty.

Paul's visit to Jerusalem as recorded in Acts 15 is his third after his conversion, whereas the same visit, as recorded in Gal. 2, is undoubtedly his second. I can see no reason to doubt that Paul's first visit to Jerusalem in Galatians is the one referred to in Acts 9.26–30; 22.17. The fact that Luke's details do not square with Galatians is further evidence that Luke was not able to consult Galatians; but the general geographical agreement, that Paul came to Jerusalem from Damascus and left Jerusalem to go to Syria and Cilicia, makes it almost certain that the two accounts are versions of the one visit. I have already argued that the framework source in Acts 15 is describing the visit to Jerusalem that Paul recalls in Gal. 2. We are left with the famine relief visit in Acts 11.30 (cf. 12.24f) to account for.

A visit to Jerusalem by Barnabas and Paul carrying alms seems to be ruled out by the wording of Gal. 2.10: μόνον τῶν πτωχῶν ἵνα μνημονεύωμεν, ὃ καὶ ἐσπούδασα αὐτὸ τοῦτο ποιῆσαι. The tight chronological account of the visits to Jerusalem as set out in Galatians, together with the general impression that Paul is giving a complete narrative of his relations with the "pillars" up to that date, make it exceedingly difficult to agree with J. B. Lightfoot that Paul's "past care for their poor prompted this request of the elder Apostles"; Galatians does not allow room for an earlier visit by Paul and Barnabas with alms for Jerusalem. But, as Lightfoot was quick to notice, the change to the singular, ἐσπούδασα, implies that Paul had parted from Barnabas before they had any opportunity to fulfil the request together.[1] The wording of Gal. 2.10 also excludes the possibility that Barnabas and Paul had brought alms from Antioch on this very visit; although ἵνα μνημονεύωμεν could be translated "that we should continue to remember", this translation is not at all obvious, and would not be a likely interpretation of either the words or

[1] *Saint Paul's Epistle to the Galatians* (7th ed., 1881), 111.

the context to anyone who was not trying to fit the visit of Acts
11.30 into the framework of Galatians.

The visit of Barnabas and Paul in Acts 11.30 is unlikely to
have taken place.[1]

LUKE'S THEOLOGY AND ITS SETTING

What have we learnt about Luke's theology, and the setting from
out of which he wrote?

First, Luke did not understand what Paul was really attempting to do. Paul was attempting to set up purely Gentile churches
instead of continuing with the usual practice up till then of
attracting Gentile converts to the existing Jewish Christian
synagogues. Luke thought that Paul stood in the succession of
Peter, with the one difference, that the organized Jewish
opposition he met with out in the Gentile world and, in the end,
in Jerusalem forced him to turn decisively to the Gentiles, to
announce to the Jews that their unresponsiveness was incor-
rigible, and to establish the Church as an organization separate
from Judaism (13.45–52; 14.2–7; 14.19; 17.5–19; 17.13; 18.6;
18.12–17; 19.8–9; 20.3; 28.25–8). Luke thought that there was
one straight pressure in history operating on the Church, a
pressure that led from Jerusalem, the capital of Judaism, to
Rome, the capital of the Gentiles. We know from Paul's Epistle
to the Romans, chapters 9 to 11, that Paul did reckon with
Jewish obduracy, but we do not find that he thought his own
strategy was a substitute for the normal strategy practised by
Peter. I conclude that Luke was writing at a time when events
had made it clear that the Church's future lay principally with
the Gentiles, and that the remaining Jewish Christian congregations would have to live with that fact. This means that Luke
was writing after the adoption of the Test Benediction by the
majority of Jewish synagogues had effectively excluded those
Jews and those synagogues that believed Jesus was the Messiah

---

[1] H. J. Holtzmann; H. H. Wendt; O. Bauernfeind; E. Haenchen;
H. Schlier. G. Strecker, "Die sogenannte zweite Jerusalemreise des Paulus
(Act 11.27–30)", *Z.N.W.*, 53 (1962), 67–77 argues that 11.29, 30 is a
Lucan invention.

from the fellowship with their own people they had previously enjoyed. (We recall the esteem in which James was held by some, at least, of the unbelieving Jews, Eusebius, *H.E.*, ii.23.10.) Luke's situation effectively set the limits within which his theology could move, and his lack of accurate understanding of Paul's intentions precluded him from realizing that his history of the early Church was oversimplified.

But why did he not know that the churches Paul founded were not simply breakaway synagogues? This leads to my second point: Luke, for all his interest in Paul, stands genuinely in the succession of Peter, and was not the heir of Pauline theology. This point can be put very simply by saying that Luke has not inherited the Pauline epistles.

Paul's epistles were treasured by the churches to which he wrote. They were not, as Goodspeed argued, locked away in the archives of the churches, to be rediscovered and republished after a period of neglect. Certainly that is how it looked, from the point of view of the churches in the Petrine tradition, and Goodspeed's evidence about the long lack of interest in Paul must be given full weight and, as I have argued in Chapter One, the period of lack of interest in Paul must be extended to include the period of Justin Martyr. But the nature of the corpus of epistles itself indicates that Paul's writings were never ignored in some circles; there was no tunnel period in the Pauline churches. This is reasonably clear from the fact that a rich growth of Pauline epistles sprang up around the original letters; some or all of the following epistles were written by disciples of Paul on the basis of Pauline traditions and reminiscences: Ephesians, Philippians, Colossians, 2 Thessalonians, 1 and 2 Timothy, Titus, and Philemon. It is hard to imagine such a proliferation of writings, very different from one another, arising simply on the basis of a rediscovery of Paul's original epistles, and much more likely that they are evidence for a continuing tradition developing over a long period. I should myself argue that the major epistles that are usually regarded as undoubtedly Paul's are in fact much-expanded and elaborated versions of what he originally wrote and, if this hypothesis be correct, we should have to conclude that Paul's epistles were the basis of meditation, preaching, and teaching over a long period of time, undoubtedly stretched back almost to the day on which the letters were first received. The epistles of Paul would then have a strikingly similar history to that of the Gospels.

The fact that Luke has no knowledge of the Pauline epistles, despite his interest in Paul and his information about Paul from other sources, can only be explained on the assumption that there were two streams of tradition in early Christianity, which did not mix. Notice how little Luke reports about the continuing life of the churches Paul founded. He knows about the foundation of most of them, although not all, because the foundation of the Galatian churches is not mentioned, assuming, as seems almost certain, that the Epistle to the Galatians was written to the churches in Galatia proper, and not to the churches in the south of the Roman province of that name. But beyond the founding period, he tells us remarkably little, and this probably indicates that he knows remarkably little, because, when he does have source material about the later life of the church, as he has from Ephesus, he gives it quite naturally as part of his story (18.24—19.7 is not so much an account of the founding events, as an account of how the Ephesian church grew and developed).

If Luke did not belong to a church in the Pauline stream, and was not aware of the rich Pauline corpus, to what stream did he belong? The consensus of opinion at the end of the nineteenth century was that Luke represented early catholicism, and that this was something that had grown up as a result of the clash and reconciliation of two sharply opposed tendencies at an earlier period, represented by Peter on the one hand and Paul on the other hand. The evidence we have examined in this chapter will not permit us to retain the picture of a clash between two sharply opposed positions in the earliest days of the Church, but neither will it permit us to retain the picture of a subsequent mingling of the two tendencies. Luke seems to have been a stranger to the traditions of the Gentile congregations Paul founded.

Yet Luke writes from the standpoint of a church in which

Gentiles are now dominant, and in which the remaining Jewish congregations are a minority. His roots are in Judaism, as became clear in Chapter Three and as I hope to show more fully in Chapter Five, but he belongs to a church that is quite independent of Judaism and expects nothing but rejection from the synagogues.

The conclusion that best fits these facts is that the believing Jewish synagogues, which had been glad to welcome Gentile converts into their fellowship, but which regarded the conversion of the rest of Israel as their main mission, were disappointed in their main hope, but unexpectedly blessed by a large accession of Gentiles. The Gentiles eventually outnumbered the Jewish Christians, and the Jewish Christians were either absorbed into the general ethos of the churches, or were content to maintain Jewish Christian churches alongside the flourishing predominantly Gentile congregations. That, at least, seems to be the church situation as Luke (and Justin Martyr) knew it.

How did Paul become Luke's hero? First, there was information available. A number of congregations which began as synagogues had records of the missionary work of Paul and Barnabas; Luke had information from Antioch, and probably from Ephesus. Second, Luke needed to explain how a movement that had been rooted in Judaism became an independent religion. His records showed that Peter and James did not act as though this was to be the future of the men who believed Jesus was Messiah, but the records about Paul were different. He had clearly gone out from the synagogues to establish Gentile congregations. Paul was the obvious typical figure to represent the actual history of Luke's church tradition. We are in a position to see that history was more complicated, and that the church tradition to which Luke belonged had become largely Gentile without the benefit of Paul's theology or Paul's strategy, but we possess Paul's epistles and can use them to help in a source-analysis of Acts. Luke's church tradition probably became largely Gentile for the very reasons Luke gives: the hostility of the Jews, who after A.D. 70 became more and more organized, and the receptiveness of the Gentiles; Paul had chosen a strategy of direct approach to the Gentiles long before these pressures became so strong, and for theological reasons, but it was not *his* strategy nor *his* theology that prepared for the success among the Gentiles to which Luke-Acts bears witness.

It still remains difficult to understand how Luke, writing in the second century, could have remained ignorant of both Paul's epistles and Paul's actual achievement of establishing independent Gentile churches. Geographical isolation may explain some of this ignorance; he seems simply not to have heard of the Galatian congregations, for example. But he knows about Christians at Rome, and Paul's Epistle to the Romans had been cherished (and, if I am right, much added to) over a long period of time. What is the answer?

When we recall that Clement of Rome was himself in much the same situation as Luke, we may be close to a solution. Clement, in writing to the Corinthians, could mention Paul's letter to them (47.1), and so knew that Paul's epistles were important (something that Luke seems not to know), but he does not write like a man who belonged to a church that treasured Paul's Epistle to the Romans.[1] If Clement in Rome could be indifferent to the teaching of Paul treasured by some congregations in that city, we need not be surprised if Luke, writing perhaps from a city with no congregations owing anything to Paul, was ignorant of the full extent of Paul's achievement.

It may also be that the congregations that used Paul's epistles as the basis of their life failed to flourish after their initial success, and there may be truth in Goodspeed's theory that the publication of Luke-Acts led to the rescue and publication of the Pauline epistles. The truth would not be, however, that the epistles had lain neglected, but that the churches in which the epistles were used had remained outside the mainstream of Christianity and had, perhaps, declined in strength and im-

[1] The alleged quotation from Rom. 1.29-32 in 1 Clement 35.3f makes no mention of a source. I suspect Rom. 1.29-32 is part of a later addition, and I conjecture that both the interpolator in Romans, and Clement, were quoting traditional ethical material.

portance. We do not know enough to say, and we must beware of generalizing about churches scattered widely across the Empire, and living under very different circumstances.

We have learnt a great deal about Luke's own situation and his theology from a new attempt to explore the old problem of the relation between Acts and Galatians. The second-century date for Luke-Acts remains the most likely date for a writer who has to rely on written sources pieced together as best he can. We have seen that he belongs to a predominantly Gentile church, but a church that goes straight back to Peter and James in Jerusalem rather than to Paul. We have also seen why he attaches such great importance to Paul, while remaining ignorant of Paul the letter-writer; and while not quite understanding the purpose Paul himself had pursued.

In the next chapters we must fix more clearly the Judaism out of which his church tradition grew. Finally, we must try to draw back from the examination of the historical setting in which Luke worked, to consider the actual aim he had in mind in writing Luke-Acts.

CHAPTER FIVE

THE DEBT TO HELLENISTIC JUDAISM

WE HAVE learnt a great deal about Luke from comparing his views with those of the Christian theologians who, we have reason to believe, were his contemporaries. Our task will not be complete, however, until we know the wider background of his thought. We need to look beyond Christianity to Judaism, which, as Luke's own theological interests have already suggested, still provided the ethos for Christian thinking.

There is a strong case for saying that the Judaism to which Luke was indebted was not Palestinian Judaism but the Judaism of the Dispersion. It rests on his use of the Septuagint. As W. K. L. Clarke has shown in his article on "The Use of the LXX in Acts",[1] a high proportion of the words peculiar to Luke-Acts (51 out of 58) and a high proportion of the words characteristic of Luke-Acts (68 out of 69) occur in the LXX. This alone might only prove that Luke was very familiar with his Greek Bible, but the number of special affinities Clarke has shown to exist between Luke-Acts and the apocryphal books of the O.T. indicates that the literature peculiar to Greek-speaking Judaism has exerted a particular influence on his thought. Not only is the LXX his authoritative text of the O.T., but those parts of it which did not exist in Hebrew have coloured the language of his narrative.[2]

The Judaism of the Dispersion had for at least three centuries been confronted with the sort of missionary problem which the Church faced in the first century of its life. It had produced a

[1] *Beginnings*, ii.66–105.
[2] Ibid., 73–80. See now Traugott Holtz, *Untersuchungen über die Alttestamentlichen Zitate bei Lukas*, *T.U.*, 104 (Berlin, 1968).

large body of missionary literature written in Greek which employed a developed apologetic to convince its Gentile readers of the truth of the Jewish faith.[1] We know that some of these writings were prized by Christians—the only remnants of Demetrius (Artapanos), Philo the Elder, Eupolemus, Ezekiel the Tragedian, and Aristobulos are to be found in Eusebius or Clement of Alexandria[2]—and one of their favourite arguments, that the Greeks learnt their philosophy from Moses, soon became a stock piece of Christian apologetic, but it is still a matter of debate how early this Hellenistic Jewish thought made its mark on Christian theology. In this chapter we shall ask whether a number of features of Acts cannot best be explained by assuming that the church to which Luke belonged had learnt much of both its missionary strategy and its missionary theology from the synagogues of the Dispersion.

Although we shall bring forward a number of detailed comparisons between Hellenistic Jewish missionary literature and Acts, it is important to note that the influence of this literature is not confined to the details but affects the whole. Luke is not only influenced in the way he describes the missionary activity of his heroes by the practice of the synagogues in proselytizing among their Gentile neighbours, but his work is itself an argument for the faith, which he hoped would be read by non-Christians as well as by Christians. It should be compared as a whole with the apologetic writings of Hellenistic Judaism.

We should not expect Luke's purpose of converting men to Christianity to be immediately obvious. He would not be an effective apologist if it was. The studied objectivity of the

[1] Peter Dalbert, *Die Theologie der hellenistisch-jüdischen Missions-literatur unter Ausschluss von Philo und Josephus* (Hamburg, 1954). To his list should be added *The Life and Confession, or Prayer of Asenath*, text edited by P. Batiffol, *Studia Patristica* (Fascicule 1,2, Paris, 1889–90); see Kaufmann Kohler, *The Jewish Encyclopedia*, ii (N.Y., 1902), 172–6; G. D. Kilpatrick, *E.T.*, 64 (1952–53), 4–8, accepted by J. Jeremias, Bultmann Festschrift (*Z.N.W.* Beiheft 21, Berlin 1954), 255, 260; Christoph Burchard, *Untersuchungen zu Joseph und Aseneth: Überlieferung—Ortsbestimmung* (Tübingen, 1965).

[2] Eusebius copied his extracts (except for Aristobulos) from Alexander Polyhistor's *Concerning the Jews*; Clement of Alexandria may have used the same source.

introduction to the whole work, and the comparisons it invites with the dedications to secular histories, guarantee the seriousness of his missionary purpose.[1] In this he is following the Hellenistic Jewish tradition. Philo begins his *Life of Moses*, a work with a similar purpose, almost casually: "I hope to bring the story of this greatest and most perfect of men to the knowledge of such as deserve not to remain in ignorance of it; for, while the fame of the laws which he left behind him has travelled throughout the civilized world and reached the ends of the earth, the man himself as he really was is known to few."[2] Josephus, in the introduction to his *Jewish Antiquities* simply asks his Greek readers to approach his work with an open mind: "to fix their thoughts on God, and to test whether our lawgiver has had a worthy conception of his nature".[3]

The mention of Josephus, a Palestinian Jew who needed help with his Greek,[4] might seem to weaken the case that Hellenistic Judaism is the main influence on Luke's method, but it should be observed that Josephus himself appeals to the apologetic writings of his Greek-speaking Dispersion compatriots in justifying his undertaking. After mentioning the traditional story about the request of Ptolemy II for the co-operation of the High Priest Eleazar in producing the Septuagint, he writes, "Accordingly, I thought that it became me also to imitate the high priest's magnanimity and to assume there are still to-day many lovers of learning like the king."[5] Josephus has also taken his model from the apologetic experience of Hellenistic Judaism.[6]

---

[1] H. J. Cadbury is right to insist that the avowed purpose of Luke 1.1–4 is "to correct misinformation about Christianity rather than, as is so often supposed, to confirm the historical basis of Theophilus's religious faith"; *The Making of Luke-Acts* (N.Y. 1927), 315; cf. *Beginnings*, ii.489–510.

[2] *De vita Mosis*, I (tr. F. H. Colson, Loeb Library, London and Cambridge, Mass., 1935), 277.

[3] Proem 3 (tr. H. St. J. Thackeray, Loeb Library, 1930), 9.

[4] Ap. i.50; see H. St. J. Thackeray, *Josephus, the Man and the Historian* (N.Y., 1929), 5th Lecture.

[5] Tr. Thackeray, op. cit., 7.

[6] Josephus has a Palestinian forerunner in Eupolemos, who lived in the middle of the second century B.C.: Eus. *Praep.Ev.*, ix.26,30–34,39 (cf. Clem.

Perhaps it is Luke's familiarity—or the familiarity of the makers of the Christian tradition to which he belonged—with the apologetic literature of Hellenistic Judaism that led him to adopt the form of a history for his work. It is, after all, not immediately obvious that a history of the Church would be the best way to commend Christianity to unbelievers. A philosophical argument or a discourse about the moral teaching of Jesus might have been more immediately attractive to a cultured audience. In choosing to write the history of the foundation period of the Church Luke has chosen the basic method which the Greek-speaking Jewish apologists had chosen before him. Demetrius (Artapanos), and Eupolemos simply recounted the history of the Patriarchs, with more or less elaboration; the writer of the Wisdom of Solomon meditated on the significance of the Exodus;[1] Aristobulus and Philo, though eager to put the discussion on a philosophical plane, started from the history and character of Moses and the other leaders of their people; Ezekiel the Tragedian wrote *The Exodus*, a historical drama; and *The Prayer of Asenath* was the story of an ideal conversion to Judaism based on the historical fact that Joseph married the daughter of an Egyptian priest. The lesson in all these works was that God had manifestly worked in the history of Israel. It has required the essays of Dibelius to drive home the simple fact that Acts is designed to show the same thing for the early history of the Church.[2] However much the theological understanding of the history of God's people belongs to the essence of Jewish and Christian faith, it must still be recognized that the decision to attempt to win converts by expounding this special history to unbelievers was a new step, and a step taken in the environment where the Septuagint was made.

The thesis that Luke has been affected by that apologetic

Alex., *Str.*, i.23.153; 21.130); W. N. Stearns, *Fragments from Graeco-Jewish Writers* (Chicago, 1908), 29–41; Dalbert, op. cit.,35–42. One of his arguments is that Moses was the πρῶτος σοφός who gave the alphabet to the Greeks through the Phoenicians (Eus., *Praep. Ev.*, ix.26).

[1] At least, the writer of Sap. Sal. 11–19; see Dalbert, op. cit., 71 f.

[2] Cadbury, *The Making of Luke-Acts* (N.Y. 1927), 303–6, made the same point.

tradition can only be sustained if it can be shown in the details that Acts is indebted to the methods employed by Jewish missionary writers who wrote in Greek. There are four points at which this is possible, although one cannot always say that Hellenistic Jewish missionary literature provides the only parallel. The four points are: the way Acts commends the heroes of the faith; the appeal to the State; the approach to the philosophers; and the theology of conversion.

On two occasions in Acts Paul is taken to be a god by a heathen people, the first time at Lystra when he is called Hermes and Barnabas Zeus (14.11f), and the second time on Malta when he suffers no ill-effects from snake-bite (28.6).

The incident at Lystra can scarcely be historical. Assuming the Lystrans to have been among the recipients of the Epistle to the Galatians, appeal has been made to Gal. 4.14 for the basis of this narrative: ὡς ἄγγελον θεοῦ ἐδέξασθέ με. In fact, the contrast between the two passages could scarely be more telling. In his Epistle Paul praises the original discernment of the Galatians in accepting him as God's messenger, ὡς Χριστὸν Ἰησοῦν, despite his weakness of the flesh; in Acts a display of wonder-working power drives the poor credulous Lystrans to do sacrifice to the two apostles. The chief difficulty which lies in the way of accepting this story as historical is the unlikelihood that either the Lystrans or the priest of Zeus would honour Barnabas and Paul as gods simply because they had performed a cure. They would have honoured successful Jewish exorcists, but not honoured them as gods.[1] If the story is unlikely to have occurred, we must try to understand how Luke came to construct it.

This is the first time in Acts that any Christian missionaries have come into contact with a Gentile audience which has not been prepared for the gospel in the Synagogue, and it is interesting to see that the teaching given to them by Paul makes no mention of Christ; this is a common apologetic opportunity which would be familiar to Hellenistic Jews, and Barnabas

---

[1] A. Loisy, *Les Actes des Apôtres* (Paris, 1920), 552; Haenchen (10th ed.), 380; (12th ed.), 374.

and Paul meet it in a typical way. The point of the speech is that there is one God, the Creator, far above all the so-called gods who are like men. Luke has given magnificent dramatic support to this argument by letting the Lycaonians demonstrate the absurdity of their worship when they try to sacrifice to Barnabas and Paul. He is dramatizing the ridicule with which Jews since Second Isaiah had regarded the religions which honoured idols and gods that were plainly unworthy of honour when compared with the "living God who made heaven and earth and the sea and all that is in them".

Part of the occasion for constructing this scene was offered by the legend that Zeus and Hermes had appeared to Baucis and Philemon in this district.[1] Luke puts Paul into the rôle of Hermes, traditionally the messenger of the gods. It is unlikely at this early stage in the work of Paul that he would do all the talking while Barnabas kept silent, but the title "leader in speaking" is a good description of Paul's status in Acts as a whole, besides having another sense which the readers of Acts would quickly see: leading exponent of the Word of God.[2] Nor is Luke deterred from applying this title to Paul here by the fact that, although Hermes carried messages for Zeus, he would not do so while Zeus was present.[3] It seems that he has begun to construct a story with the intention of showing both that Paul's position as a preacher was recognized by pagans, and that the recognition of his position was spoiled by their propensity to worship the creature in place of the Creator. The local legend about Zeus and Hermes was probably the means by which the story was elaborated, but a basic element is still unexplained. Why should Luke ever imagine that pagans would honour the heroes of the faith as gods?

Ovid, *Metamorphoses*, viii.611–724. The Lystran inscriptions discovered by Prof. W. M. Calder which link Zeus and Hermes show that Ovid's legend had a basis in the religious practice of the area, but do not prove that the story in Acts is historical; cf. F. F. Bruce, *The Acts of the Apostles* (London, 1951), 281f.

[2] Hermes is called θεὸς ὁ τῶν λόγων ἡγεμών in Jamblichus, *De mysteriis Aegypt.*, 1; for further parallels see Bauer-Arndt-Gingrich, 310, 344.

[3] Loisy, op. cit., 551; Haenchen (10th ed.), 379; (12th ed.), 373.

The legendary account of Moses in the Hellenistic Jewish missionary story by Artapanos called *Concerning the Jews* offers an analogy and an explanation.[1] Artapanos makes a great deal of the achievement of Moses in ruling over the Egyptians; he says that he taught Orpheus, invented ships and machines for use in peace and war, and invented philosophy.[2] Even more surprising is his reorganization of the religious life of Egypt, in which he provided the priests with their sacred writings so that the kingdom would be safe and law-abiding. "For these reasons, then, Moses was beloved by the multitudes, and being deemed by the priests worthy to be honoured like a god, was named Hermes, because of his interpretation of the Hieroglyphics (διὰ τὴν τῶν ἱερῶν γραμμάτων ἑρμηνείαν)."[3]

Artapanos's book is a good example of the apologetic desire to show that the great leaders in the history of the Jews were highly honoured, even deified, by the non-Jews they met. Luke's two accounts of the way pagans honoured Paul as a god, particularly the second occasion on Malta, serve the same purpose, and both the motive and the device may well have been inherited from the Hellenistic Jewish tradition of apologetics. Certainly, if he knew the old legend that the Egyptians called Moses Hermes, he would then have to hand the suggestion necessary for constructing the scene which he sets in Lystra.

Artapanos provides another possible parallel to Acts in his account of Moses' miraculous release from prison.

"And when the king of Egypt heard of the arrival of Moses, he called him before him, and asked what he had come for: and he said, Because the Lord of the world (τῆς οἰκουμένης δεσπότην) commanded him to deliver the Jews.

"And when the king heard this, he shut him up in prison. But when it was night, all the doors of the prison-house opened of their own accord (τάς τε θύρας πάσας αὐτομάτως ἀνοιχθῆναι τοῦ δεσμωτηρίου), and of the guards some died, and some were sunk in sleep, and their weapons broken in pieces."[4]

---

[1] Eus., *Praep. Ev.*, ix.18,23,27; cf. Clem. Alex., *Strom.*, i.23.154; Stearns, op. cit., 42–56; see Dalbert, op. cit., 42–52.   [2] Eus., ix.27.
[3] Ibid., tr. Gifford (Oxford, 1903), iii. 463.   [4] Ibid., tr. Gifford, 465.

Acts contains three miraculous releases from prison (5.18ff, the Apostles; 12.5–10, Peter; 16.22–8, Paul and Silas) and the account in Artapanos is similar to the first two.[1] Clarke has pointed out the similarity between the language of the third and the *Testament of Joseph*, though this of course contains no miraculous release.[2] We may conclude that, at least in the telling of the stories, Luke is in debt to Hellenistic Jewish literature.

Acts is designed to show that Christianity is a law-abiding religion and that it should be recognized as such by the Roman state.[3] The Hellenistic synagogues had everywhere been officially recognized, but they could never be sure that their political privileges would not at any moment be disregarded or withdrawn. Their apologetic writings reflect this uncertainty and can profitably be compared with Acts.

Philo and Josephus both had direct dealings with the Romans and both wrote books which, in part at least, were intended to regain and confirm Roman toleration for the Jewish people. Philo's immediate concern was to avert the pogrom which was about to be launched on the Jewish settlement in Alexandria and which the prefect Flaccus was permitting and even encouraging. Larger issues immediately became involved, and Philo found himself writing on behalf of all Jewry to defend them from the necessity of worshipping the Emperor.[4] Josephus is writing under more difficult conditions, after the destruction of Jerusalem in A.D. 70, and his first attempt to regain the confidence of the Romans in his people had to be a warning to all subject peoples not to follow the example of the Jews and revolt against the Empire.[5] His *Antiquities*, on the other hand, was

[1] E. Preuschen, *Die Apg.*, *Hdb.z.N.T.* (Tübingen, 1912), 77: "This might have been the model here" (12.10).

[2] *Beginnings*, ii.77f.

[3] One of the firmly established points in the history of the criticism of Acts, it was early agreed upon by both sides of the Tübingen controversy: Schneckenburger and Zeller.

[4] *In Flaccum* and *De legatione ad Caium*; see E. R. Goodenough, *The Politics of Philo Judaeus, Practice and Theory* (New Haven, 1938).

[5] H. St J. Thackeray, op. cit., 2nd lecture, esp. 27–30.

"designed to magnify the Jewish race in the eyes of the Graeco-Roman world by a record of their ancient and glorious history".[1] In it he took care to mention the Roman records relating to the privileges which had been bestowed on the Jews.

Theology is not far from the surface in the apologies. Philo, particularly in *Against Flaccus*, makes it clear that any official who allows the Jews to be persecuted does so at his own risk. God defends his own, as Josephus reminds his readers in the Preface to the *Antiquities*. In the *Wisdom of Solomon* the "rulers of the earth" who are addressed in 1.1ff and 6.1ff might well ponder the fate of the Egyptians who persecuted the Jews.

> For they deserved to be deprived of light and kept
>   in darkness,
> They who kept imprisoned thy children
> Through whom the incorruptible light of the Law was
>   to be given to the world. (18.4)[2]

Acts itself gives a purely Jewish account of the fate suffered by Herod Agrippa I. He is struck down because men had begun to deify him and, it may be inferred, because he persecuted the Church (Acts 12. esp. 20–3). No Roman official suffers because he harms the Church, but no Roman official persecutes the Church except from weakness or cupidity. Luke is not in the position of his Hellenistic Jewish fore-runners, who could appeal to a long history of legal recognition; he is asking for something the Church has never had, and is in no position to threaten the wrath of God if it is not granted.

The Apologists were not only defending their people and trying to show that God had defended them and would defend them. They carried their missionary zeal into the realm of politics, and dared to preach to their heathen overlords that only in the service of the true and living God could they learn how to rule properly. From the crude glorification of Joseph and Moses as model rulers who reorganized the whole system of Egyptian government in Artapanos, to Philo's philosophical

---

[1] Ibid., 51.
[2] Dalbert, op. cit., 72f.

argument that Moses was the ideal king, [1] the Jewish apologists again and again put forward their law as the proper law for the ordering of human society.

The *Wisdom of Solomon*, though cast in markedly Greek terms, makes a strong appeal to rulers to recognize that their power stemmed from the one true God. It begins "Love righteousness, you judges of the earth", and in chapter six we read:

> Hear then, O kings, and consider,
> Learn, you judges of the earth.
> Listen, you who rule many peoples
> And have boasted of hosts of nations.
> Because your dominion was bestowed by the Lord,
> And your sovereignty by the Most High,
> He will put your works under review and
>   find out your plans,
> For you, who are servants of his Kingdom,
>   have not judged rightly,
> Have not kept the Law,
> And have not followed the will of God. . . .
> My words are for you, O rulers,
> So that you may learn wisdom and not
>   err. (6.1–4,9)

The *Letter of Aristeas* is another interesting example of the same sort of claim. It relates how the ruler of Egypt desired to have a copy of the Hebrew scriptures in his library and sent to Jerusalem to the high priest to provide him with a translation. The supposed author of the book, who is writing this account for his friend Philocrates, is sent to Jerusalem with the king's request. He had previously prevailed on Pharaoh to release the Jews who were kept as slaves in Egypt, as a sign of devotion to the God whose scriptures he wanted to have translated. "Since the law which we want not only to transcribe but to

---

[1] "In God's foreknowledge he became king and lawgiver and high priest and prophet, and in each he was supreme (τὰ πρωτεῖα)"; *de vita Mosis*, ii.3.

translate belongs to all the Jews, how can we justify our mission while so many of them are kept in slavery in your kingdom? But in the perfection and bounty of your being, release those who are oppressed and suffer great hardship, for the God who holds you responsible for this kingdom is the God who gave them the Law (κατευθύνοντός σου τὴν βασιλείαν τοῦ τεθεικότος αὐτοῖς θεοῦ τὸν νόμον), as I have taken trouble to confirm. For they worship God the Guardian and Creator of all, whom all men, including ourselves, O king, call by different names, such as Zeus or Dis" . . . (15,16). This is very close to syncretism, but the boldness of writing Jewish propaganda under the name of a cultured Egyptian court official justifies the risk. The learned discourse of the seventy translators at the king's banquets, which occupies the bulk of the rest of the work, shows quite clearly that the Jews are the only exponents of the wisdom of the true God. At the end of one day's after-dinner discussions Aristeas writes: "The king saluted them in a loud voice and congratulated them, all present joining in the applause, especially the philosophers. For they greatly excelled the philosophers both in conduct and in argument because they made God their starting point (τὴν καταρχήν)" (235). The purpose is to show that in questions of conduct, especially the conduct of rulers and men of position, the Law of the God of the Jews is the best guide.

We may seem to have wandered away from the Book of Acts, but the distance is not as great as it appears. In Acts we find Paul evangelizing among rulers and using the highest ideals of conduct and the central concerns of religion to lead them to Christianity: when Felix and Drusilla asked Paul to talk about this religion, "he discoursed about righteousness and self-control and the future judgement" (24.24f). No Roman official is yet told that the Christians' God is the one from whom they derive their authority (cf. John 19.11), but it is made clear in the story of the shipwreck that the Roman escort owed their lives to the God who is bringing Paul to Jerusalem. "Have no fear, Paul. It is necessary for you to stand before Caesar, and, behold, God has given you the lives of all who sail with you" (27.24). If Acts is a plea for the recognition of Christianity, Luke in return offers to the State the protection of the true and living God.

Gärtner's exhaustive study of the Areopagus speech has established Luke's debt to the missionary methods of Hellen- istic Judaism.[1] Gärtner's anxiety to show the Jewish and O.T. affinities of the speech has led him, however, to underrate the essential ambiguity of the apologetics. The object is to convert the hearers to faith in the one living God of the O.T., but the method is to appeal to accepted philosophical notions so that the Greeks may be led by their own philosophy to true worship. The closest example of the method used in Acts 14 and 17 is to be found in the Wisdom of Solomon 13—15; in both cases the absurdity of worshipping idols (or gods who are like man) is shown up by contrasting these creaturely things with God the Creator of all, and it is assumed that everyone should be able to recognize the absurdity. There is, as Gärtner rightly main- tains, no essential difference between the passages in Acts and the Wisdom of Solomon and Romans 1.[2] Our purpose here is not to discuss whether the Areopagus speech is Pauline, but to reaffirm that it owes its form and content to Diaspora propa- ganda. This is one more debt of Luke to the missionary tradi- tion of Hellenistic Judaism. Whether or not Paul spoke like this in Lystra and Athens, Luke himself was addressing his

[1] Bertil Gärtner, *The Areopagus Speech and Natural Revelation*, Acta Semin- arii Neotestamentici Upsaliensis XXI (Uppsala, 1955); e.g., 252, on the similarities between Sap. Sal. 13–15, Rom. 1, Acts 17: "This tradition can, in all essentials, be classified as Jewish Diaspora propaganda." See now Chapter Six.

[2] H. P. Owen, "The Scope of Natural Revelation in Rom. I and Acts XVII", *N.T.S.*, v (1958–9), 133–43, tries to distinguish between Sap. Sal. 13 on the one hand and Rom. 1 and Acts 17 on the other. His main point, that neither Rom. nor Acts assumes that God can be known as Creator of the world through the exercise of natural reason, is not supported by his exegesis; the argument against idolatry in Rom. and Acts only has force on the assumption that the Gentiles have failed to recognize what it was possible for them to know, viz., that it was wrong to worship created things in place of the Creator. This is also the assumption behind Sap. Sal. 13–15, and any variations on the theme, about the extent to which natural revela- tion was understood, are unimportant.

non-Christian readers through these two speeches, using the well-tried arguments developed by Greek-speaking Jewish apologists. The only specifically Christian element is the mention of Christ who will come to judge in Acts 17.31; the resurrection of "the divinely appointed man" has made the judgement certain, and gives a new urgency to the old arguments.

Finally, a key theological idea in Luke-Acts derives from the vocabulary of Hellenistic Judaism. Professor G. D. Kilpatrick has pointed out that two Lucan technical words, ἔλευσις and εὐαγγελίζεσθαι, come from this environment and no other;[1] we shall try now to show that Luke's theology of repentance comes from the same Jewish background.

The words μετανοέω and μετάνοια occur very frequently in Luke-Acts in comparison with the rest of the N.T.[2] Although Luke uses these terms to apply to repentance from individual sins (Luke 17.3f; Acts 8.22) as well as to signify the change of heart that Israel is called on to undergo (Luke 3.3, following Mark 1.4; 16.30; Acts 2.38; 3.19; 5.31), his usage is dominated by the idea that repentance is the great step a Gentile takes when he leaves behind his old religious or philosophical beliefs and turns to the living God. Repentance is for Luke primarily a term of proselytism, and this makes him use it both more frequently than other N.T. writers and in a more restricted sense.

Luke adopts the term "preaching of repentance", and similar phrases, as the best way to describe the Gentile mission. Luke 24.44ff, Jesus' exposition of the scriptures to his disciples after the Resurrection, is a thoroughly Lucan passage. It emphasizes, in the Lucan manner, that everything that has happened was foretold in the scriptures, particularly that "the Messiah should suffer" (cf. Luke 24.26; Acts 3.18; 17.3). The conclusion states that "it is written . . . that repentance for the forgiveness of sins is to be preached in the Messiah's name to all the Gentiles

---

[1] "Acts VII.52 ΕΛΕΥΣΙΣ", *J.T.S.*, xlvi (1945), 136–45; the comment on εὐαγγελίζεσθαι is to be found in an article, "Scribes, Lawyers, and Lucan Origins", *J.T.S.*, N.S., i (1950), 58.

[2] See Behm, Wurthwein in Kittel, *Th.Wb.z.N.T.*, iv (Stuttgart, 1942), 972–1004.

—beginning from Jerusalem". Luke has applied the summary of John the Baptist's preaching (Luke 3.3; Mark 1.4) to the Gentile mission. After Peter told the Jerusalem Church about the first and crucial Gentile conversion, the conversion of Cornelius, they used the word "repentance" to sum up what had happened: "Why, God has given repentance unto life to the Gentiles also" (11.18). Paul at Athens proclaimed that God was now calling "all men everywhere to repent", and the context makes it plain that the term is drawn from the vocabulary of Jewish proselytism rather than from a specifically Christian idea of repentance. God has not overlooked times of ignorance of the Christian gospel—there was nothing to overlook, because Jesus had not yet come—but he has overlooked the Gentile ignorance of him as Creator, which it had always been possible for them to know.[1] The new fact, that Christ is to come as judge, merely adds urgency to an old challenge.

This leads us to see the limitation on the meaning of the term which Luke must maintain because of its Jewish origin. As repentance is something that could be achieved under the old dispensation, in Christian times it can only be the first step on the way from unbelief to belief. Luke is forced to change the words about the mission of the Twelve in Mark 6.12, καὶ ἐξελθόντες ἐκήρυξαν ἵνα μετανοῶσιν, to ἐξερχόμενοι δὲ διήρχοντο κατὰ τὰς κώμας εὐαγγελιζόμενοι (9.6). Repentance for Luke is something preliminary, and he is here bound to substitute for it the word for the comprehensive proclamation of the gospel.[2] Similarly, in the words of Jesus which we have already mentioned (Luke 24.47), the proclamation of repentance to the Gentiles was qualified by the phrase "in the Messiah's name", and the Jerusalem Church to which Peter reported Cornelius's conversion called it repentance "unto life" (εἰς ζωήν).

Luke believed that the preliminary proclamation of repentance was of importance in the Gentile mission. When Paul, in

[1] But see H. P. Owen, op. cit.
[2] Conzelmann, *Die Mitte der Zeit* (Tübingen, 1954), 84, Eng. tr., 99.

his efforts to convert King Agrippa, described the preaching he undertook in obedience to the heavenly vision he said that he urged Jews and Gentiles "to repent and turn to God, performing works worthy of repentance" (26.20). Only the vision is specifically Christian; the vocabulary he adopts to explain what he did as a result of the vision is deliberately couched in terms of general religious significance so that Agrippa would understand, and perhaps accept for himself, the conversion he is preaching. Conversion to the living God and the good works that follow conversion are the important first steps, and the Christian content of conversion can be added to this in good time. The two stages were carefully distinguished by Paul in his farewell speech to the Ephesian elders when he said that he had witnessed "to Jews and the Greeks repentance towards God, and faith in our Lord Jesus Christ" (20.21; cf. 19.4 and Heb. 6.1-4). If the Jews now need to repent, that is because they have forgotten Moses and the prophets and put themselves in the position of the Gentiles, as poor Dives realized too late (Luke 16.30f).

In most, but not all, cases, Luke's use of the term seems to be drawn from the language of proselytism developed in Hellenistic Judaism. The Rabbis also developed a technical term for repentance which had no precise O.T. equivalent (תְּשׁוּבָה), but they never seem to have used it to designate the step a Gentile took when he became a proselyte. One of the few passages about repentance in which the Gentiles are mentioned is Pesikt. R. 156 a/b: "Gentiles who have not become proselytes are excluded from repentance";[1] repentance and becoming a proselyte are completely different things. Repentance is the resumption of a right attitude to God, which Israel is called on to make before the Messiah can come.[2] It is not the first step from heathen belief to be taken by Gentile proselytes.[3]

In Hellenistic Judaism, on the other hand, μετανοέω and

[1] Quoted by Wurthwein in Kittel, *Th.Wb.z.N.T.*, iv.992.
[2] The doctrine of one school of Rabbis is admirably summed up by Peter in Acts 3.19ff.
[3] See Wurthwein, op. cit., 991ff; Billerbeck, i.162-72.

μετάνοια came to be used to serve the Gentile mission in the period following the making of the LXX translation.[1]

In the three cases of the use of μετάνοια in the Wisdom of Solomon it refers to God's offer of repentance to Gentiles as well as to Jews.

> Thou hast mercy on all, because thou art able
> to do all,
> And thou overlookest men's sins that they may
> repent.
> For thou lovest all that is,
> And abhorrest nothing thou hast made;
> Thou wouldest never have fashioned anything
> thou hatest.
>
> (11.23f; cf. 12.10,19)

The Sibylline Oracles, while much more nationalist in tone, still remain true to their missionary purpose in offering repentance to the Gentiles. In the Fourth Book the phrase δοῦναι μετάνοιαν occurs, which is used twice in Acts. (Cf. 2 Tim. 2.25, and in the Apostolic Fathers.)[2] "O ill-starred mortals, let not these things be, and drive not the Great God to divers deeds of wrath; but have done with swords and moanings and killings of men, and deeds of violence, and wash your bodies whole in ever-running rivers, and, stretching your hands to heaven, seek forgiveness for your former deeds, and with praises ask pardon (ἱλάσκεσθε) for your bitter ungodliness. God will grant repentance (θεὸς δώσει μετάνοιαν) and will not slay: He will stay his wrath once more if with one accord ye practise godliness in your heart" (lines 163–70).[3] This is an appeal to

---

[1] The word μετάνοια is not used in the full religious sense of "repentance" in the LXX translation of the Hebrew scriptures. The verb μετανοέω is sometimes used to translate נחם.

[2] See Conzelmann in Dibelius, *Die Pastoralbriefe, Hdb.z.N.T.* (3rd ed., Tübingen, 1955), 85f. Conzelmann's assertion, *Die Mitte der Zeit* (Tübingen 1954), 85 (Eng. tr., 100), that this expression in Acts is merely a stock phrase which has lost its original meaning, is unwarranted.

[3] Text ed. Geffcken (Leipzig, 1902); tr. H. C. O. Lanchester in Charles *Apocrypha and Pseudepigrapha* (Oxford, 1913), ii.396.

men to become proselytes, to renounce violence, to be baptized and to pray. In this way all men can receive the reward of God's gift of repentance.

Besides these scattered occurrences of μετάνοια, which illustrate its special use in appealing to Gentiles to become Jews, there are two long passages in the missionary literature of Hellenistic Judaism devoted to its praise.

The first occurs in the *Prayer of Asenath*, which tells how Asenath, the daughter of Pentephres the Priest, turned from the Egyptian gods and became a Jewish proselyte in order that she might marry Joseph.[1] She smashed up her idols and began to fast after Joseph had refused to kiss her because her mouth was polluted with food offered to idols. "And she broke into a great sweat as she heard these words from Joseph, and as he spoke to her in the name of the Most High God. Then she wept with long and bitter weeping and repented from her gods which she worshipped and the idols to which she prayed . . ."(ix). After seven days fasting she prayed a long prayer of repentance, remembering that the God of the Hebrews was true and living and merciful, and that he did not take account of the sin of the humble, particularly when they had sinned in ignorance (xi). At the end of her prayer the Archangel Michael appeared to her and told her that God had heard her prayer and that her name was written in the Book of Life.

> And your name will no longer be called "Asenath",
> But your name will be " City of Refuge ",
> Because many nations will flee to you,
> For the Lord God Most High;
> And many peoples will be sheltered under your wings,
> Trusting in the Lord God;
> And those who devote themselves to God the Most High
>   in the name of Repentence
> Will be preserved by your walls.   (xv)[2]

---

[1] Burchard, op. cit., 112–21.

[2] Ibid., 67, for Burchard's reconstruction of the text, which is followed here (61.9–13, citing by page and line in Batiffol, op. cit.).

Asenath is portrayed as the guardian and type of all proselytes,[1] and is admitted to Israel by eating the bread of life and drinking the cup of immortality and being anointed with the ointment of incorruption.

Immediately after Michael has announced Asenath's new name we find this hymn to Repentance.

> For Repentance is in heaven
> As the noble and exceedingly good daughter of the Most High;
> And she earnestly entreats God the Most High for you every hour,
> And for all who repent in the name of God the Most High.
>
> So He is the Father of Repentance,
> And she is the guardian of all virgins;
> And she loves you exceedingly,
> And makes requests for you every hour from the Most High;
> And she receives all who repent,
> And she has prepared for them a place of rest in heaven;
> And she restores all who repent,
> And she herself will minister to them for ever.   (xv)[2]

It is clear from the context that repentance is the great response to the mercy of God which proselytes make, and that the writer of the story is praising repentance, and showing the honour in which God holds those who repent, in order to win new converts.

The concluding two sections of Philo's *Concerning the Virtues*, on Repentance and on Nobility, are designed to show the Gentile reader the way to enter "the best of commonwealths" (175) and to assure him that his status in Israel will be equal to that of the best of the Jews, for the law values each man for his own sake and disregards his ancestry in awarding praise and blame (227).[3] Again Repentance is painted in glowing colours; it means passing from darkness to light. Those who turn their

---

[1] Burchard, op. cit., 120: "Asenath, the City of Refuge, does not only *signify*, she *is* the company of proselytes, and the proselytes are in her."

[2] Ibid., 67.

[3] Cf. Rom. 2.5–12, etc.

back on vanity and the mythical fables on which they have been brought up, and honour God the Creator in place of those who were no gods, are joyfully welcomed into the family of the Jewish people. "So therefore all those who did not at the first acknowledge their duty to reverence the Founder and Father of all, yet afterwards embraced the creed of one instead of a multiplicity of sovereigns, must be held to be our dearest friends and closest kinsmen. They have shown the godliness of heart which above all leads to friendship and affinity, and we must rejoice with them. As if, though blind at the first they had recovered their sight and had come from the deepest darkness to behold the most radiant light" (179).[1] Repentance is like a decisive change from sickness to health (176; cf. *Abr.* 26); it is the way the proselyte must follow.

It seems clear that μετάνοια is a term used in Hellenistic Judaism in its mission to the Gentiles and that "repentance" does not have this strong and particular association in Rabbinic Judaism. In the N.T. repentance is used like this by later writers, especially by Luke, who seems to be employing the term to show his non-Christian readers the way into Christianity and to show his Christian readers how to begin to evangelize their neighbours. We conclude that this is a further debt he owes to Hellenistic Judaism.

With a short note we may close. In Acts 24.25 there is a curious summary of the topics covered by Paul when he was asked to tell Felix and Drusilla about faith in the Messiah: διαλεγομένου δὲ αὐτοῦ περὶ δικαιοσύνης καὶ ἐγκρατείας καὶ τοῦ κρίματος τοῦ μέλλοντος. . . . This type of apologetic, where moral virtues are pressed on the hearers with urgency because the judgement is coming, is naturally found in Hellenistic Jewish missionary literature. The passages already quoted from the Wisdom of Solomon (6.1–9) and the Sibylline Oracles (iv.163–78) are good examples. "God will grant repentance and will not slay: he will stay his wrath once more if with one accord ye practise precious godliness (εὐσεβίην περίτιμον) in your hearts" (Sib. Or. iv.168–70). The two virtues

---

[1] Tr. F. H. Colson, Leob Classical Library, Philo, viii (London, 1939), 273.

mentioned in Acts, however, are not the obvious ones to choose, either for themselves or in combination.[1] For that reason it is significant that they occur together in two apologetic books of Diaspora Judaism. In the Epistle of Aristeas 277, Pharaoh asked why the majority of men never became virtuous. The answer he was given by one of the Jewish translators ended, "The habit of virtue is a hindrance to those who are devoted to a life of pleasure because it enjoins upon them the preference of *temperance* and *righteousness*. For it is God who is the master of these things (ἐγκράτειαν δὲ κελεύει καὶ δικαιοσύνην προτιμᾶν. ὁ δὲ θεὸς πάντων ἡγεῖται τούτων) " (278).[2] Self-control and righteousness are brought forward in an apologetic situation as the two virtues enjoined by God. The same combination is found in Philo. In his discourse on Repentance he says that a man must not only turn to revere the Creator before his creatures, but should also change to virtue from "that malignant mistress, vice". "This means passing from ignorance to knowledge of things which it is disgraceful not to know, from senselessness to good sense, from incontinence to *continence*, from injustice to *justice*, from timidity to boldness (ἐξ ἀκρατείας εἰς ἐγκράτειαν, ἐξ ἀδικίας εἰς δικαιοσύνην, ἐξ ἀτολμίας εἰς θαρραλεότητα) " (*De virtutibus*, 180).[3] The final transition, from timidity to confidence or boldness, is significant; it probably represents the confidence which comes to a man who knows that he is both God-loving and God-beloved (θεοφιλὴς καὶ φιλόθεος, 184). We may contrast it with the fear with which Felix heard about the judgement to come (ἔμφοβος γενόμενος), and speculate whether the two virtues of self-control and righteousness might not have been combined in Jewish missionary practice with a warning about God's judgement, to produce either fear or godly confidence in those who heard. There is

---

[1] ἐγκράτεια is not precise enough to provide a reference to Felix's sexual irregularities; *Beginnings*, iv.305.

[2] Text ed. P. Wendland (Leipzig, 1900); tr. H. T. Andrews in Charles, op. cit., ii (Oxford, 1913), 118.

[3] Tr. F. H. Colson, Loeb, viii (London, 1939). Cf. the list of the most necessary virtues, *De Josepho*, 153: σωφροσύνη, αἰδώς, ἐγκράτεια, and δικαιοσύνη.

not enough evidence to decide whether or not Luke has reproduced completely a common missionary formula, but we can
affirm that the summary of Paul's preaching given here is
typical of a certain approach to Gentiles which was made by
Jews of the Dispersion.

CHAPTER SIX

ATHENS

THROUGHOUT this book we have been examining the ideas contained in Acts in an attempt to discern three distinct, if inseparable, layers of ideas.

The first layer is that contained in Luke's sources; these ideas he simply handed on because he was an historian, and so handed on entire the old accounts he judged to be trustworthy.[1] Of course, he realized that these old accounts could be incomplete, and he knew that they needed to be put in order, but, once he had accepted a particular source as trustworthy, he would probably give it in full, with explanatory additions as necessary; it would not have occurred to him to imagine that a source could be both good evidence of the truth and, at the same time, a false account. These sources inevitably embodied ideas which Luke accepted and passed on because he was a Christian, but which were not necessarily expressed in the words he would have chosen if left to himself.

The second layer of ideas is that presupposed by Luke because he was a man of his own particular time and situation; if I am right in my arguments, a Gentile Christian historian who wrote in the first quarter of the second century, living in a church whose traditions went straight back to a Jewish Christian Church that had proved remarkably successful in attracting Gentile converts. This layer of ideas embodied the questions Luke naturally asked himself, and the assumptions he shared with

[1] There were sources about the early Church to be handed on. Jacob Jervell, "Zur Frage der Traditionsgrundlage der Apg.", *Studia Theologica*, 16 (1962), 25–41, rightly challenges Dibelius's assumption that the early Church had no interest in recording the doings of the Apostles and the progress of the mission.

fellow-Christians of the same era and the same situation. These ideas might be betrayed by a detail, but they are best seen in the structure and scope of Luke's work when taken as a whole.

The third layer of ideas is the result of the conscious intentions of Luke as he composed Luke-Acts. These ideas are the lessons he wished to teach, and the effects he wished to produce, by composing this work and no other.

Any historical work must contain these three layers of ideas, the ideas transmitted from the past, the ideas presupposed as true by the historian, and the ideas the historian is putting forward in the specific work of his under examination, but it is not at all easy to distinguish one layer from another, particularly in an ancient work like Luke-Acts. In this case the author does not explicitly mark off his sources from each other and from his own additions; we do not know from external evidence who he was; and we are given only a brief and enigmatic account of his purpose (Luke 1.1–4).

That is why it is important to recognize the existence of all three layers, and why it is dangerous to search for exact knowledge of one layer without trying to know about the other layers at the same time. If Luke had indicated the exact limits of his sources and had plausibly guaranteed that he was copying them word for word, we could happily forget about him and his purposes if our aim was to write our own account of the events to which the sources referred, or we could happily forget about his sources if our aim was to write about him; if we knew who Luke was, we should know his presuppositions, his immediate purpose in writing, and his probable sources; if we possessed the clear information about the purpose of Luke-Acts that the publisher's blurb or even the name of the publisher alone can convey to a modern reader, we should scarcely need to ask about the author's presuppositions, because his cultural *milieu* would be immediately obvious. But we do not have clear answers to any of these questions; consequently, we cannot afford to ignore any of them.

In the previous chapters I have paid particular attention to the second layer of ideas, the ideas which Luke presupposed because he was the man he was, living and working in the circumstances in which he was. I have inevitably uncovered ideas that belong to the set of his conscious intentions in writing Luke-Acts (for, naturally, his conscious intentions arose out of his less conscious presuppositions), and the final chapter will be devoted to an attempt to decide his dominant aim, and to distinguish this aim as sharply as possible from the underlying presuppositions. I have also suggested the existence of sources.

In this chapter I wish to take an incident and a theme that stands almost completely isolated in Acts, and use it as a test case of the conclusions that have already emerged. The isolated incident is Paul's visit to Athens, where he speaks not just to Gentiles (that he has done before), but to Gentile intellectuals. I shall try to distinguish the ideas contained in Luke's source from his own use of the source, and to distinguish his presuppositions as an historian and a theologian from his specific purpose in writing this passage in this particular way.

There is little doubt that Luke had a source. If he had been writing a free account of Paul's movements on the basis of general oral information, he would scarcely have conjectured that Paul was waiting for Silas and Timothy (17.16), without explaining why Paul left Athens before they came, and why they did not join Paul until he had been a little time in Corinth (18.5). Either Luke was using a written source, or he was himself the source of the information. A romancer is unlikely to leave the loose ends that commonly occur in factual reports. But this account is unlikely to have been drawn from Luke's own experience or the experience of an eyewitness, since it is inaccurate. Timothy, and probably Silas (Silvanus), were in Athens with Paul on this occasion, according to 1 Thess. 3.1. Acts is not far out, since Timothy and Silas were with Paul subsequently in Corinth (1 Cor. 1.19), but the discrepancy makes it likely that Luke was relying on a written source that had been compiled some time after the missionary journey had taken place.

What was the extent of Luke's source? If, say, verses 16, 17,

and 34 belong to an itinerary source,[1] is there any connection
that might suggest that the written source extended still further?
In verse 16 it is reported that Paul's "spirit was angry within
him" at the idolatry of the city. This indignation led him to go
down to the market place every day to reason with the people
he met. That connects up with verses 24 to 29 of the speech, the
section in which Paul attacked the manufacture of representa-
tions of the Godhead in gold and silver and stone. On the
evidence of this connection alone we could not decide between
two possible hypotheses, that Luke had made up a suitable
speech, or that Luke had copied out a source which contained
a suitable speech. But there is a further piece of evidence that
positively excludes the first hypothesis, although it does not
finally establish the second.

Luke can hardly have composed the words in verses 24 to 29,
because this section of the speech has been embedded by a later
editor in a framework of another kind. Luke can have been the
author of the framework, but not of the original piece around
which the framework has been built. This framework shows
itself in the introduction to the speech, verses 22 and 23. In
this introduction Paul draws attention to an altar that cannot,
by its nature, have included any representation of the god in
whose honour it was erected. This god was unknown. Therefore
the polemic against idolatry in verses 24 to 29 would be completely beside the point. We must conclude that verses 22f and
verses 24 to 29 came from two different hands, and it seems
reasonable to assume that the former was added to the latter,
rather than the other way round.

The source in verses 24 to 29 extends further than these verses,
and the framework is also longer than verses 22f alone. Verse
30 clearly belongs with verses 24 to 29, rather than with the
framework. Verse 30 implies that the ignorance is culpable, and
therefore entails an argument to show that God should have

---

[1] Dibelius, *Aufsätze*, 67ff, 114; *Essays*, 73ff, 130, ascribes verses 17 and 34
to the itinerary source; Bultmann, *Gnomon*, 16 (1940), 336 and Hommel,
Z.N.W., 46 (1955), 173–6, give rather more to the source: verses 16–18 and
34.

been recognized and worshipped, but has not been recognized and worshipped. This argument is given in verses 24 to 29, especially in verses 26 and 27.[1] The framework, on the other hand, implies that the Athenians, in so far as they worship at the shrine of the Unknown God, already worship God unwittingly, but need to have revealed to them who the God is they worship without knowing. But God cannot be said to overlook an ignorance that needs revelation to enlighten. He can only overlook culpable ignorance. It follows that verse 30 goes with verses 24 to 29, and not with verses 22f.

The framework must extend back to include verse 18, the reference to the Epicureans and Stoics. They would almost certainly have accepted the point that God was not to be at all adequately represented in objects made of gold and silver and stone. The argument that they worshipped a God they did not know would be much more fittingly addressed to them than to idolaters. In fact, the argument that Paul could reveal to them the Unknown God contained an implicit claim that a greater than Socrates was here. As I pointed out in Chapter One, Luke was able to assume (like Justin Martyr, Appendix to the Apology 10.6) that Socrates had taught the Athenians to seek full knowledge of the God who was unknown to them. The Epicureans and Stoics, both of whom, especially the Stoics, revered Socrates, are confronted by a man who knows the secret that Socrates could not, or would not, divulge. It is ironic that these Epicureans and Stoics call Paul a σπερμολόγος, in the same manner as Aristophanes in the *Clouds* had ridiculed Socratic philosophy,[2] and that they wonder whether he has not been trying to introduce strange divinities, the charge upon which Socrates was condemned to death (Xenophon, *Memorabilia*, i.1; Plato, *Apology*, 24B).

[1] The words κατοικεῖν . . . αὐτῶν in verse 26 intolerably overload the sentence, and are probably a gloss. The glossator took ἐξ ἑνός to refer to Adam (an unlikely supposition in a context that emphasizes the fact that all men are God's offspring, verses 28f). The phrase ἐξ ἑνός probably meant "unanimously". The argument, which prefectly fits the context without distracting from the flow of ideas, is that God made all races of men, without exception, to seek him; they were given both the instinct and the possibility.

[2] F. C. Baur, *Paul*, i (London, 1876), 170.

The intervening verses, verses 19 to 21, also belong to the
framework, as they emphasize the eagerness with which the
philosophically minded Athenians wish to hear Paul; and the
place to which they take him (perhaps in mockery, to pretend
that they are being serious[1]) is the place where Socrates had
been tried. These verses contrast with verses 16 and 17, where an
angry Paul goes to the market place to combat idolatry. The
framework consists of verses 18 to 23.

Does the end of the speech belong to the same framework?
It has often been remarked that the whole speech, down to the
middle of verse 31, is not specifically Christian, and could well
have been derived from Hellenistic Jewish apologetics. Perhaps,
then, we should separate the reference to the resurrection from
the preceding verses; if so, the conclusion would seem to lie
close at hand that verse 31b belonged to the framework, because
the last clause of verse 18 in the framework explained that the
strange divinities were "Jesus" and "Anastasis". But, before
we jump to this conclusion, we should notice that verse 18c is by
no means secure in its context. If the point of the reference to
"strange divinities" is a literary device to allude to Socrates'
trial and to prepare for Paul's revelation of the Unknown God,
the author would not wish to distract his readers' attention by
providing a rather feeble explanation of why Paul should be
taken for a polytheist. Just as with Socrates, the point was not
the polytheism but the novelty. The explanation looks very
much like the work of an inferior glossator, and this conjecture
is supported by the fact that the words are omitted in D d gig.

Although it is true that Paul's speech is not specifically
Christian until the last few words, there is no reason to assume
that the Jewish apologetics and the reference to Jesus as the
Judge raised from the dead could not have been combined in
one source. Paul's creedal statement in 1 Thess. 1.9f contains
precisely the same combination of ideas.

However, verses 32 and 33 probably belong to the framework.
They imply that the Athenians have arranged the hearing
("We shall hear you about this again"), and that is the domi-
nant theme in the framework, and does not appear in the source,

[1] Ibid., i.171.

as far as we have it. Furthermore, the laughter at the idea of resurrection would be much more likely from philosophers, particularly from the Epicureans, who did not believe in existence after death, than from ordinary idolaters, whose religions were full of resurrections.[1]

The result of this investigation is to suggest that someone, probably Luke, has added verses 18 to 23 and 32, 33 to a source consisting of verses 16, 17, 24 to 31, and 34. It is possible that the source originally consisted of two parts, the itinerary and the speech, but that added hypothesis is not necessary: we have already argued that the itinerary is slightly inaccurate, and the lapse of time that would account for the inaccuracy of the itinerary would also account for the fact that the speech, although representing "the general sense of what was actually spoken",[2] as we know from 1 Thess. 1.9f, contains expressions and even arguments that do not fit so well with Paul's own theology as we know it from the epistles. Whether or not the source was always a unit, it almost certainly came to Luke as a unit, and we are now in a position to discuss the use he made of this traditional material.

There is one assumption of Luke that stands out immediately as soon as we observe that he has inserted a small detail into the second sentence of the source. In verse 17 we read that Paul conducted discussions in the synagogue with Jews and those who feared God, as well as with those he met in the market place. The reader of Acts is accustomed to hearing that Paul went to the synagogue first, but a closer examination of this verse makes it plain that Luke's source said no such thing. The words ἐν τῇ συναγωγῇ τοῖς Ἰουδαίοις καὶ τοῖς σεβομένοις καί were added to the source, probably by Luke himself. Notice, first, that the word οὖν represents a *non sequitur*, as far as the Jews and God-fearers were concerned; the idolatry of the city would not "therefore" lead Paul to hold discussions with them. Second, the construction after διελέγετο in the source differs

[1] Cf. F. C. Baur, op. cit., i.175f.

[2] Thucydides, *Peloponnesian War*, i.22; see T. Francis Glasson's salutary note, *E.T.*, lxxvi (1964–5), 165.

from the construction in the interpolated words; the interpolated words use the simple dative, whereas the source has πρός with the accusative. This fine difference possibly represents the difference in temperature between the discussion in the synagogue and the discussion in the market place (cf. Mark 9.34, πρὸς ἀλλήλους γὰρ διελέχθησαν τίς μείζων), but the fact remains that a sentence beginning διελέγετο μὲν οὖν after a sentence like the one preceding, verse 16, would more naturally continue πρός τινας than τισι; if the different constructions do convey slightly different senses, we should not expect to find both used together in this sort of context.

The reason these difficulties did not bother Luke and do not bother us, until we think about them, is that we expect Paul to go first to the synagogue, for did not the predominantly Gentile Church grow organically out of the Synagogue? But this assumption is one of Luke's presuppositions that we have found reason to question. Luke's own sources and Paul's epistles show that Paul had deliberately attempted to set up Gentile congregations independently of Jewish Christian synagogues. If he did go to a synagogue first, it was in order to find a Gentile who would form the nucleus of a Gentile congregation, not in order to build more Gentiles into the existing synagogue.[1] Therefore it is perfectly possible that Paul went straight into the market place in Athens to try to win Gentiles from idolatry and to persuade them to believe in Jesus Christ. He may, of course, have visited the synagogue, but the source does not mention this, and does not think that Dionysius, Damaris, and the others had joined Paul and believed because they had first been attached to the synagogue. But Luke assumed that the Synagogue was the basis of the Church, and added the reference in verse 17, although it has no organic relationship to the rest of the events in Athens as reported in his source.

Luke's chief addition, however, is the magnificent framework to the speech, which he provided in verses 18 to 23 and 32f. Well might he feel called on to produce his best, because the speech he found in his source is already a gem of precise and telling

[1] Acts 18.1–11, and the discussion in Chapter Four above.

apologetics. If men are God's offspring, not only is it inappropriate that they should try to represent the Godhead in gold or silver or stone, an image formed by the art and imagination of man, but it is most appropriate that men, whoever they be and wherever they live, should be judged in righteousness by a man; and the resurrection is the not entirely unexpected sign of God's designation. The argument of the source is coherent and pointed, and reflects the long tradition of apologetic skill that had been developed in Hellenistic Judaism.[1] Luke, as I have argued in the previous chapter, belonged in this tradition, and our task now is to discover how he used the source in order to carry forward his purposes.

What exactly has Luke achieved by adding verses 18 to 23 and 32f? He has enlarged a speech against idolatry to suggest that philosophers who were concerned with the most serious issue of philosophy should see in this attack on idolatry the revelation of what they were pursuing. He makes the point vivid by supposing that the well-known altar to the unknown gods in fact embodied the philosophical tradition that began when Socrates used to speak about the unknown God (Justin, Appendix to the Apology, 10.16; cf. Plato, Timaeus, 29C). His point would not have told against Socrates, who presumably thought he knew God as clearly as man is permitted to know God, but it would tell in a later age, when the oriental mystery religions had flooded across into Greece and Rome.[2] The Epicureans and Stoics are out-trumped by a man who can speak openly to everyone of what Socrates, the greatest philospher of all, had only hinted. The Athenians, who had a reputation for seeking novelty (verse 21), are given knowledge which is both

[1] See the list of books and articles in Gärtner, *The Areopagus Speech and Natural Revelation* (Uppsala, 1955), 253–72; Haenchen, *Die Apostelgeschichte* (12th ed., Göttingen, 1969), 453f; Dupont, "Le Salut des Gentils et la Signification Théologique du Livre des Actes", *N.T.S.*, 6 (1959–60), 152f n 4; repr. in *Études sur les Actes des Apôtres* (Paris, 1967), 416f n 79; and add Jürgen-Christian Lebram, "Der Aufbau der Areopagrede", *Z.N.W.*, 55 (1964), 221–43; Timothy D. Barnes, "An Apostle on Trial", *J.T.S.*, n.s. xx (1969), 407–19.

[2] Cf. Loisy, *Les Actes des Apôtres* (Paris, 1921), 669f.

new, in that it tells of the appointment of a man to judge the world, and old, in that it concerns the true God whom Socrates had long ago perceived, and whom Athens still hankered after.

Luke has clearly assumed that Athens is the philosophical capital of the world. His imagination is fired by the significance of Athens in human thought, and he has taken it for granted that the life of the city is dominated by philosophy still. The source he was using provided him with a skilful and apposite attack on idolatry, and the information that Dionysius the Areopagite had been among Paul's converts. This suggested to him, I think, that Paul's speech might well have occurred before the Council of the Areopagus, acting not as a court, but as a gathering of leading citizens who had no function, as far as Luke was concerned, except to represent what Athens stood for, philosophical curiosity. In order to get Paul before the Council, he further conjectured that some Epicurean and Stoic philosophers had met him in the market place, and that they had brought him to the Areopagus.[1]

Luke has also assumed that the speech Paul made at Athens to answer idolatry was capable also of answering the philosophical search of men who were too sophisticated to think that idol worship was the real point of religion. We might be shocked that an historian would invent a vivid occasion for the speech that stood in his source, and write a new introduction to extend the application of the speech, but we should remember that ancient historians gave themselves greater liberties than we would allow. In defence of Luke, we should remember that he has preserved the speech as given in his source, and that his addition is only designed to show that the revelation contained in the original speech was the answer to further philosophical problems. The original source had already appealed to the best traditions of Athens, by quoting Aratus, in order to spur

[1] I do not think the suggestion likely, in *Beginnings*, iv.211, that the Epicurean and Stoic philosophers are left hanging in the air at the opening of verse 18, and that the people who make the mocking remarks and who bring Paul to the Areopagus are "Athenians in general".

the Athenians to abandon idolatry; Luke would feel fully justified in appealing to the best philosophical tradition of Athens in order to lead the Epicureans and Stoics to discover the truth for which they were groping.

Now a second assumption of Luke becomes clear. Luke assumes that when Paul comes to Athens he will confront philosophy with its central challenge. If Athens represents Philosophy to Luke's imagination, Paul represents the greatest missionary of the Christian faith. It is dramatically necessary to Luke that when Paul speaks at Athens he should speak the crucial word to Philosophy.

These two assumptions mark Luke off as a man of his time. He belongs to the age of the Apologists, and this is one more indication that he lived in the second century rather than in the first.

But if Luke's assumptions are clear, his specific purpose is clearer still. It was not only *Luke's* imagination that seized on Athens as the representative City of Philosophy, but this must have been the picture in the minds of his audience as well. His readers would expect Paul's visit to Athens to be philosophically significant. Luke had a source which reported Paul as having made a telling speech in Athens, but he owed it to his readers to make the philosophical significance as dramatically explicit as possible. The readers governed Luke's efforts; his audience called forth his utmost skill. They can hardly have been simply Christians seeking information about the early days of the Church, for Luke could not assume that many of them were set alight by the image of Athens, or were interested in Epicurean and Stoic philosophies. The readers must have been members of the educated reading public. Athens would have great meaning for them; many of them would be inclined towards either Epicureanism or Stoicism, or at least well aware of their tenets; all of them would be infected with a longing to know the Unknown God. If this was Luke's audience, he can have written his history of Paul at Athens with but one purpose in mind: to persuade them to follow Dionysius the Areopagite, a woman named Damaris, and certain others, in believing in

Jesus and worshipping the God, once unknown but now known, who had appointed Jesus to judge the world in righteousness.

We have found confirmation in this one short passage for the thesis that the author of Acts was a man who shared the presuppositions of the era otherwise represented by Justin Martyr, and we have once more been able to observe him at work on his sources. Now we must see whether the specific intention that shines through the drama of Paul's encounter with the philosophers in Athens, the intention to convert the educated reader who might pick up his book and read this passage, is also the pervasive purpose in the whole of Luke-Acts.

CHAPTER SEVEN

THE CENTRAL THEOLOGICAL PURPOSE OF ACTS

THERE has been no attempt in the previous chapters to provide a comprehensive exposition of the theology of Acts; the aim has been to try to fix the historical setting in which this theology arose in the life of the Church. The theology is that represented in Acts, but we are really looking for the theology of the author of "Luke-Acts", one work in two volumes.[1] A full theology of the author of Luke-Acts would have to deal with Christology, the doctrines of the Spirit and the Church and baptism, the place and conception of the common meals, the function and authority of various ministers, eschatology, the uses of the Law, and so on. And the question might well be raised, Would it not be both more complete and more fruitful, in investigating the theology of Luke, to start with these doctrines, for, after all, theology is primarily concerned with doctrines?

There are two difficulties in the way of this approach, difficulties that have become more and more obvious since the publication of Conzelmann's important book on Lucan theology, *Die Mitte der Zeit*.[2]

The first is that the obvious starting-point for a study of Luke's distinctive doctrines, the observation of precisely how he uses Mark's Gospel, and a comparison of his use of Q with the use of Q in Matthew's Gospel, has run up against the old difficulties, which had somehow been forgotten. It is as little established as ever that Luke's copy of Mark was the same as our

[1] See Hans Conzelmann's perceptive criticism of the first edition of this book, *Theologische Literaturzeitung* 87 (1962), columns 753–5.

[2] (Tübingen, 1954 and many subsequent editions); English tr., *The Theology of St Luke* (London, 1960).

copy of Mark;[1] I now think it most likely that our Mark has been enlarged from the Mark used by Luke.[2] Nor can we agree on the limits and contents of Q; Q was probably a good deal shorter than the reconstructions put forward by most scholars,[3] although I do not see the need to dispense with Q.[4] Further, even if we could decide about Q, there is still no safe way of deciding whether Matthew or Luke has changed the source, where they disagree. Finally, questions about the earliest text of the Gospels, and the possibility of that early text's having been glossed, are still open. I do not wish to deny that important observations about Luke's theology have been made by comparing his Gospel with the Gospels of Matthew and Mark, but extreme caution is necessary, to see that tentative results are not made into unshakeable conclusions.

But there is a second difficulty in attempting to characterize Luke's theology by seeing how he handles key doctrines. Behind such an attempt usually lies the assumption that doctrines developed organically from the common beginning, and that once we know the inner law of development and the external pressures that have been applied to the organism we can determine the age and generalize about the character of a document. The favourite test case for organic development is eschatology, and it is usually supposed that an imminent eschatology at the beginning of the Church's life changed into a

[1] W. Bussmann, *Synoptische Studien*. 3 vols. Halle, 1925–31.

[2] The fact that Matthew's copy of Mark was longer than Luke's might be used to argue for an earlier date for Luke than the date I suggest. However (a) Matthew's Gospel was probably not used by Ignatius (see J. Smit Sibinga, "Ignatius and Matthew", *Novum Testamentum*, viii (1966), 263–83), and may have to be dated even later than Ignatius; and (b) the gradual expansion of Mark, before the canonical text was standardized, probably occurred at different rates in different centres, so that we cannot even give relative dates to Matthew and Luke by comparing their relationship to Marcan development.

[3] Cf. H.-Th. Wrege, *Die Überlieferungsgeschichte der Bergpredigt* (Tübingen, 1968), who denies, to my mind convincingly, that Matthew was indebted to Q in the Sermon on the Mount. See Ernst Bammel, "Das Ende von Q", in *Verborum Veritas: Gustav Stählin zum 70 Geburtstag* (Wuppertal, 1970), 39–50.

[4] A. M. Farrer, "On Dispensing with Q" in *Studies in the Gospels: Essays in Memory of R. H. Lightfoot*, ed. D. E. Nineham (Oxford, 1955), 55–88.

realized eschatology on the one hand and an indefinitely postponed eschatology on the other hand. But almost every assumption behind this supposed "law" is open to question— the terms in which the "law" is stated as well as the movement it presupposes.[1]

Hans Conzelmann has attempted to use a subtle and detailed form of this approach in order to fix Luke's place in the development of early Christianity.[2] He argues that "in comparison with Mark, Luke appears advanced; compared with Justin he appears relatively primitive".[3] The difficulty is that all the criteria he proposes for the "early catholicism" to which Justin is supposed to belong and which are "lacking in Luke or can be found only as initial traces"[4] break down on examination. I can detect no fundamental difference between Justin and Luke over the Church as an institution of salvation; neither Justin nor Luke gives a strongly marked "institutional definition of the ecclesiastical office (priesthood)", and the lack of reports about a regular weekly Eucharist in Luke-Acts (cf. Justin, Apology 65; but note Acts 20.7) is open to a variety of explanations; and although Luke may not tie the Spirit to the institution, he is careful to show that the Spirit's work always had institutional consequences. If "making the tradition secure through apostolic succession" is a necessary mark of "early catholicism", neither Ignatius of Antioch nor Justin Martyr would qualify.

For the most part I have tried to avoid such comparison of doctrines. I have attempted rather to isolate the preoccupations of Luke as shown in the broad structure of his work and in the themes to which he returns again and again. At this level we may hope to uncover the basic presuppositions held by Luke, and at this level it is possible to discern an affinity between Luke and Justin Martyr, which differences in detail or in doctrine need not disturb. The point I am making becomes clear when we reflect

[1] E. Bammel, "Erwägungen zur Eschatologie Jesu", *Studia Evangelica III*, ed. F. L. Cross, *T.U.*, 88 (1964), 3–32, at 3–6.
[2] "Luke's Place in the Development of Early Christianity", *S.L.A.*, 298–316.
[3] Ibid., 305.
[4] Ibid., 304.

on an extreme case: two men who are bitter enemies, and think they disagree with each other completely, may still share a common interest in the same issues, and a common assumption about what questions are important and what arguments are valid.

Justin and Luke were different men, writing their own works in their own ways, unaware of each other's existence, yet their shared presuppositions mark them clearly as men of the same generation, as clearly as Milton belonged to the generation of Marvell and not to the generation of Spenser, or as Wordsworth belonged to the generation of Coleridge and not to the generation of Pope.

I have concentrated on Acts rather than on Luke's Gospel because the very idea of adding Acts to the Gospel is significant, and because a history of the Church is more likely to betray the author's place in the developing life of the Church than a history of Jesus' death and resurrection.

In this study I have come to see that we are still grappling with the thesis put forward by Ferdinand Christian Baur. Baur argued that Luke was attempting to reconcile the Gospel of the Judaizers and the free Gospel of Paul. By the end of the last century this picture of a self-conscious Lucan pro-gramme was abandoned, and scholars were fond of quoting Jülicher's aphorism, " Paul is not Judaized and Peter Paulinized, but both are Lucanized, that is, Catholicized ".[1] The great virtue of this picture, in either Baur's form or the later form, is that it recognizes that there is a difference between Paul's epistles on the one hand, and the rest of the New Testament on the other hand. The great difficulty of this picture is that it does not con-vincingly explain the fact that Luke constructed his synthesis without taking into account Paul's epistles.

---

[1] *Einleitung in das N.T.* (1894; 7th ed., Tübingen, 1931), 431; tr. by McGiffert, *Beginnings*, ii.384 n 2. This was the point of view adopted by, among others, Bruno Bauer; A. Ritschl; F. Overbeck; H. J. Holtzmann, *Hand-Commentar z. N.T.*, 1.2 (Freiburg, 1899), 321; P. Wendland, *Die Urchr. Literaturformen, Hdb.z.N.T.*, 1.3 (2nd and 3rd ed., Tübingen, 1912), 320f; H. Windisch, *Beginnings*, ii.298–348.

The discussion of the old questions raised by Baur, particularly the question of the relationship of the Jewish Christians and the Gentile Christians, has led me to question whether Baur was right in his description of how Paul saw his distinctive mission, and to suggest that Luke, far from being a synthesizer of the two streams, is simply a late member of the Church that had developed organically out of the Synagogue. He possessed accounts of Paul's missionary work, but not Paul's legacy to the churches he founded, the epistles. The synthesis was to come later still, when Paul's epistles were combined with the rest of the New Testament writings.

Our picture of Luke cannot be complete until, in addition to describing his basic presuppositions, we also attempt to state his specific theological intention in writing Luke-Acts. Yet a description of the basic assumptions he held and the deep issues that concerned him has already put the key into our hands. We have slowly realized, as we began to discern a structure and a persistent set of themes, that we were handling a piece of literature, and a piece of literature designed to take its place beside other histories. Here, not later, lies the beginning of Christian literature, because here, for the first time, a Christian addressed the general reading public with a major work.[1]

The conclusion to which we have been driven is that Luke-Acts was primarily an attempt to persuade an educated reading public to become Christians; it was an "apology" in outward form but, like all true apologies, it had the burning inner purpose of bringing men to the faith. The use of the term "apology" does not imply that Acts was chiefly designed to gain official recognition for Christianity. That would clearly be an inadequate description of the central purpose of the book, because it would leave large portions out of account, as well as excluding most of Luke's Gospel. Attempts have been made to avoid this objection to the view that Acts was narrowly apologetic by supposing that a full statement of the nature of Christianity was a necessary part of the case to be presented to the Romans.

[1] Cf. Overbeck's stimulating essay, *Über die Anfänge der patristischen Literatur* (1882, repr. Basel, n.d. [1960]).

B. S. Easton, for example, has argued that Luke was a liberal Jew who was asking for Christianity to be recognized as a *religio licita* because it was, despite its large Gentile member-ship, still part of Judaism.[1] There is truth in this contention, but it fails to do justice to the evangelical purpose of the work as a whole. The neutrality of the dedication to the two volumes in Luke 1.1–4, which explains to an educated public that Luke is about to set out an accurate account of Christianity's history from the beginning in order to correct and supplement the knowledge they had already gathered,[2] should not mislead us into thinking that he was on the defensive. As we have seen in the fifth chapter, studied objectivity characterized the prefaces to Hellenistic Jewish attempts to win educated converts for the faith, and Luke-Acts in this, as in other ways, belongs to the same *genre*. A work which was concerned with the irresistible progress of the Word of God from Jerusalem to Rome can hardly be said to be defensive. All the stylistic indications that Luke had shaped his history according to his intention to preach the gospel,[3] together with the nature of the dedicatory introduction, show that the primary purpose of Luke-Acts was to lead an educated reading public to embrace the Christian faith.[4]

Once this is established, the other suggestions about Luke's purpose fall into place. They can be shown to depend on the theme which he has adopted to give unity to his evangelistic treatise: the movement up to Jerusalem, and from Jerusalem to Rome.

First, he used this scheme of events to show that the fortunes of Jesus and the Church were governed at every turn by the

[1] "The Purpose of Acts" (1936), reprinted in *Early Christianity: The Purpose of Acts and Other Papers* (London, 1955), 33–118.

[2] See H. J. Cadbury, *Beginnings*, ii.489–510.

[3] See Dibelius, *Studies* (London, 1956), 102, 136f, and *passim*. Dibelius has failed to see that Luke was primarily concerned with preaching to unbelievers; cf. 135.

[4] Not, of course, just Theophilus; the dedication does not imply that he was the chief target of the work, but that Luke intended to publish his book for the educated world to read; see Cadbury, *The Making of Luke-Acts* (N.Y., 1927; repr. London, 1958), 204, and A. D. Nock, Review of Dibel-ius's *Aufsätze, Gnomen*, 25 (1953), 501.

hand of God. Everything that happened was inevitable and fore-ordained, and could be discovered, in the last resort, in the pages of the O.T.[1] It was no accident that Jesus died in Jerusalem or that the rejection of the gospel by Jerusalem led to Paul's arrival in Rome. Human decision was almost completely excluded at the crucial moments of the story, and Peter and Paul's movements were controlled by supernatural direction from the Holy Spirit and angels and visions whenever a decisive step had to be taken. To anyone who was prepared to see the signs of God's activity in the success of a religious movement, it could be seen here in the unprecedented growth of Christianity from the smallest beginnings, a growth which depended entirely on God's initiative. The success of Christianity, despite all the sets-backs it encountered, was used to support its claim to be the only true religion.

Second, as we have seen in Chapter Two, the movement from Jerusalem to Rome was not meant to be the story of the first preaching of the gospel in the main cities of the Empire. Acts is not primarily a history of Christian missions. It is the account of how the Church discovered its true nature in the way God dealt with it on the path from Jerusalem to Rome; the Church discovered its independent destiny when Paul reached Rome and finally turned from the Jews to the Gentiles. The educated Roman reader was being told, first and foremost, that the Church had been designed for him by God, rather than that the gospel had been brought to him by Paul. Although Jerusalem remained the city where his salvation had been achieved in the death and resurrection of Jesus Christ, Rome had been chosen as the city where the Church discovered its true rôle in the world. The Church was not simply a genuine form of the old Jewish religion which the Roman authorities had recognized and even protected; it was the only true Israel. It alone could understand the riddles in the Bible, the book which was the distinguishing mark of Judaism, and it alone should be recognized as the true organized representative of Jewish monotheism. But Acts was not only designed to show that

[1] Cadbury, op. cit., 303–6; Dibelius, op. cit., passim.

Christianity had a far greater claim to recognition than Judaism; it demonstrated by the examples of Cornelius and Sergius Paulus (and Publius?, Acts 28.7ff) that some well-placed Romans had already adopted it as their faith in the earliest days. The divinely ordained movement from Jerusalem to Rome corresponded to the current of missionary success; what the Jews had rejected was now an open possibility for the Romans. The fact that educated Romans could believe and had believed was a strong argument for others to follow their example. Luke-Acts not only showed that God had prepared the Church for them by his intervention in history, but it also taught the salient points of the faith which it was asking them to accept. The speeches in Acts fulfil many functions, but not the least important is that of repeating over and over again the framework of the Christian faith as understood by Luke and his Church.[1]

We have seen that Luke's history of the Church demonstrated the power of the true and living God, and that it opened up to educated citizens of the Empire the possibility of belief. It also demonstrated the innocence of the Christians of any revolutionary political tendencies, and this is the third point.[2] The political accusations made against Jesus and the Christian leaders were completely groundless, as the decisions of Pilate and Herod and the rest showed. The accusations arose either from fear in certain quarters that the adoption of Christianity would involve financial loss, or from the hostility of the Jews. The Jews often linked the political charge with a religious one, that Christians were teaching the violation of the Law of Moses; Roman officials always judged Christians innocent of the first and, if they held themselves incompetent to decide the

[1] Dibelius, "The Speeches in Acts and Ancient Historiography", op. cit., 138–85; U. Wilckens, *Die Missionsreden der Apg.* (Neukirchen Kreis Moers, 1961); C. F. Evans, " 'Speeches' in Acts " in *Mélanges Bibliques en hommage au R. P. Béda Rigaux* (Gembloux, 1970), 287–302.

[2] The classic statement of the argument is by Joh. Weiss, *Ueber die Absicht und den litterarischen Charakter der Apg.* (Göttingen, 1897); see also Overbeck, Introduction to de Wette's commentary (Eng. tr., London, 1875), 23ff, and B. S. Easton, op. cit. Weiss argues that the twin political and religious question of the recognition of Christianity was the chief concern of Acts, 54–60.

second, the accused Christians always made it clear that it, too, had no substance. The Church came to maturity in Rome by way of Paul's suffering as a Roman prisoner, just as Jesus had come to reign in Jerusalem by way of death on a Roman cross, but in both cases it was innocent suffering, and the central position given to Jerusalem, with the emphasis on the fulfillings of O.T. prophecies there, showed that this innocent religion was also the true Judaism. Johannes Weiss has rightly emphasized the connection between the establishment of the Church's political innocence and the establishment of its undeviating adherence to the true beliefs of Judaism, but it is drawing too narrow a conclusion to infer that Luke's argument was simply that "the State should confer on the new religion the protection granted to the old".[1] Luke may have incidentally desired legal recognition, but his primary aim was something greater; a legal case could have been better presented in a shorter and more direct form. The repeated and dramatic demonstration that Christianity was both politically innocent and religiously the true fulfilment of the expectations of Judaism was not a legal but an evangelistic argument. Luke wanted to persuade Romans that, as Christianity was not a subversive movement and was the consummation of an ancient and honourable monotheism, it was eminently worthy of their allegiance. In doing so, he has put the leaders of unrepentant Judaism in a bad light by showing how they used the mob to stir up

[1] Op. cit., 59. Conzelmann in a review of the third edition of Haenchen's Commentary, *Theologische Literaturzeitung*, 85 (1960), 241–50 at 244f, points out that there was no such thing as the legal concept of a *religio licita*; it was constructed on one occasion, *ad hoc*, by Tertullian (*Apol.* 21.1?). This additional evidence confirms an earlier observation, *Die Mitte der Zeit* (Tübingen, 1954), 117–24, Eng. tr. (London, 1960), 138–44, that Christians in Acts never sought acquittal in a Roman court by appealing to any religious toleration which may have been extended to Jews; the relation between Christianity and Judaism was, from a legal point of view, irrelevant (Acts 18.14ff). Conzelmann goes on to argue, however, that Luke was employing a double argument, emphasizing the Church's continuity with Israel (for ecclesiastical consumption) and the gulf between the Church and "the Jews" (for imperial consumption). This distinction of audience seems artificial; both ideas were, in the end, important for both audiences. See Conzelmann, *Die Apostelgeschichte, Hdb.z.N.T.*, 7 (1963), 10.

trouble against innocent men. If Acts was written between A.D. 115 and 130, it was written between the Jewish rising in the East in 116 and the Bar Cochba rebellion in 132; in those circumstances Luke's dissociation of Christianity from disaffected Judaism would have been a prudent step, and a necessary one if Romans were to be converted. He showed that the earthly Jerusalem, representing Jewish aspirations for political independence, was to remain in subjection, while the salvation worked out in the heavenly city, despite the malevolence of the earthly, had been handed over to the Gentiles in Rome (cf. Luke 21.24). The account of the movement from Jerusalem to Rome is again made to express in symbolic form an important part of Luke's apologetic theology.

It is important to see that Luke's primary aim was to preach the gospel to unbelievers. Although a theological message for the Church inevitably flowed from this venture in apologetics, that was strictly a subsidiary concern. This should not surprise Christians in the twentieth century, for the most far-reaching contemporary examination of the Church's theology has come from a man who began by finding that he did not know how to preach to an unbelieving world. Karl Barth has in fact defined the discipline of dogmatic theology by subordinating it to the Church's preaching mission: dogmatic theology is the Church's continual attempt to criticize its own proclamation of the gospel by the standards God has given it. The important theological positions to which Luke called the attention of his Church in Luke-Acts followed directly from his central purpose. In drawing the attention of educated Romans to the magnitude of what God had done in Jesus' death and resurrection, he was at the same time reminding the Church of the power to which it owed its existence, and warning it not to betray its trust.

A number of specific warnings to the Church flow from Luke's apologetic and evangelistic arguments. First, he warned Christians not to pin their hopes on a literal and immediate fulfilment of the apocalyptic expectations inherited from Judaism. Not only might such beliefs lure them into joining in Jewish insurrections, but they would frustrate God's purpose for them by turning their attention away from the ordinary world of men. Romans holding influential positions would not be impressed by such religious enthusiasm. So we read that, when the disciples asked Jesus just before his ascension whether he would then restore the kingdom to Israel, he firmly prohibited all such speculation and told them to prepare themselves instead to receive the power which would drive them out from Jerusalem to Rome as his witnesses (Acts 1.6–8). This was Jesus' last and, in some ways, his most important command. Luke believed that Jesus' intention was to establish the Church as a power in the Gentile world, and his own attempt in Luke-Acts to further this destiny inevitably meant reminding the Church of where its responsibilities lay: not in nourishing apocalyptic hopes centred on Jerusalem, but in witnessing to the Gentiles.

Second, part of the gospel which Luke proclaimed to Gentiles was that God had established his Church as an independent entity for them. Paul fully discovered this only when he was forced to turn from the Jews to the Gentiles in Rome, but this discovery lends added weight to his last testimony to the leaders of the Church, the speech addressed to the Ephesian elders in Miletus (Acts 20.17–38).[1] When Paul came to Rome to die for the faith, he set the seal on the Church's recognition that it had superseded Judaism, and the Testament of Paul to the Church leaders was designed to fit the Church to perform this newly realized function. The local churches were the congregations into which the Gentiles were to be welcomed, and for that reason Paul warned the appointed leaders, the elders or bishops, to be on their guard against the internal disruptive forces of heresy (20.28–30). Similarly, in Chapter Four we saw that Luke has assumed that the early Church had arrived at an orderly arrangement for settling the potentially disruptive relations

---

[1] Johannes Munck, "Discours d'adieu dans le N.T. et dans la littérature biblique", *Goguel Festschrift* (Neuchatel and Paris, 1950), 155–70, esp. 159–61, 164, 169: "The death of the Apostles marks the advent of the Antichrist."

between Jewish and Gentile Christians. This was a problem which faced his own Church, to which he believed the apostolic age offered the solution. We also suggested that the Jerusalem Decree, besides codifying the terms of this agreement, was probably meant to provide a test for use against antinomian heresy. Acts shows the Church discovering itself as the only true heir to the universal promises in the O.T., but in discovering that it was a people separate from Judaism, it also had to discover ways of guarding the purity of its faith and the integrity of its organization. Luke's insistence on this point sprang from his desire to win the allegiance of Romans to the only religion foretold and established by God, and his apologetic arguments necessarily involved him in showing to the Church the means by which it should preserve the unity achieved in the apostolic age. Luke's own attempts to forward the Church's mission involved his preaching the Church's unity.

Finally, by finishing his work when Paul arrived at Rome, Luke has tried to show the Church where its future lay. He believed Christianity was fitted by nature to be the religion of the world. This seems to be the reason why he made Paul his hero. The usual reasons which have been advanced to explain Paul's prominence do not seem to explain the evidence. Luke can hardly have belonged to a specifically Pauline party in the Church, because he made no distinction between Paul's theological position and that of the other Church leaders. He knew that there were some characteristic features in Pauline theology to do with justification and grace, but he represented such features as merely additions to the standard preaching (13.38) which, in any case, the Apostles also believed (15.10f). He took trouble to make it clear that Paul did not advocate the abandonment of the Law by Jews and, on the other hand, he insisted that there was nothing specifically Pauline in the insistence by all the Church leaders that Gentile Christians should be free from circumcision. Luke did not know Paul's epistles, and it is unlikely that he made Paul his hero because he wished to support a specifically Pauline theology, or even because he wished to explain how Gentile Christianity, deeply influenced by Christian Judaism, had been founded by Paul.[1] There is no evidence before 2 Polycarp that the Church was particularly conscious of Paul as a theologian, and the only evidence we do possess suggests that Paul was honoured for something far more practical. In Clement of Rome's epistle to the Corinthians, as we have seen in Chapter One, Paul was honoured not only for his martyrdom, but for the fact that he had reached "the western goal"—Rome—to die. It is almost certain that Peter was also martyred in Rome, but Clement did not seem to attach the same significance to the place where Peter died. He noted two things about Paul's arrival in the capital: it was the end of a preaching mission to the whole world, and it was the place where he witnessed to the rulers. The same significance is attached to Paul's last days in Rome in 2 Tim. 4.16–18.[2] The author of the Pastoral epistles has emphasized that Paul's defence before the Imperial court in Rome completed the preaching. In principle the Gentile mission was over.

Acts assumed the same view of Paul's martyrdom. As we have already seen, the book was constructed according to the pattern laid down in Jesus' last commission to his disciples: to be his witnesses in Jerusalem, and in all Judea and Samaria, and to the end of the earth. The pattern was complete, according to Luke, when Paul came to Rome to die, and whole of Acts was a plea to the Gentiles in general, and to educated Romans in particular, to accept the heritage which was prepared for them in this way. Luke has taken the traditional view of the significance of Paul's martyrdom and extended it to embrace the whole of the central period of the history of salvation. From the time when God sent Gabriel to Nazareth in Galilee to announce to Mary that she would bear Jesus who would rule over the house of Israel for ever, until the time when Paul was brought to Rome to witness to what had happened in Jerusalem, salvation was being prepared for the Gentiles; every decision made and every journey undertaken served this one

[1] Overbeck, Introduction to de Wette's Commentary, published in the Eng. tr. of Zeller's Commentary (London, 1875), 22.

[2] See the discussion, 6–9 above.

end. In Rome the witness to the rulers was made and, in principle, the Gospel was preached to all the Gentiles. The Church assumed the rôle official Judaism had forfeited.

Acts affords no indication that Paul was singled out to serve a party interest. Although the author seems to be indebted to the traditional view of the significance of Paul's mission and martyrdom preserved in 1 Clement and the Pastoral epistles, he obviously believed that this was also the significance of the work of Christ and the Apostles. He was careful to show that Paul was only carrying on what Peter had begun and, by omitting an actual account of Paul's martyrdom, to emphasize that the establishment of the Church in Rome was the fruit of Christ's death and resurrection in Jerusalem. His aim was to convert his readers to Christianity, not to defend one party in the Church; the corresponding message to the Church was that its future lay in the very centre of the political world. Luke was looking forward to the time when Christianity would become the religion of the Empire, and he wanted the Church to prepare itself for the rôle.

We have come by devious routes to see the unique place which Acts occupies in the N.T. The evidence which has emerged from the previous chapters has led us to one conclusion: Luke's background, his theology, and his understanding of the Church's situation made him, in the fullest sense of the word, an apologist. The book of Acts, together with Luke's Gospel, is probably the only work in the N.T. which was specifically addressed to unbelievers. Luke believed that God had prepared the Church to receive the educated and the politically powerful as well as the poor and the outcast, and he wrote Luke-Acts to persuade men at the centre of power to abandon their lives to the service of the kingdom of God.

187

4. EARLY CHRISTIAN WRITINGS

Roman numerals refer to the Tables, 48–58

5. OTHER ANCIENT WRITINGS

6. MODERN WRITERS